IV.

Key Approaches to Criminology

The new Sage *Key Approaches to Criminology* series is intended to celebrate the removal of traditional barriers between disciplines and bring together some of the leading scholars working at the intersections of different, yet related subjects. Each book in the series will help readers to make intellectual connections between fields and disciplines, and to understand the importance of studying crime and criminal justice within a broader context of their relation to policy, law, ethics, and so on.

This first contribution to the series, *Media and Crime*, reflects the symbiotic relationship between two of the most pervasive features of late-modern life. Fortunately few of us will be victims of serious crime but all of us know much (some would say too much) about every aspect of offending, victimhood and crime detection. But, as this book makes clear, the 'picture' of crime that most of us hold is highly skewed by a range of subtle and not-so-subtle biases, prejudices and false assumptions that permeate the mediation of crime and justice at every stage from media production to media consumption.

Yvonne Jewkes
Series Editor

Media and Crime

Yvonne Jewkes

SAGE Publications
London ● Thousand Oaks ● New Delhi

SAGE Publications Ltd
1 Oliver's Yard
55 City Road
London EC1Y 1SP

SAGE Publications Inc
2455 Teller Road
Thousand Oaks
California 91320

SAGE Publications India Pvt. Ltd
B–42 Panchsheel Enclave
PO Box 4109
New Delhi 110 017

British Library Cataloguing in Publication data
A catalogue record for this book is available from the British Library

ISBN-10 0-7619-4764-7   ISBN-13 978-0-7619-4764-6
ISBN-10 0-7619-4765-5 (pbk)   ISBN-13 978-0-7619-4765-3 (pbk)

Typeset by C&M Digitals Pvt. Ltd., Chennai, India
Printed and bound in Great Britain by
Cromwell Press Limited, Trowbridge, Wiltshire
Printed on paper from sustainable sources

Contents

For my brothers, Michael and Martin,
and my sister, Sarah

Preface

The last decade has seen the rise, not just of university-taught criminology degrees in general, but also of specialist modules teaching 'Media and Crime' to undergraduate and postgraduate students. These developments are to be welcomed by those of us who have been teaching such courses for some time, especially as it means that there is a new, emerging literature on all things related to media and crime which will hopefully continue to inspire students and lead to further research in these areas. My own contribution is aimed predominantly at students on criminology degrees who are studying specialist courses in media and crime, and related subjects, or who are conducting their own research for dissertations in areas that are covered in this volume.

I hope that *Media and Crime* will also stand up to scrutiny by scholars in media studies, cultural studies, sociology, gender studies and law, whose interests lie at the intersections of crime and media. While the book is intended to explore controversies and debates of historical, contemporary and future relevance in a critically and, at times, theoretically challenging way, it is nonetheless primarily a textbook. It therefore includes a number of pedagogic features (overviews, key terms, summaries, study questions, suggestions for further reading, and a glossary) which, it is hoped, will make it engaging and accessible–as well as being stimulating and intellectually challenging – to students and researchers alike. Key terms are also highlighted at their first appearance in the chapter.

The book is organized into seven chapters. The first two chapters provide the foundation for what follows, and many of the themes and debates introduced here are then picked up and developed in relation to specific subjects and case studies in the remainder of the volume. Chapter 1 brings together theoretical analysis from criminology, sociology, media studies and cultural studies in order to provide a critical understanding of the relationships between these areas of academic study, and to synthesize their contributions to our understanding of the relationship between media and crime. Chapter 2 then discusses the 'manufacture' of crime news, and considers why crime has always been, and remains, so eminently 'newsworthy'. The chapter introduces a set of 'news values' which shape the selection and presentation of stories involving crime, deviance and punishment in contemporary news production. Although the chapter concentrates solely on news, these criteria – which alert us to the subtle biases that inform public perceptions of crime – extend beyond the newsroom, and underpin much of our mediated picture of crime in contemporary Britain.

The remaining chapters of the book illustrate the extent to which crime and justice are constructed according to prevailing cultural assumptions and ideologies by examining a number of different issues that have gained significant media attention. Although divergent in terms of subject, the overriding theme of the book is that contemporary media deal only in binary oppositions, polarizing public responses to criminals and victims of crime, perpetuating psychically held notions of 'self' and 'other' and contributing to the formation of identities based on 'insider' and 'outsider' status. The book thus argues that the media, in all its forms, is one of the primary sites of social inclusion and exclusion, a theme that is explored in Chapter 3 in relation to 'moral panics'. So influential has Stanley Cohen's *Folk Devils and Moral Panics* been (now in its 3rd edition, 1972/2002), that a book about media and crime could not have omitted the concept he made famous. The moral panic thesis is therefore discussed, but in such a way as to move beyond the faithful re-writing of Cohen's famous study of Mods and Rockers that is favoured by many commentators, and problematize moral panics as they have traditionally been conceived.

Chapter 4 develops the previous chapter's examination of moral panics over youth, by considering the extent to which, in today's media landscape, children and young people are viewed both as folk devils, and as the victims of folk devils – notably paedophiles. The chapter discusses the extent to which mediated constructions of children in the 21st century are still seen through the lens of 19th century idealized images of childhood as a time of innocence – a (mis)representation that only serves to fuel public hysteria when children commit very serious offences or are themselves the victims of such crimes.

Chapter 5 is also concerned with constructions of offenders (and, peripherally, victims) which remain curiously embedded in the Victorian age, only here the focus is on deviant women, especially those who murder and commit serious sexual crimes. Using psychoanalytical and feminist theories, this chapter introduces a psychosocial perspective to argue that the media reinforce misogynist images of females who fail to conform to deeply-held cultural beliefs about 'ideal' womanhood. For such women their construction as 'others' renders them subject to hostile censure and their crimes can come to occupy a peculiarly symbolic place in the collective psyche.

Our gendered analysis continues in Chapter 6, which considers the ways in which victims, offenders and the police are constructed on British television. The chapter concludes that, in the main, crime narratives are constructed around female victims (usually either very young or elderly), male offenders (often black, usually strangers), either in the victim's home (increasing the impression of personal violation and female vulnerability) or in public places ('the streets', where we are all at risk), and are investigated and brought to a successful and 'just' conclusion by a caring and efficient police force that can trace its lineage back to everyone's favourite policeman, PC George Dixon. The salience of this archetypal narrative is explored via a detailed study of *Crimewatch UK*, which also gives rise to a discussion about the extent to which media texts such as this amplify fears about crime, especially among certain sections of the audience.

Chapter 7 continues developing the theme of demonized 'others' in its examination of the extent to which surveillance technologies are employed as repressive forms of regulation and social control – but only in relation to certain sections of society. This suggestion is ultimately challenged, but it does raise important questions about social exclusion and 'otherness' which are especially meaningful given the preponderance of surveillance images on television and in popular culture. It also forcefully brings home an issue that is finally debated in the Conclusion to the book, which is that the media's stigmatization – not only of offenders, but also of those who simply look 'different' – is a necessary counterpoint to their sentimentalization and even sanctification of certain victims of the most serious crimes, and their families. Without 'others', 'outsiders', 'strangers' and 'enemies within', the media would not succeed in constructing the moral consensus required to sell newspapers, gain audiences and, most importantly, maintain a world at one with itself.

Acknowledgements

The last couple of years have been an exceptionally busy and exciting period of my career and there are many people I would like to thank – not only for their help, advice and support in the writing of this book, but also for their presence more generally in my work and my life. A special debt of gratitude goes to Chris Greer who has provided scholarly wisdom, invaluable references, warm friendship and sufficient entertainment to restore my sense of humour in moments when I thought I'd never reach the end of this project. He has also read drafts of every chapter, for which I am particularly indebted. Thanks too to colleagues in criminology at the University of Hull for providing such a civilized and stimulating environment in which to work, and to Helen Johnston and Simon Green in particular for talking through some of the ideas contained in this volume. For their helpful comments on draft chapters I'd also like to thank Mike McCahill and Russell Waterman.

Throughout my career, I have been fortunate to work in various capacities with many people who inspired and encouraged me. Among those whose influence is particularly evident in this book are Rinella Cere, Steve Chibnall, Jeff Ferrell, Ros Minsky, John Muncie, Tim O'Sullivan, Mike Presdee, Terry Willits and Maggie Wykes. Thanks also go to the many students who have undertaken my 'Media and Crime' courses over the years at Leicester, De Montfort and Hull Universities, and to my own lecturers who first inspired my interest in the subject at the now sadly-defunct Centre for Mass Communications Research, especially Graham Murdock, Peter Golding, Jim Halloran, Paul Hartman and Peggy Gray. A debt of gratitude long overdue also goes to my former English teacher, Charles Conquest, who instilled in me an enthusiasm for writing and was instrumental in my choice to pursue a higher degree at the CMCR, a decision that I suppose ultimately, if somewhat belatedly, resulted in this book. To Miranda Nunhofer and Caroline Porter at Sage, thank you for your generous support of this and other projects. And, finally, thanks to my partner, David Wright, for managing to get through some draft chapters without entirely losing the will to live.

1

Theorizing Media and Crime

Chapter Contents

OVERVIEW

Chapter 1 provides:

- An overview of the theoretical contours that have shaped the academic fields of criminology and media studies during the modern period.

- A discussion of the 'media effects' debate; its origins, its epistemological value and its influence on contemporary debates about media, crime and violence.

- An analysis of the theories - both individual (behaviourism, positivism) and social (anomie, dominant ideology) - which have dominated debates about the relationship between media and crime within the academy.

- An analysis of the theories (pluralism, left realism) which have emerged from within the academy but which have explicitly addressed the implications of theory for practitioners and policy-makers.

- An exploration of new, emerging theories which can broadly be called 'postmodern', including cultural criminology.

KEY TERMS

anomie	functionalism	paradigm
behaviourism	hegemony	pluralism
crime	hypodermic syringe model	political economy
criminalization	ideology	positivism
critical criminology	Marxism	postmodernism
cultural criminology	mass media	realism (left and right)
'effects' research	mass society	reception analysis
stereotyping	mediated	

It's a cold November night as I pull up on their turf, heading towards my destiny. A sense of dread comes over me as I approach the abandoned warehouse. There's no going back now. I'm in too deep. I have to see this through to the end, no matter what. The silence is eerie – only broken by my rapid heartbeat which shows no signs of slowing. I pause to check the gun, knowing that this is the moment I've been chasing for three years, ever since the day they took everything from me. It's payback time.

NOW!! I kick the door down and burst in. They don't expect me, they're just sitting round a table smoking and drinking. Round after round flies, empty cartridges hit the floor and the screams of the wounded ring out.

Some of them go down, others scatter across the floor. I dive behind some boxes to my right, taking a moment to recompose myself. I see blood spilling from my left shoulder. The adrenaline's kicked in, there's no pain and no time to think about it now. Rage engulfs my mind and I come out running. Bullets fly all around my head but I keep shooting. I'm hit again. My chest fills with lead. Everything's going black and I know it's all over. Those infuriating little words fill the screen once more. GAME OVER!

(Thanks to Michael Jewkes for permission to use this.)

Every day newspaper headlines scream for our attention with stories about crime designed to shock, frighten, titillate and entertain. Politicians of every political party campaign on law and order issues, reducing complex crime problems to easily digestible 'sound bites' for the forthcoming news bulletins on radio and television. Crime is ubiquitous in film genres from the Keystone Cops of the 1920s to the gangster-chic flicks of today. Video and computer games such as *Grand Theft Auto* and *The Getaway* (narrated above) allow us vicariously to indulge in violent criminal acts, while contemporary popular music such as rap and hip hop frequently glorify crime and violence both in the music itself and in the street gang style adopted by the artists. The Internet has fuelled interest in all things crime-related, providing both a forum for people to exchange their views on crime and facilitating new ways to commit crimes such as fraud, theft, trespass and harassment. 'Reality' television shows, in which the police and television companies form unique partnerships to try to catch offenders, are proliferating in number, as are those which employ a 'hidden camera' to record unwitting citizens being robbed, defrauded or otherwise swindled by 'cowboy' traders. Soap operas regularly use stories centred around serious and violent crime in order to boost ratings, and the court trial has become a staple of television drama. Television schedules are crammed with programmes about the police, criminals, prisoners and the courts, and American detective shows from *Murder, She Wrote* to *CSI: Crime Scene Investigation* are syndicated around the world. How do we account for their popularity? Why are we – the audience – so fascinated by crime and deviance? And if the media can so successfully engage the public's fascination, can they equally tap into – and increase – people's fears about crime? Is the media's interest in – some would say, obsession with – crime *harmful*? What exactly *is* the relationship between the mass media and crime?

Students and researchers of both criminology and media studies have sought to understand the connections between media and crime for well over a century. It's interesting to note that, although rarely working together, striking parallels can be found between the efforts of criminologists and media theorists to understand and 'unpack' the relationships between crime, deviance and criminal justice on the one hand, and media and popular culture on the other. Indeed, it is not just at the interface between crime and media that we find similarities between the two disciplines. Parallels between criminology and media studies are evident even when we consider some of the most fundamental questions that have concerned academics in each field, such as 'what *makes* a criminal?' and 'why do the mass media *matter*?' The reason for this is that as criminology and media studies have developed as areas of interest, they have been shaped by a number of different theoretical and empirical perspectives which have, in turn, been heavily influenced by developments in related fields, notably sociology and psychology, but also other disciplines across the arts, sciences and social sciences. Equally, academic research is almost always shaped by external forces and events from the social, political, economic and cultural worlds. Consequently we can look back through history and note how major episodes and developments – for example, Freud's 'discovery' of the unconscious, or the exile of Jewish intellectuals to America at the time of Nazi ascendancy in Germany – have influenced the intellectual contours of both criminology and media studies in ways that, at times, have synthesized the concerns of each. In addition, the interdisciplinary nature of both subject areas and their shared origins in the social sciences, has meant that, since the 1960s when they were introduced as degree studies at universities, a number of key figures working at the nexus between criminology and media/cultural studies have succeeded in bringing their work to readerships in both subject areas – Steve Chibnall, Stanley Cohen, Richard Ericson, Stuart Hall and Jock Young to name just a few.

The purpose of this first chapter is to introduce some of this cross-disciplinary scholarship and to develop a theoretical context for what follows in the remainder of the book. The chapter is not intended to provide a comprehensive overview of all the theoretical perspectives that have shaped media research and criminology in the modern era – an endeavour that could fill at least an entire book on its own. Instead, it will draw from each tradition a few of the major theoretical 'pegs' upon which we can hang our consideration of the relationship between media and crime. These approaches are presented in an analogous fashion with an emphasis on the points of similarity and convergence between the two fields of study (but remember that, in the main, scholars in media studies have worked entirely independently of those in criminology, and vice versa). In addition, the theoretical perspectives discussed in this chapter are presented in the broadly chronological order in which they were developed, although it is important to stress that theories do not simply appear and then, at some later date, disappear, to be replaced by something altogether more sophisticated and enlightening. While we can take an overview of the development of an academic discipline and detect some degree of linearity in so far as we can see fundamental shifts in critical thinking, this linearity does not mean that there were always decisive breaks in opinion as each theoretical phase came and went. In fact, there is a great deal of overlap in the approaches that follow, with many points of correspondence as well as conflict. Nor does it necessarily indicate a coherence of opinion within each theoretical position or, even any real sense of progress in our understanding and knowledge of certain issues. As Tierney puts it:

> There is always a danger of oversimplification when trying to paint in some historical background, of ending up with such broad brushstrokes that the past becomes a caricature of itself, smoothed out and shed of all those irksome details that confound an apparent coherence and elegant simplicity. (1996: 49)

However, notwithstanding the fact that what follows is of necessity selective, condensed and painted with a very broad brush, this chapter seeks to locate the last 40 years of university-taught media studies and criminology within over 100 years of intellectual discourse about the theoretical and empirical connections between media and crime. The theoretical perspectives that will be discussed in this chapter include strain theory and anomie; Marxism, critical criminology and the dominant ideology approach; pluralism and ideological struggle; realism and reception analysis; and postmodernism and cultural criminology.

However, it is with one of the most enduring areas of research that our discussion of theory begins: that of media 'effects'.

Media 'effects'

One of the most persistent debates in academic and lay circles concerning the mass media is the extent to which media can be said to cause anti-social, deviant or criminal behaviour: in other words, to what degree do media images bring about *negative* effects in their viewers? The academic study of this phenomenon – 'effects research' as it has come to be known – developed from two main sources: **mass society** theory and **behaviourism**. Although deriving from different disciplines – sociology and psychology respectively – these two approaches find compatibility in their essentially pessimistic view of society and their belief that human nature is unstable and susceptible to external influences. This section explores the combined impact of mass society theory and psychological behaviourism and outlines how they gave rise to the notion that has become something of a truism: that media images are responsible for eroding moral standards, subverting consensual codes of behaviour and corrupting young minds.

It is often taken as an unassailable fact that society has become more violent since the advent of the modern media industry. The arrival and growth of film, television and, latterly, computer technologies, have served to intensify public anxieties but there are few *crime* waves which are genuinely new phenomena, despite the media's efforts to present them as such. For many observers, it is a matter of 'common sense' that society has become increasingly characterized by crime – especially violent crime – since the advent of film and television, resulting in a persistent mythology that the two phenomena – media and violent crime – are 'naturally' linked. Yet as Pearson (1983) illustrates, the history of respectable fears goes back several hundred years, and public outrage at perceived crime waves has become more intensely focused with the introduction of each new media innovation. From theatrical productions in the 18th century, the birth of commercial cinema and the emergence of cheap, sensationalistic publications known as 'Penny Dreadfuls' at the end of the 19th century, to jazz and 'pulp fiction' in the early 20th century, popular fears about the influence of visual images on vulnerable minds have been well rehearsed in this country and elsewhere. Anxieties were frequently crystallised in the notion of 'the crowd' and it became a popular 19th-century myth that when people mass together they are suggestible to outside influences and become irrational, even animalistic (Murdock, 1997; Blackman and Walkerdine, 2001). The most influential exponent of this view was Gustave Le Bon, a French royalist writing at the time of the revolution, who believed that when a man forms part of a crowd he 'descends several rungs in the ladder of civilisation' (Le Bon, 1895/1960: 32). Le Bon himself alluded to the persuasive powers of the media of the day when he said that:

> Crowds being only capable of thinking in images are only to be impressed by images. It is only images that attract them and become motives for action ... Nothing has a greater effect on the imagination of crowds than theatrical representations ... Sometimes the sentiments suggested by the images are so strong that they tend, like habitual suggestions, to transform themselves into acts. (1895/1960: 68)

This statement was one of the first public airings of a view that rapidly gained credibility with the significant advancements in photography, cinema and the popular press which occurred at the turn of the 20th century. Put simply, it became increasingly common for writers and thinkers to mourn the passing of a literate culture, which was believed to require a degree of critical thinking, and bemoan its replacement, a visual popular culture which was believed to plug directly into the mind without need for rational thought or interpretation (Murdock, 1997).

Mass society theory

Fears about 'the crowd' precipitated mass society theory, which developed in the latter years of the 19th century and early 20th century, becoming firmly established as a sociological theory after the Second World War. Mass society theory usually carries negative connotations, referring to the masses or the 'common people' who are characterized by their lack of individuality, their alienation from the moral and ethical values to be gained from work and religion, their political apathy, and their taste for 'low' culture. In most versions of the theory, individuals are seen as uneducated, ignorant, potentially unruly and prone to violence (McQuail, 2000). The late 19th and early 20th centuries marked a period of tremendous turbulence and uncertainty, and mass society theorists held that social upheavals associated with industrialization, urbanization and the Great War had made people feel increasingly vulnerable. Within this atomized society, two important strands of thought can be detected. First, it was believed that as communities fragmented and traditional social ties were dismantled, society became a mass of isolated individuals cut adrift from kinship and organic ties and lacking moral cohesion. An increase in crime and anti-social behaviour seemed inevitable, and as mass society took hold – in all its complex, over-bureaucratized incomprehensibility – citizens turned away from the authorities who were seen as remote, indifferent and incompetent. Instead they sought solutions to crime at a personal, community-orientated, 'micro' level, which included vigilantism, personal security devices and, in some countries, guns. The second significant development that emerged from conceptualizations of mass society was that the media were seen as both an aid to people's psychic survival under difficult circumstances (McQuail, 2000) and as a powerful force for controlling people's thoughts and diverting them from political action.

Mass society theory has been described as more a diagnosis of the sickness of the times than a fully coherent social theory (McQuail, 2000); a fact borne out by the paradox that it views society as both 'atomized' and centrally controlled, and individuals as similar and undifferentiated, yet isolated and lacking social cohesion. However, the importance of mass society theory in the current context is that it gave rise to a number of theoretical and empirical models claiming that the mass media can be used subversively as a powerful means of manipulating vulnerable minds.

Behaviourism and positivism

In addition to mass society theory, models of media effects have been strongly influenced by a second strand of research – behaviourism – an empiricist approach to psychology pioneered by J.B. Watson in the first decade of the 20th century. Deriving from a philosophy known as *positivism*, which emerged from the natural sciences and regards the world as fixed and quantifiable, behaviourism represented a major challenge to the more dominant perspective of *psychoanalysis*. Shifting the research focus away from the realm of the mind with its emphasis on introspection and individual interpretation, behavioural psychologists argued that an individual's identity was shaped by their responses to the external environment which formed stable and recognizable patterns of behaviour that could be publicly observed. In addition to emulating the scientific examination of relations between organisms in the natural world, Watson was inspired by Ivan Pavlov, who was famously conducting experiments with dogs, producing 'conditioned responses' (salivating) to external stimuli (a bell ringing). The impact of these developments led to a belief that the complex structures and systems that make up human behaviour could be observed and measured in a generaliz-able manner so that predictions of future behaviour could be made. In addition to stimulus-response experiments in psychology and the natural sciences, developments were occurring elsewhere which took a similar view of human behaviour. For example, the modern education system was being established with learning being seen as something to be tested and examined. The consumerist society was also just beginning to take hold amid rising levels of affluence, and advertisers were to become regarded as the 'hidden persuaders' who could influence people to purchase consumer goods almost against their better judgement.

Meanwhile, in criminology, the search for objective knowledge through the positive application of science was also having a significant impact. The endeav-our to observe and measure the relationship between 'cause and effect' led to a belief that criminality is not a matter of free will, but is caused by a biological, psychological or social disposition over which the offender has little or no con-trol. Through gaining knowledge about how behaviour is determined by such conditions – be they genetic deficiencies or disadvantages associated with their social environments – it was believed that problems such as crime and deviance could be examined and treated. The most famous name in positivist criminology is Cesare Lombroso, who published *The Criminal Man* (1876) and *The Female Offender* (Lombroso and Ferrero, 1895), outlining his commitment to the notion that the causes of crime are to be found in individual biology. An Italian physi-cian whose ideas were much influenced by Darwin's theory of evolution, Lombroso studied the bodies of executed criminals and came to the conclusion that law-breakers were physically different to non-offenders. He claimed that criminals were atavistic throwbacks to an earlier stage of biological development and could be identified by physical abnormalities such as prominent jaws, strong canine teeth, sloping foreheads, unusual ear size and so on. Although in more recent years positivist forms of criminology have become theoretically more sophisticated (see, for example, the work of Wilson and Herrnstein, 1985), Lombroso's rather crude approach to biological criminology is still evident today, particularly in popular media discourses about women and children who commit serious and violent crime (see Chapters 4 and 5).

While criminologists in the early decades of the 20th century were concern-ing themselves with isolating the variables most likely to be found in criminals as distinct from non-criminals, media researchers were also developing new theories based on positivist assumptions and behaviourist methods. The notion that all human action is modelled on the condition reflex, so that one's action is precipitated by responses to stimuli in one's environment rather than being a matter of individual agency, made the new media of mass communications an obvious candidate for concern. In the context of research into media effects, this approach most often resulted in experiments being carried out under laboratory conditions to try to establish a direct causal link between media images of a violent or potentially harmful nature and resultant changes in actual behaviour, notably an inclination among the research participants to demonstrate markedly agitated or aggressive tendencies.

One of the most famous series of experiments was that conducted by Albert Bandura and colleagues at Stanford University, California in the 1950s and 1960s, in which children were shown a film or cartoon depicting some kind of violent act and were then given 'Bobo' dolls to play with (these were large inflatable dolls with weighted bases to ensure that they wobble but do not stay down when struck). Their behaviour towards the dolls was used as a measure of the programme's effect, and when the children were observed behaving aggressively (compared to a control group who did not watch the violent content) it was taken as evidence that a direct relationship existed between 'screen violence' and juvenile aggression. Although these studies were undoubtedly influential and, indeed, have attained a certain notoriety, they are hugely problematic. Despite the 'scientific' status they claim, behaviourist methods have been rejected by most contemporary media scholars on the grounds of their great many flaws and inconsistencies. Bandura and his colleagues have been widely discredited for, among other things: failing to replicate a 'real life' media environment; reducing complex patterns of human behaviour to a single factor among a wide network of mediating influences and therefore treating children as unsophisticated 'lab rats'; being able to measure only immediate responses to media content and having nothing to say about the long-term, cumulative effects of exposure to violent material; using dolls that were designed to frustrate; praising or rewarding children when they behaved as 'expected'; and overlooking the fact that children who had not been shown any film stimulus were nevertheless found to behave aggressively towards the Bobo doll if left with it – and especially if they felt it was expected of them by the experimenter. (For a more extensive critical review of these experiments and later research inspired by Bandura, see Gauntlett, 1995: 17–23.)

This first major phase of media research is sometimes called *functionalism* because its advocates were interested in accounting for the functions of the mass media, or what the media *do* to people. Effects research is also sometimes collectively termed the **hypodermic syringe model** because the relationship between media and audiences is conceived as a mechanistic and unsophisticated process, by which the media 'inject' values, ideas and information directly into the passive receiver, producing direct and unmediated 'effects' which, in turn, have a negative influence on thoughts and actions. Anxieties about media effects have traditionally taken one of three forms. The first is a moral or religious anxiety that exposure to the popular media encourages lewd behaviour and corrupts established norms of decency and moral certitude. A second anxiety, from the intellectual right, is that the mass media undermine the civilizing influence of high culture (great literature, art and so on) and debase tastes. A third concern, which has traditionally been associated with the intellectual left, was that the mass media represent the ruling élite, and manipulate mass consciousness in their interests. This view was given a particular impetus by the emergence of fascist and totalitarian governments across Europe in the 1920s and 1930s, which used propaganda to great effect in winning the hearts and minds of the people. The belief that the new media of mass communications were among the most powerful weapons of these political regimes was given academic attention by members of the Frankfurt School – a group of predominantly Jewish scholars who themselves fled Hitler's Germany for America.

A famous example from America that appears to support mass society theory's belief in an omnipresent and potentially harmful media and behaviourism's assumptions about the observable reactions of a susceptible audience, concerns the radio transmission of H.G. Wells's *War of the Worlds* on Halloween Night in October 1938. The broadcast was a fictitious drama concerning the invasion of aliens from Mars, but many believed they were listening to a *real* report of a Martian attack. While the broadcast was on air, panic broke out. People all over the US prayed, cried, fled their homes and telephoned loved ones to say emotional farewells (Cantril, 1940, in O'Sullivan and Jewkes, 1997). One in six listeners were said to have been very frightened by the broadcast, a fear that was exacerbated by the gravitas of the narrator, Orson Wells, and by the cast of 'experts' giving orders for evacuation and attack. As one listener said: 'I believed the broadcast as soon as I heard the professor from Princeton and the officials in Washington' (1997: 9). The example of the *War of the Worlds* broadcast provides a powerfully resonant metaphor for the belief that the modern media are capable of exerting harmful influences, of triggering mass outbreaks of negative social consequence and of causing damaging psychological effects. However, to characterize the episode as 'proof' of the hypodermic syringe effect of the media would be very misleading. The relationship between stimulus and response was not simple or direct because, quite simply, the panic experienced by some listeners was not without context. It was the time of the Depression, and American citizens were experiencing a prolonged period of economic unrest and widespread unemployment and were looking to their leaders for reassurance and direction. War was breaking out in Europe and many believed that an attack by a foreign power was imminent (1997). It is of little surprise, then, that the realistic quality of the broadcast – played out as an extended news report in which the radio announcer appeared to be actually witnessing terrible events unfolding before him – powerfully tapped into the feelings of insecurity, change and loss being experienced by many American people, to produce a panic of this magnitude.

The legacy of 'effects' research

Scholars in the UK have, for many years, strongly resisted attempts to assert a direct, causal link between media images and deviant behaviour. The idea of isolating television, film or any other medium as a variable and ignoring all the other factors that might influence a person's behaviour, is considered too crude and reductive an idea to be of any epistemological value. Much effects research cannot adequately address the subtleties of media meanings, the polysemy of media *texts* (that is, they are open to multiple interpretations), the unique characteristics and identity of the audience member, or the social and cultural context within which the encounter between media text and audience member occurs. It mistakenly assumes that we all have the same ideas about what constitutes 'aggression', 'violence' and 'deviance', and that those who are susceptible to harmful portrayals can be affected by a 'one-off' media incident, regardless of the wider context of a lifetime of meaning-making (Boyd-Barrett, 2002). It also ignores the possibility that influence travels the opposite way; that is, that the characteristics, interests and concerns of the audience may determine what media producers produce.

But despite the obvious flaws in effects research, behaviourist assumptions about the power of the media to influence criminal and anti-social behaviour persist, especially – and somewhat ironically – in discussions within the popular media, which are frequently intended to bring pressure on governments and other authorities to tighten up controls on other elements of the media. For example, it is surprising to witness how much contemporary popular discourse about the power of the media rests on assumptions that are very close to those underpinning the hypodermic syringe model. Such assumptions draw on distinctly Lombrosian ideas about the kinds of individuals most likely to be affected by harmful media content (see below). In addition, they dovetail neatly with mass society theorists' fears that institutions such as the family and religion are losing their power to shape young minds, and that socialization happens instead via external forces such as the *mass media*. Whether assessing the effects of advertising, measuring the usefulness of political campaigns in predicting voting behaviour, deciding film and video classifications or introducing software to aid parents in controlling their children's exposure to certain forms of Internet content, much policy in these areas is underpinned by media-centric, message-specific, micro-orientated, positivist, authoritarian, short-term assumptions of human behaviour.

The ongoing political debate about censorship and control of the media tends to periodically reach an apotheosis when serious, high-profile crimes occur, especially those perpetrated by children or young people. For example, following the tragic death of two-year-old James Bulger at the hands of two older boys in February 1993, there was a great deal of speculation in the popular press that the murderers had watched and imitated *Child's Play 3*, a mildly violent 'video nasty' about a psychopathic doll. Despite there being no evidence that the boys ever saw the film, and consistent denials from the police that there was a connection, the insidious features of *Child's Play 3* were soon ingrained in the public consciousness. Television presenter Anne Diamond summed up the feelings of the 'common-sense brigade' in her tabloid newspaper column:

> Our gut tells us they *must* have seen the evil doll Chucky. They *must* have loved the film. And they *must* have seen it over and over again, because some of the things they did are almost exact copies of the screenplay ... We all know that violence begets violence.

> (*Mirror*, 1 December 1993, quoted in Petley, 1997: 188)

This appeal to common sense ('we all know ...') is a perennial feature of what has come to be known as the 'copycat' theory of crime and is seen by its adherents as natural and unassailable. However, it is instructive here to remember Gramsci's definition of the term 'common sense': 'a reservoir of historically discontinuous and disjointed ideas that functions as the philosophy of nonphilosophers,' a folklore whose fundamental distinction is its 'fragmentary, incoherent and inconsequential character' (Gramsci, 1971: 419). Others, meanwhile, have demonstrated how the unquestioned truths which we accept as common sense are, in fact, culturally derived mythologies specific not only to individual cultures but also to particular points in time (see, for example, Barthes, 1973; Foucault, 1977; Geertz, 1983).

The link between screen violence and real-life violence was given a gloss of academic respectability when, in the aftermath of the Bulger case, Professor Elizabeth Newson, head of the Child Development Unit at Nottingham University, produced a report that was endorsed by 25 psychologists, paediatricians and other academics. Despite extensive and sustained publicity in the media, it turned out that Newson's report was just nine pages long, contained no original research, and concluded – as these things inevitably do – that more research was needed (McQueen, 1998). But despite the highly-questionable evidence for the potentially harmful effects of media content, the proposition that media portrayals of crime and violence desensitize the viewer to 'real' pain and suffering, and may excite or arouse some people to commit similar acts, persists in the popular imagination where it is rarely applied universally, but tends to be tinged with a distinct class-edged bias. Echoes of both mass society theory and criminological positivism can be detected in most discourses about crime and the media where there lingers a notion of an inferior class hampered by some degree of mental deficiency that precludes them from being able to distinguish between media images and real life. For example, middle-class columnists like Anne Diamond do not consider their own children to be at risk from television and video content (computer technologies are somewhat different because of their interactive nature), but rather it is the offspring of the already threatening 'under-class' who pose the greatest threat to society. This view, appealing to common-sense notions of 'intelligent people' versus the dark shapeless mass that forms the residue of society, also has a gendered bias. The contemporary culture of blame is frequently directed at the 'monstrous offspring' of 'bad mothers', a construc-tion that combines two contemporary *folk devils* and taps into cultural fears of the 'other', which will be explored further in Chapters 4 and 5. Consequently, when particularly horrific crimes come to light, the knee-jerk reaction of a society unwilling to concede that depravity and cruelty reside within its midst, is frequently to turn to the familiar scapegoat of the mass media to attribute blame.

Another version of this approach, which also has its roots in mass society the-ory, concerns a broader preoccupation with the globalization of cultural forms and products and, in particular, the American origin of much popular global culture. Television, cinema, video and latterly the Internet, have come in for particular criticism by those who view anything American in origin as intrinsically cheap, trashy and alien to British culture and identity. Fears dating back more than a cen-tury concerning the fragmentation of traditional hierarchies of class and taste, together with the secularization and democratization of society, have become crys-tallised in the view that the popular visual media are slowly corrupting the 'British' way of life by importing values that are altogether more vulgar and trashy from the other side of the Atlantic. The concerns of the Frankfurt School theorists Adorno and Horkheimer about the debasement of 'high' culture by 'low' popular cultural forms found synthesis in the UK with élitist expressions of concern about the *youth* culture surrounding American-style 'milk bars' in post-War Britain. Since that time, a variety of moral panics have reached these shores only months after their appearance in America, and a wide range of phenomena – rock and roll music, mugging, dangerous dogs, car-jacking, satanic child abuse, gun crime and gang warfare – have been characterized by our media as essentially 'un-British'; an unwelcome and alien crime-wave from the US (see Chapter 3).

Strain theory and anomie

By the 1960s academic scholars were turning their backs on positivist, behav-iourist research. Media researchers viewed behaviourism as attributing too much power to the media and underestimating the importance of the social contexts of media consumption, the social structures which mediate the relationship between the state and the individual, and the sophistication and diversity of the audience. Similarly, positivist approaches to explaining crime in terms of its individual, biological roots were giving way to more sociologically informed approaches which originated in the work of the Chicago School in the 1920s and 1930s. The overriding concern of Chicago School sociology, and those who were influenced by it, was to understand the role of social environment and social interaction on deviant and criminal behaviour. In other words, it was recognized that where people grow up and who they associate with is closely linked to their likelihood of involvement in crime and anti-social behaviour.

Limitations of space preclude a full discussion of sociological approaches to crime here, but one important early theory that has a bearing on the present discussion of the relationship between media and crime is Robert Merton's (1938) strain theory, or *'anomie'*. Merton borrowed the term 'anomie' (meaning 'normlessness') from Durkheim and followed the Chicago School in rejecting individualistic explanations of crime and looking instead to social and structural factors. Like mass society theory, strain theory takes as its starting point a decline of community and social order and its replacement by alienation and disorder. Whole sections of society are cut adrift, unable to conform to the norms that traditionally bind communities together. Yet, within this state of normlessness, society as a whole remains more or less intact. As Durkheim (1893/1933) notes, social cohesion persists despite periodic economic crises (such as rapid increases in prosperity for some sections of society and the concomitant impoverishment of others in relative terms). Social cohesion may be partly accounted for by the pursuit of common objectives, and anomie draws attention to the goals that people are encouraged to aspire to, such as a comfortable level of wealth or status. The majority of people will conform to the socially acceptable means of attaining those goals; for example, hard work and a commitment to traditional, consensual values. Through socialization, most come to accept both the goals *and* the legitimate means of achieving them; a process summed up in the notion of the 'American Dream'. But an overemphasis on either the cultural goals or the institutionalized means of attaining them can lead to social strains, and anomie usually describes a situation where a society places strong emphasis on a particular goal, but far less emphasis on the appropriate means of achieving that goal. It is this imbalance that can lead some individuals who Merton terms 'innovators' to pursue nonconformist or illegal paths to achieve the culturally sanctioned goals of success and wealth.

Merton's theory – which paved the way for much of the later research on delinquent subcultures (Cohen, 1955; Cloward and Ohlin, 1960) as well as the contemporary notion of relative deprivation (Lea and Young, 1984; 1993; Young, 1992) – proved attractive in so far as it appeared to offer a way of reducing crime by improving the legitimate life chances of those who otherwise might pursue culturally-approved goals by illegitimate means. However, one of the key factors involved in the internalization of cultural goals is the mass media which, it might be argued, instil in people needs and desires that may not be gratifiable by means other than criminal. In particular, it has been suggested that advertising exploits anomie by offering a false sense of community to those isolated and fragmented from society (Osborne, 2002). It is they who, in an era of rampant media-fuelled global consumerism, are arguably most likely to pursue society's rewards by innovative means. Some do so in desperation: in his classic 1972 study of the clashes between mods and rockers in the 1960s, Stanley Cohen claims that the participants were driven in part by their anguished feelings of alienation from the mass consumer culture directed at the new wave of 'teenagers'. It has also been suggested that much youth crime is committed out of a sense of 'calculating hedonism'; the pursuit of excitement and an attempt to assert control in the face of the banality and boredom of everyday life (a theory that chimes with the new *cultural criminology*, see below; cf. Fenwick and Hayward, 2000; cf. Morrison, 1995).

For others, the anomic drive might be less concerned with feelings of desperation and more to do with conspicuous consumption and the desire for peer approval. In her study of street robbery, Elizabeth Burney notes that the outstanding characteristic of young street offenders is their 'avid adherence to a group "style", which dictates a very expensive level of brand-name dressing, financed by crime' (1990: 63). Elsewhere, I have noted a similar tendency among young men serving long prison sentences who attain anomic gratification by keeping up to date with the latest, and most expensive, designs in footwear (Jewkes, 2002). A further application of the theory is found in the debate about the *effects* of viewing violence, reviewed earlier in this chapter, where it is frequently suggested that it is vulnerable, marginalized members of society who are most susceptible to harmful consequences instigated by glamorized portrayals of violence by the mass media (2002). Coleman and Norris (2000) even suggest that strain theory may help to explain serial killing, a phenomenon that is usually associated with modern America. Using Leyton's (1989) study of multiple murderers, they argue that the growth of the American economy since the 1960s has resulted in a commensurate rise in the numbers of serial killings. Inevitably, some sections of the population will be excluded from the general rise in living standards which, in a culture that glorifies violence, may lead some disaffected individuals to a (usually misdirected) desire for revenge.

Anomie has fallen in and out of favour with remarkable fluidity over the years, but from its nadir in the 1970s when Rock and McIntosh referred to the 'exhaustion of the anomie tradition' (in Downes and Rock, 1988: 110) it has recently enjoyed something of a revival thanks to two diverse phenomena. The first is the emergence of interest, within both criminology and cultural studies, in transgressive forms of excitement, ranging from extreme sports to violent crime, as a means of combating the routinized alienation that besets contemporary life (activities that are central to the approach known as 'cultural criminology'; see below). The second is the growth of electronic communications, such as the Internet, which seem to offer a solution to the problems of dislocation by fostering a sense of community across time and space. In the world of virtual reality, anomie is both 'a condition and a pleasure' (Osborne, 2002: 29).

Marxism, critical criminology and the 'dominant ideology' approach

It is clear from the discussion so far that the mid-20th century saw a change in focus from the individual to society. This *paradigm* shift led to the predominance of Marxist-inspired models of media power and, in particular, to the writings of Karl Marx (1818–83) himself and Antonio Gramsci (1891–1937). Their theories of social structure led to the development of an approach known as the 'dominant ideology' or 'media-as-hegemony' model, which was taken up enthusiastically by both criminologists and media researchers in the 1960s and dominated academic discussions of media power for over 20 years.

Marxism proposes that the media – like all other capitalist institutions – are owned by the ruling bourgeois élite and operate in the interests of that class, denying access to oppositional or alternative views. Although the media were far from being the mass phenomena in Marx's lifetime that they are today, their position as a key capitalist industry, and their power to widely disseminate messages which affirm the validity and legitimacy of a stratified society, made his theories seem very relevant at a later time when the mass media was going through a combined process of expansion, deregulation and concentration of ownership and control. Gramsci developed Marx's theories to incorporate the concept of *hegemony*, which has played a central role in theorizing about the media's portrayal of crime, deviance, and law and order. In brief, hegemony refers to the process by which the ruling classes win approval for their actions by consent rather than by coercion. This is largely achieved through social and cultural institutions such as the law, the family, the education system and the mass media. All such institutions reproduce everyday representations, meanings and activities in such a way as to render the class interests of those in power into an apparently natural, inevitable and hence unarguable general interest with a claim on everybody. In short, media representations may support or (more rarely) challenge the dominant definitions of a situation, and they can extend, legitimize, celebrate or criticize the prevailing discourses at any given time. The media thus play a crucial role in the winning of consent for a social system, its values and its dominant interests, or in the rejection of them. This is an important refinement of Marx's original formulation, for Gramsci dispensed with the idea that people passively take on the ideas *in toto* of the ruling élite (a position usually termed 'false consciousness'), and instead established a model of power in which different cultural elements are subtly articulated together to appeal to the widest possible spectrum of opinion.

The writings of Marx and Gramsci inform the theoretical organization of much of the most important and influential work which emerged within the social sciences in the 1970s and 1980s. For example, although Marx himself had little to say about crime, the rediscovery of his theories of social structure gave impetus to a new 'radical' criminology that sought to expose the significance of structural inequalities upon crime and, crucially, upon **criminalization**. Also drawing heavily on labelling theory, which posits that crime and deviance are not the product of either a 'sick individual' or a 'sick society' but that 'deviant behaviour is behaviour that people so label' (Becker, 1963: 8), a new generation of radical criminologists such as Taylor, Walton and Young (who, in 1973, published the hugely influential *The New Criminology*) took this proposition and gave it a Marxist edge, arguing that the power to label people as deviants or criminals and prosecute and punish them accordingly was a function of the state. In other words, acts are defined as criminal because it is in the interests of the ruling class to define them as such, and while the powerful will violate laws with impunity, working-class crimes will be punished.

Inspired by the 'new criminology', a number of further 'radical' studies emerged which drew attention to the criminogenic function of the state and the role of the media in orchestrating public panics about crime and deflecting concerns away from the social problems that emanate from capitalism. This work became known as **critical criminology** and of particular importance is Stuart Hall et al.'s *Policing the Crisis: Mugging, the State and Law and Order* (1978), which remains one of the most important texts on the **ideological** role of the media in defining and reporting crime and deviance. In media research, the work of the Glasgow University Media Group (GUMG) is also of note. The GUMG produced a series of studies based on empirical and semiotic analysis (collectively known as the *Bad News* books and now collected in one edition; see Philo, 1995) looking at bias in television news coverage of industrial conflicts, political disputes and acts of war. The central finding in these studies is that television news represses the diversity of opinions in any given situation, reproduces a dominant ideology (based on, for example, middle-class, anti-dissent and pro-family views) and silences contradictory voices. Another important perspective that influenced studies of media power throughout the 1980s and beyond was the **political economy** approach, which claims that the undisputed fact of increasing concentration of media ownership in recent years makes Marx's analysis all the more relevant to contemporary debates about the power of the media

(McQueen, 1998). Political economy focuses on relations between media and other economic and political institutions and argues that, since the mass media are largely privately owned, the drive for profit will shape their output and political position. Concentration of ownership, it is suggested, leads to a decline in the material available (albeit that there are more channels in which to communicate), a preoccupation with ratings at the expense of quality and choice, and a preference for previously successful formulae over innovation and risk-taking. The net result of these processes is that the material offered is reduced to the commercially viable, popular, easily understood and largely unchallenging (Golding and Murdock, 2000). Some writers go as far as to suggest that the 'dumbing down' of culture is part of a wider manipulative strategy on the part of the military-industrial complex to prevent people from engaging in serious political thought or activity. For example, Noam Chomsky's 'propaganda-model' demonstrates how certain stories are underrepresented in the media because of powerful military-industrial interests. In a content analysis of the *New York Times* he shows how atrocities committed by Indonesia in East Timor received a fraction of the coverage devoted to the Khmer Rouge killings in Cambodia. Chomsky claims that the reason for this imbalanced coverage is that the weaponry used to slaughter the people of East Timor was supplied by America, Britain and Holland (Herman and Chomsky, 1992; see also Pilger, 1999).

Although not without their critics, these bodies of work were among the first to systematically and rigorously interrogate the role of the mass media in shaping our understanding, not only of crime and deviance, but also of the processes of criminalization. The common theme in all these studies is that information flows from the top down, with the media representing the views of political leaders, military leaders, police chiefs, judges, prominent intellectuals, advertisers and big business, newspaper owners and vocal opinion leaders. At the same time, they reduce the viewer, reader or listener to the role of passive receiver, overshadowing his or her opinions, concerns and beliefs. Thus, a hierarchy of credibility is established in which the opinions and definitions of powerful members of society are privileged, while the 'ordinary' viewer or reader is prevented by lack of comparative material from engaging in critical or comparative thinking (Ericson et al., 1987).

This structured relationship between the media and its 'powerful' sources has important consequences for the representation of crime, criminals and criminal justice, particularly with respect to those whose lifestyle or behaviour deviates from the norms established by a white, male, heterosexual, educationally privileged élite. For example, in the aforementioned *Policing the Crisis*, Hall and his colleagues demonstrate how hegemony is achieved through the media. In brief, the book details how the press significantly over-reacted to the perceived threat of violent crime in the early 1970s and created a moral panic about 'mugging', but only *after* there had been an intensification of police mobilization against black offenders. The net result of these forces – public fear and hostility fuelled by sensationalized media reporting and heavy-handed treatment of black people by the police – combined to produce a situation where more black people were arrested and put before the courts, which in turn set the spiral for continuing media attention. But as Hall et al. explain, this episode can be set against a backdrop of economic and structural crisis in 1970s' Britain, whereby the disintegration of traditional, regulated forms of life led to a displaced reaction onto black and Asian immigrants and their descendants. The central thesis of the book is that by the 1970s, the consent that might previously have been won by the ruling classes was being severely undermined, and the state was struggling to retain power. The birth of the 'law and order' society, evidenced in the development of a pre-emptive escalation of social control directed at a minority population, served to divert public attention from the looming economic and structural crisis, crystallize public fears in the figure of the black mugger, create a coherent popular discourse that sanctioned tougher penal measures, and ultimately justify the drift towards ideological repression. All these developments were disclosed, supported and made acceptable by a media that had become one of the most important instruments in maintaining hegemonic power (Hall et al., 1978).

Critics of the hegemonic approach suggest that it overstates the *intent* of powerful institutions to deceive the public. They argue that it is not the case that media industries maintain a policy of deliberately ignoring or marginalizing significant portions of their audience. The tendency of professional communicators to perpetuate the taken-for-granted assumptions of consensus politics is not something that is necessarily overt, deliberate or even conscious, and certainly can rarely be described with any certainty as conspiracy. Rather, it may be attributed to an underlying frame of mind that characterizes news organizations (Halloran, 1970). In other words, journalists are like those who work within any organization or institution in that they are gradually socialized into the ways and ethos of that environment and come to recognize the appropriate ways of responding to the subtle pressures which are always there but rarely become overtly apparent. In a news room these 'ways of responding' range from the individual reporter's intuitive 'hunch' through perceptions about what constitutes a 'good story' and 'giving the public what it wants' to more structured ideological biases, which predispose the media to focus on certain events and turn them into 'news' (Cohen, 1972/2002; see also Chapter 2). But hegemonists maintain that alternative definitions of any given situation may not get aired simply because there is no longer the spread of sources that there once was. The ownership and control of the mass media is concentrated in the hands of fewer and fewer individuals, and there is a reliance among editors on a relatively limited pool of expert and readily available sources. These official sources and accredited 'experts', together with the journalists themselves, thus become the 'primary definers' of much news and information; a kind of deviance-defining élite

(Ericson et al., 1987). Consequently, according to proponents of the 'dominant ideology' approach, there is an increasing risk that culturally dominant groups impose patterns of belief and behaviour which conflict with those of ethnic, cultural and religious minorities. Feminists have argued that gender inequalities in society are also reproduced ideologically by a patriarchal media industry; an issue that will be examined further in Chapter 5.

The legacy of the Marxist dominant ideology approach

As we have seen, the dominant ideology approach has successfully highlighted the extent to which those in power manipulate the media agenda to harness support for policies that criminalize those with least power in society. But Marxist inspired criminologies have also been useful in raising awareness of the crimes of the powerful themselves; in other words, the offences committed by corporations, business people, governments and states. Critical criminologists whose intellectual roots lie in Marxism, such as Steven Box, have noted that the media rarely covers 'white collar' or 'corporate' crime unless it has a 'big bang' element and contains several features considered conventionally newsworthy (see Chapter 2). This reluctance to portray corporate wrongs contrasts with the manufacturing of 'street' crime waves and reflects a pervasive bias in the labelling of criminals. Although this inclination extends beyond the media and arguably constitutes a 'collective ignorance' towards corporate crime on the part of all social institutions (Box, 1983: 31), there is little doubt that the media are among the most guilty in perpetuating very narrow definitions of crime. In fact, the media might be said to be doubly culpable: first for portraying affluence as the ultimate (anomic) goal and glamorizing images of offending and, second, for pandering to public tastes for drama and immediacy over complexity. As Box says, 'the public understands more easily what it means for an old lady to have £5 snatched from her purse than to grasp the financial significance of corporate crime' (1983: 31).

As Chapter 2 will demonstrate, crime is portrayed by the media as a matter of individual pathology which mitigates against the investigation and reporting of wrongdoings in a large organization. On the whole, corporate crimes are not the stuff of catchy headlines and tend to be reported, if at all, in such a way as to reinforce impressions of their exceptional nature and distinction from 'ordinary crime' (Slapper and Tombs, 1999; Croall, 2001; Hughes and Langan, 2001). The underdeveloped vocabulary of corporate crime compounds the difficulty of regarding it as an offence. Words such as 'accident' and 'disaster' appear in contexts where 'crime' and 'negligence' might be more accurate. Where they succeed in making the news agenda, corporate crimes are frequently treated not as offences, but as 'scandals' or 'abuses of power', terminology which implies 'sexy upper-world intrigue' (Punch, 1996). Alternatively, they may be presented as 'acts of God', thus reinforcing the notion that modern life is beset by risks and that actions that result in casualties and/or fatalities are random or preordained, depending on your religious convictions. The choice of this kind of language not only serves the purposes of a commercial media steeped in circulation and ratings wars, but it also suits corporations themselves who are able to secure powerful political allies and carefully control and manage information about damning incidents (Herman and Chomsky, 1992). So, while a few journalists uphold the investigative tradition and are prepared to act as whistleblowers when they uncover corporate offences, the vast majority of media institutions – according to radical crime and media theorists – either ignore the crimes of the powerful or misrepresent them. As a consequence, news reporting remains coupled to state definitions of crime and criminal law.

Pluralism, competition and ideological struggle

The theoretical models outlined so far share a belief in the omnipresence of the media and hold assumptions about a passive and stratified audience, with those at the bottom of the socio-economic strata being the most vulnerable to media influences, whether they be 'effects' caused by media content or, conversely, discrimination at the hands of a powerful élite that uses the mass media as its mouthpiece. By contrast, the 'competitive' or 'pluralist' paradigm that emerged during the 1980s and 1990s tends to be a more positive reading of the mass media as an embodiment of intellectual freedom and diversity offered to a knowledgeable and sceptical audience. Given this favourable characterization of the media industry, it is unsurprising that, while the 'dominant ideology' perspective has been influential within the academy, *pluralism* has been championed by practitioners and policy-makers (Greer, 2003a).

Pluralists argue that the processes of deregulation and privatization which have gone on over the last two decades in the media industries (especially, although by no means exclusively, in North America and Western Europe) have succeeded in removing the media from state regulation and censorship, and encouraging open competition between media institutions. Advocates of these processes have heralded a new age of freedom in which the greatly increased number of new television and radio channels, magazine titles and computer-based services have offered a previously unimaginable extension of public choice in a media market of plurality and openness. The result of this has been that, in addition to the primary definers already mentioned – politicians, police chiefs and so on – there also exists the possibility of 'counter definers'; people with views and ideas which conflict with those of official commentators, and which are given voice by the media. Consequently it is suggested, while we can still identify a dominant economic class in an abstract, materialistic sense, it rarely acts as a coherent political force and is consistently challenged by individuals and organizations which campaign for policy changes in areas such as criminal justice. Furthermore, traditional ideological inequalities formed along lines of class, gender and race no longer inhabit the static positions suggested by those who favour the dominant ideology approach outlined previously. Thanks to mass education, social mobility and the rise of the 'celebrity culture', the contemporary 'ruling class' is more culturally diverse than at any time previously, and the modern media has been at the forefront of the erosion of traditional élitist values (McNair, 1998).

The expansion and proliferation of media channels has certainly made more accessible the views and ideas of a greater diversity of people. However, the pluralist perspective could be said to be limited by its sheer idealism. Although the media may be regarded as a potential site of ideological struggle, proponents of the competitive, pluralist paradigm believe that *all* minority interests can be served by the plurality of channels of communication available. While theoretically true, this is a somewhat unrealistic vision because it does not take account of the many vested interests in media ownership and control or of the fact that, for all the proliferation of new channels, media industries are still predominantly owned and controlled by a small handful of white, wealthy, middle-class men (or corporations started by such men). Nor does this perspective pay much attention to the increasingly profit-oriented nature of much media output which denies a form of public participation to those who cannot afford to pay for it. It might also be argued that competition and deregulation pose a serious threat to informed, analytical programming. An accusation frequently directed at media organizations in the increasingly commercial marketplace is that the competition for audience share leads to 'soundbite' journalism, in which there is little room for background, explanation or context. Consequently, it is argued, while there may be greater public engagement with shocking or visually dramatic events, there is little evidence of extensive public participation in the issues of policy, politics and reform that underlie such stories, or of a media willing to communicate such a context to the public (Barak, 1994b; Manning, 2001). Public participation in **mediated** discourse may *appear* to be more inclusive: after all, more people can air their views on the serious issues of the day via talk radio, television audience shows and newspaper polls, while telephone and computer resources have broadened traditional channels of communication to the extent where even television news broadcasts now encourage viewers to phone, text or e-mail their thoughts and opinions into the studio to be transmitted almost instantaneously on air. But the 20- or 30-second viewer contribution has arguably been introduced at the expense of complex analysis or detailed critique, and *media* pluralism – that is, many channels – does not necessarily result in *message* pluralism – diversity of content (Barak, 1994b; Manning, 2001). Critics argue that the media continue to provide homogenized versions of reality that avoid controversy and preserve the status quo. Consequently, ignorance among audiences is perpetuated, and the labelling, *stereotyping* and criminalization of certain groups (often along lines of class, race and gender) persists.

Political economists have also highlighted the potential disadvantages of a market-based system for the facilitation of democratic participation, arguing that the increasingly commercialized character of media institutions results in tried and tested formulae, with an entertainment bias, aimed at a 'lowest common denominator' audience who are easily identifiable and potentially lucrative targets for advertisers. The tendency to 'play it safe' by offering the shocking, the sensational and the 'real' is becoming increasingly evident in the British television schedules where mainstream programming is dominated by seemingly endless and increasingly stale imitations of once innovative ideas. Even 24-hour rolling news services on cable and satellite, such as CNN, are restricted by the news values to which they have to conform (see Chapter 2) and by the pressures of having to succeed in a commercial environment. As Blumler observes of American broadcast news media, while they may have a tradition of professional political journalism, it can nonetheless be the case that 'heightened competition tempts national network news ... to avoid complexity and hit only those highlights that will gain and keep viewers' attention' (Blumler, 1991: 207). These 'highlights' will rarely involve in-depth political commentary or sustained analysis. Instead, viewers are fed a diet of 'infotainment' which may have a strong 'human interest' angle or a particularly dramatic or violent component. This trend – often described by its critics as the 'dumbing down' of news and current affairs media – privileges audience ratings over analysis and debate and results in 'a flawed process of public accountability, with few forums in which issues can be regularly explored from multiple perspectives' (1991: 207). Crime is a subject that is especially limited and constrained by a media agenda on an endless quest for populist, profitable programming. One of the few strands of 'documentary' film making that has survived the wave of deregulation celebrated by pluralists is the 'true crime' genre where a serious criminal case is re-examined via a predictable formula, starting with a dramatized reconstruction of the crime itself and then a smug-with-hindsight examination of the sometimes bungled, frequently tortuous police investigation, before the dramatic denouement when the culprit is captured and convicted. These programmes – which are commonly concerned with highly unusual yet high-profile cases involving rapists and serial killers – pander to the thrill-seeking, *voyeuristic* element of the audience, while at the same time quenching their thirst for retribution.

Although computer-based technologies such as the Internet might seem to support the pluralist belief in a media that facilitates dialogue and the free exchange of ideas and ideologies, they are only available to those who can afford the necessary hardware, software and subscription fees. For critics of deregulation and privatization, information becomes a commodity for sale to those who are able to purchase it, rather than a public service available to all, and infotainment is all that is on offer to the masses. Furthermore, the Internet arguably encourages the public to retreat from arenas of national debate and reject the messages of the traditional political parties, preferring instead to inhabit specialist communities rooted in identity, lifestyle, **subculture** or single-issue politics. While this might be seen as a positive outcome of pluralism, new social movements and identity politics may be more vulnerable to media sensationalism and stigmatization (Manning, 2001). Pluralism, then, might best be viewed as an expression of how things could be, rather than how things are. On the other hand, pluralism reminds us that a degree of openness *is* achievable; albeit that it is an openness that must be squared with a recognition of dominant groups enjoying structural advantages and that there are ongoing conflictual processes both inside social institutions and within the media themselves (Schlesinger et al., 1991; Manning, 2001).

Realism and reception analysis

Throughout the 1980s established theories were being challenged by new approaches which turned on their heads some previously held assumptions and altered the focus of scholars in both criminology and media studies. In criminology a new perspective called *'left realism'* emerged as both a product of, and reaction to, what it saw as the idealistic stance of the left represented in works like *Policing the Crisis* (Hall et al., 1978). Accusing writers on the left of adopting reductionist arguments about crime, and romanticizing working-class offenders, left realists claimed that the political arena had been left open to conservative campaigns on law and order which chose to overlook the fact that most crime is not inter-class (that is, perpetrated by working-class people on middle-class victims), but is *intra*-class (that is, largely perpetrated on members of one's own class and community). Writers such as Lea and Young (1984) urged criminologists to 'get real' about crime, to focus on the seriousness of its effects – especially for women and ethnic minorities – and to elevate the experiences of victims of crime in their analyses (see section on 'The mass media and fear of crime', Chapter 6). After all, if there was no rational core to the proposition that crime is a serious problem, the media would have no power of leverage to the public consciousness, and the numerous attempts to theorize the relationship between media and crime, as discussed in this chapter, would simply never have materialized (Young, 1992).

Meanwhile in media and cultural studies a form of audience research called *'reception analysis'* dominated the agenda throughout the early 1980s and early

1990s. Researchers reconceptualized media influence, seeing it no longer as a force beyond an individual's control, but as a resource that is consciously *used* by people (Morley, 1992). In the modern communications environment where there is a proliferation of media, and the omniscience of any single medium or channel has diminished, most audience members will select images and meanings that relate to their wider experiences of work, family and social relationships. Furthermore, in an age of democratic, interactive, technology-driven communications, it is argued that media and popular culture are made from 'within' and 'below', not imposed from without and above as has been traditionally conceptualized (Fiske, 1989). By the mid-1990s, researchers had dismissed concerns about what the media *do* to people, and turned the question around, asking instead, 'what do people do *with* the media?'

Postmodernism and cultural criminology

There is a clear trajectory that links the theories discussed so far, even if development has come from antagonism as well as agreement between different schools of thought. *Postmodernism* is the latest paradigm shift in social science and can be seen as a response to significant new patterns in global cultural, political and economic life, which are replacing the structural characteristics associated with 'modern' society; class structure, capitalism, industrialism, militarism, the nation state and so on. Postmodernism is thus frequently presented as a decisive break with what went before. Large-scale theories such as Marxism are rejected for their all-embracing claims to knowledge and 'truth', and their failure to address the ways in which control of language systems privileges some viewpoints over others. For example, the 'dominant' language of the courts can lead defendants to experience the system as alienating and oppressive (Walklate, 2001; Bowling and Phillips, 2002).

However, traces of earlier theories can be found in postmodern accounts. Like reception analysts, postmodernist writers view audiences as active and creative meaning-makers. In common with realists, they share a concern with fear of crime and victimization, and make problematic concepts such as 'crime' and 'deviance' just as labelling theorists did in an earlier period. Furthermore, like advocates of the pluralist approach, postmodernists suggest that the media market has been deregulated, leading to an explosion of programmes, titles and formats to choose from. All tastes and interests are now catered for, and it is the consumer who ultimately has the power to choose what he or she watches, listens to, reads and engages with, but equally what he or she ignores or rejects. In this glossy, interactive media market place, anything goes – so long as it doesn't strain an attention span of three minutes, and is packaged as 'entertainment'.

Postmodernism, then, is concerned with the excesses of information and entertainment now available, and it emphasises the style and packaging of media output in addition to the actual substance of its content. This is the 'society of the spectacle' (Debord, 1967/1997) a hyperreality in which media domination suffuses to such an extent that the distinction between image and reality no longer exists (Baudrillard, 1981; 1983). Mass media and the collapse of meaning have produced a culture centred on immediate consumption and sensationalized impact but with little depth of analysis or contextualization (Osborne, 2002). It is the fragmentary, ephemeral and ambiguous that are observed, and pleasure, spectacle, pastiche, parody and irony are the staples of postmodern media output. It is the media's responsibility to entertain, and audience gratification is the only impact worth striving for.

This abandonment of a distinction between information and entertainment raises two problems, however. The first is the threat to meaningful debate that postmodernism seems to imply. A media marketplace based on a pluralist model of ideological struggle may suffice as a forum for debate, but it relies on the public's ability to discriminate between what is true and what is not; between fact and interpretation. In an early critique of postmodernism, Dick Hebdige warns that:

> The idea of a verifiable information order, however precarious and shifting, however subject to negotiation and contestation by competing ideologies, does not survive the transition to this version of new times ... today aliens from Mars kidnap joggers, yesterday Auschwitz didn't happen, tomorrow who cares what happens? Here the so-called 'depthlessness' of the postmodern era extends beyond ... the tendency of the media to feed more and more greedily off each other, to affect the function and status of information itself. (1989: 51)

The second difficulty with postmodernism lies in how we define 'entertainment'. As Hall et al. (1978) suggest, violence – including violent crime – is often regarded as intrinsically entertaining to an audience who, it is argued, have become more emotionally detached and desensitized to the vast array of visual images bombarding them from every corner of the world. Many see this as an escalating problem. Jerry Mander sums it up thus:

> Press conferences got coverage once. Rallies brought more attention than press conferences. Marches more than rallies. Sit-ins more than marches. Violence more than sit-ins. A theory evolved: accelerate the drama of each successive action to maintain the same level of coverage. (1980: 32)

It is usually organizations that fall outside mainstream consensus politics which best understand this theory of acceleration. Groups with a radical political agenda are well practised in the art of manipulating the media and will frequently 'create' a story through the use of controversial, but stage-managed, techniques, knowing that it will make 'good copy'. Greenpeace, the Animal Liberation Front and anti-globalization, anti-capitalist movements are examples of pressure groups which have been extremely successful in garnering media attention and ensuring attention-grabbing headlines. Even the police have adopted the techniques of heightened drama and suspense to produce spectacular, even voyeuristic television, with stage-managed press conferences involving 'victims' of serious crimes whom they suspect of foul play, and dramatic raids on the homes of suspected burglars and drug dealers in which police officers are accompanied by television cameras.

But it is arguably terrorists who have taken the lesson of sensationalized impact to heart to the greatest and most devastating effect:

> The spectacularly violent acts of terrorists can be viewed as performances for the benefit of a journalistic culture addicted to high drama ... the terrorist act is the ultimate 'pseudo-event' – a politically and militarily meaningless act unless it receives recognition and coverage in the news media. (McNair, 1998: 142)

However, the desire to 'play up to the cameras' may be no less true of state aggressors as it is terrorists and dissidents. For example, military campaigns may also be planned as media episodes, as was witnessed in the 2003 Allied War on Iraq when journalists were 'embedded' with military personnel and were allowed unprecedented access to troops and operations. Similarly:

> When President Reagan bombed Libya [in 1986], he didn't do it at the most effective time of day, from a military point of view. The timing of the raid was principally determined by the timing of the American television news; it was planned in such a way as to maximize its television impact. It was timed to enable Reagan to announce on the main evening news that it had 'just happened' – it was planned as a television event. (Morley, 1992: 63–4)

But the most compelling example to date of a postmodern media 'performance' occurred on 11 September 2001. The terrorist attacks on the World Trade Center took place when millions of Americans would be tuned into the breakfast news programmes on television. The timing of the actions ensured that viewers across the world who missed the terrifying aftermath of the first attack on the north tower would tune in to see 'live' pictures of the second hijacked aircraft being flown into the south tower 16 minutes later. The television pictures from that day – transmitted immediately around the globe – have arguably become the most visually arresting and memorable news images ever seen, evoking countless cinematic representations from *The Towering Inferno* to *Independence Day*. The 'event that shook the world' had such an overwhelming impact because of the immediacy and dramatic potency of its image on screen; it was truly a postmodern spectacle.

Terrorist attacks on 'innocent' civilians chime with the postmodern idea that we are all potential victims. Postmodern analyses reject traditional criminological concerns with the causes and consequences of crime, pointing instead to the fragmentation of societies, the fear that paralyses many communities, the random violence that seems to erupt at all levels of society, and the apparent inability of governments to do anything about these problems. This concern with a lurking, unpredictable danger is fortified by an omnipresent media. Postmodernist critic Richard Osborne suggests that the ubiquity of mediated crime reinforces our sense of being victims: 'media discourses about crime now constitute all viewers as equally subject to the fragmented and random danger of criminality, and in so doing provide the preconditions for endless narratives of criminality that rehearse this everpresent danger' (Osborne, 1995: 27). Perversely, then, the media's inclination to make all audience members equal in their potential 'victimness' lies at the core of the postmodern fascination with crime. For Osborne, there is 'something obsessive in the media's, and the viewer's, love of such narratives, an hysterical replaying of the possibility of being a victim and staving it off' (1995: 29).

Another aspect of the hysteria that surrounds criminal cases, fusing the fear of becoming a victim with the postmodern imperative for entertaining the audience, is the media's inability, or unwillingness, to separate the ordinary from the extraordinary. The audience is bombarded in both factual media and in fictional representations, by crimes that are very rare, such as serial killings and abductions of children by strangers. The presentation of the atypical as typical serves to exacerbate public anxiety and deflect attention from much more commonplace offences such as street crime, corporate crime and abuse of children within the family. Reporting of the 'ever-present danger' of the predatory paedophile or young thug who preys on pensioners and is prepared to kill for a handful of change are the stock in trade of a media industry which understands that shock, outrage and fear sell newspapers. In recent years, interest has turned to the collective outpouring of grief that has been witnessed in relation to certain violent and/or criminal acts, which has resulted in them occupying a particular symbolic place in the popular imagination. It has been suggested that the 'coming together' of individuals to express collective anguish and to gaze upon the scene of crimes in a gesture of empathy and solidarity with those who have been victimized, is a sign of the desire for community; a hearkening back to pre-mass society collectivity or to use the parlance of New Labour – an assertion of 'people power' (Blackman and Walkerdine, 2001: 2). But equally it might be regarded as a voyeuristic desire to be part of the hyperreal, to take part in a globally mediated event and say 'I was there'.

The populist, entertainment imperative of the postmodernist approach is central to the developing perspective known as *cultural criminology* (Ferrell and Sanders, 1995; Fenwick and Hayward, 2000; Presdee, 2000). This approach seeks to understand both the public's fascination with violence and crime via the mass media, and also the enactment of violence and crime *as* pleasure or spectacle. Its debt to earlier work by Stuart Hall, Stanley Cohen, Phil Cohen, Jock Young and others is evident in its proposition that all crime is grounded in culture and that cultural practices are embedded in dominant processes of power. It therefore supports the early Marxist-influenced, critical criminological view that criminal acts are acts of resistance to authority. But unlike earlier accounts that conceptualized resistance as something that was internalized and expressed through personal and subcultural style (Hall and Jefferson, 1975; Hebdige, 1979), cultural criminologists emphasize the externalization of excitement and ecstasy involved in resistance. Many criminal activities involve risk-taking and danger, but may in fact represent an attempt to break free of one's demeaning and restraining circumstances, to exercise control and take responsibility for one's own destiny. In a world in which individuals find themselves over-controlled and yet without control, crime offers the possibility of excitement *and* control (Fenwick and Hayward, 2000; cf. Morrison, 1995). The rising number of gun crimes and gangland style killings in the UK might be conceived in these terms; as an act of self-expression which, somewhat ironically, makes the individuals involved feel alive.

In cultural criminology crime becomes a participatory performance, a 'carnival', and the streets become theatre (Presdee, 2000). Some commentators have found this a refreshing antidote to Marxist-inspired studies such as *Policing the Crisis*, in so far as cultural criminology avoids the 'condescension of criminal-as-victim (of disadvantageous circumstances)' (Jefferson, 2002). One of the most compelling examples from Britain of the carnival of crime is that of joyriding. Describing the large-scale ritualized joyriding that occurred on the Blackbird Leys estate in Oxford in the early 1990s, Mike Presdee comments:

> [T]heir joyriding became a celebration of a particular form of car culture that was carnivalesque in nature, performance centred and criminal. The sport of joyriding went something like this: a team of local youths would spot a hot hatch (the car of choice) and steal it (or arrange with others to have it stolen). It would be delivered to another team who would do it up, delivering it finally to the drivers. In the evenings, the cars were raced around the estate, not aimlessly but in a way designed to show off skill. Furthermore, two competing groups (teams) attempted to outdo the other. These displays were watched by certain residents of the estate who, the story goes, were charged a pound for the pleasure, sitting in picnic chairs at the sides of the road. Often after these races the cars were burned on deserted land. (2000: 49)

Riots, protests and other outbreaks of disorder can also be viewed in this way. It is not the case that all carnivalesque performances involve crime, but it can be said with some certainty that participation in them can lead to criminalization. Raves and dance culture, the weekly rollerblade rally through the streets of Paris, and the annual protests against global capitalism in London and other major cities around the world, are all examples of carnival performances that the authorities continue to try and prohibit via the law. It is therefore not just the cultural significance of crime, but the criminalization of certain cultural practices that postmodern cultural criminologists are interested in.

Cultural criminology is still in its relative infancy and its long-term influence remains to be seen. However, it is already having a significant impact on the ways in which connections between crime, media and culture are made. For example, the subject of policing remains central to criminological inquiry, but the theoretical and empirical frameworks within which policing is understood have been broadened to encompass the complex, reciprocal dynamics of power between criminal justice and mediated texts. As Ferrell observes, policing has increasingly come to be understood not simply in its political or social context, but as a set of semiotic practices entangled with 'reality' television programmes, everyday public surveillance, and the symbolism and aesthetics of police sub-cultures themselves (in McLaughlin and Muncie, 2001: 76; see also Leishman and Mason, 2003, and Chapter 6 of this volume).

Criminologists are thus encouraged to look beyond the traditional bound-aries of their field and broaden their intellectual horizons to include the worlds of art, media, culture and style (South, 1997). Cultural criminology cel-ebrates postmodern notions of difference, discontinuity and diversity, and breaks down restrictive stereotypes. What were formerly regarded as uncon-ventional interest groups have been embraced amid a renewed verve for ethnographic enquiry (see, for example, Ferrell and Sanders, 1995; Ferrell and Websdale, 1999; Ferrell and Hamm, 1998). At the same time, the postmodern project of diversity and alternative voices has enfranchised a 'new body of intellectuals ... [who] are increasingly speaking from positions of difference' (Whiteacre, undated: 21). In part, the emergence of a postmodernist paradigm within criminology can be characterized as a challenge to the lingering influ-ence of positivism which, it is suggested, has led to a vacuum in so-called 'expert' knowledge surrounding the pursuit of pleasure. The overriding con-cern with reason and scientific rationality means that traditional criminology has been unable to account for 'feelings' such as excitement, pleasure and desire. For example, some critics have called for the establishment of a 'gay criminology' on the grounds that criminology has historically ignored gay peo-ple, other than constructing a positivistic discourse that unites homosexuality with a genetic predisposition to deviance (Groombridge, 1999; Taylor, undated). Meanwhile, in a study that has echoes of Jock Young's earlier (1971) work on marijuana users, Kevin Whiteacre argues that the idea that people use drugs unproblematically and without regrets is anathema to a science embed-ded in cultural expectations about proper fulfilment of desire (Ian Taylor also attempted to open up the debate on the omnipresence and normalization of recreational drugs; see Taylor, 1999: 81–6).

Postmodernist theory suggests that aspects of identity such as sexuality and lifestyle choices have superseded traditional identifications based on gender, class and ethnicity, rendering the latter irrelevant and redundant. The growth and expansion of computer mediated communications such as the Internet have provided a playground for experimenting with aspects of identity and thus also open up new areas of interest for criminologists. As I describe elsewhere, cyberspace facilitates infinitely new possibilities to the deviant imagination:

> With the right equipment and sufficient technical know-how you can – if you are so inclined – buy a bride, cruise gay bars, go an a global shopping spree with someone else's credit card, break into a bank's security system, plan a demonstration in another country and hack into the Pentagon – all on the same day ... Anonymity, disembodiment, outreach and speed are the hallmarks of Internet communication and combined, they can make us feel daring, liberated, infallible. (Jewkes, 2003a: 2)

These activities convey the sense of excitement and desire that are at the heart of many cybercrimes, but also hint at the possibility that such pleasures can be transmuted into something darker and more distorted. Postmodern media merge 'fun' and 'hate', 'cruelty' and 'playfulness', 'inclusive' and 'exploitative', 'accessible' and 'extremist' (Presdee, 2000; Jewkes, 2003a). The Internet celebrates a world of entertainment, spectacle, narcissism and performance, and – when it comes to privatized pleasure – is surely the cardinal site of the carnival of crime.

Summary

While of necessity a distillation of the historical development of two fields of inquiry (in addition to noting the importance of the broader terrain of sociology), this chapter has traced the origins and development of the major theories that have shaped the contours of both criminology and media studies, and attempted to provide a broad overview of points of convergence and conflict between the two. In so doing, it has established that there is no body of relatively consistent, agreed upon and formalized assertions that can readily be termed 'media theory' or 'criminological theory'. Although such phrases are widely used, neither field has been unified by the development of a standard set of concepts, an inter-related body of hypotheses or an overall explanatory framework. However, it has proposed that a sense of progressive development is nevertheless evident in ideas concerning media and crime. Despite their obvious aetiological and methodological differences, the theoretical approaches discussed in this chapter have clear points of convergence which have enabled us to locate them in the wider context of social, cultural, political and economic developments that were concomitantly taking place. In summary, the theoretical 'pegs' upon which our analysis has been hung are as follows:

- *Media effects:* Early theories connecting media and crime were characterized by an overwhelmingly negative view of both the role of the media and the susceptibility of the audience. In an age of uncertainty and instability, when it was believed that social action was heavily determined by external forces rather than being a matter of personal choice, the emerging mass media became the focus of many theories about the harmful effects of powerful stimuli. Like Martians with their ray guns, the new media of mass communications were perceived through early 20th century eyes as alien invaders injecting their messages directly into the minds of a captive audience. Although academic researchers in the UK have strongly resisted attempts to assert the existence of a causal link between media and crime, rendering the debate all but redundant in media scholarship, notions of a potentially harmful media capable of eliciting negative or anti-social consequences remain at the heart of popular or mainstream discourses, including those that have been incorporated into policy.
- *Strain theory and anomie:* Merton's development of anomie helps us to understand the strain caused by a disjuncture between the cultural goals of wealth and status, and legitimate means of achieving those goals. For those with few means of attaining success through normal, legal channels, the mass media – especially the advertising industry – might be said to place incalculable pressure, creating a huge ungratified well of desire with little opportunity of fulfilment. It is in such circumstances that some individuals pursue the culturally desirable objectives of success and material wealth via illegitimate paths. Merton's work follows Durkheim's theories concerning the characteristics of society and how individuals struggle to achieve social solidarity despite the atomization they face. Recent commentators on anomie have suggested that disaffected individuals overcome feelings of isolation and normlessness by forming communities based on shared tastes and opinions, and that the Internet has, for some, countered the sense of dislocation that gaps in wealth and status inevitably produce.
- *Dominant ideology:* With the rediscovery of Marx's writings on social structure, scholars in the 1960s and 1970s focused their attentions on the extent to which consent is 'manufactured' by the powerful along ideological lines. According to the dominant ideology approach, the power to criminalize and decriminalize certain groups and behaviours lies with the ruling élite who – in a process known as 'hegemony' – win popular approval for their actions via social institutions, including the media. In short, powerful groups achieve public consensus on definitions of crime and deviance, and gain mass support for increasingly draconian measures of control and containment, not by force or coercion, but by using the media to subtly construct a web of meaning from a number of ideological threads which are then articulated into a coherent popular discourse (Stevenson, 1995). Crime and deviance could potentially pose a

dilemma for the authorities and threaten to destroy their careful construction of consensus. But hegemony ensures that anything that threatens the status quo (as crime, deviance and disorder do) will be regarded as a temporary interlude in a world otherwise at one with itself.

- *Pluralism:* This perspective emerged as a challenge to hegemonic models of media power. Pluralism emphasizes the diversity and plurality of media channels available, thus countering the notion that any ideology can be dominant for any length of time if it does not reflect what people experience to be true. Although there is undoubtedly a firm alliance between most politicians and sections of the journalistic media (indeed the Labour government of Tony Blair has taken media manipulation to a degree where political 'spin' is itself often the subject of news reports) the public like defiance, and counter-ideologies will always emerge (Manning, 2001). Pluralists argue that the media's tendency to ignore, ridicule or demonize those whose politics and lifestyle lie beyond the consensual norm is changing, precisely because public sentiments have changed. There is growing antipathy to the apparatus of political communication and people's responses to crime will always be much more complex and diverse than any headline or soundbite might suggest (Sparks, 2001). In addition, it might be argued that the quantity and rapidity of contemporary news-making undermines the notion of élite power and ensures that governments are accountable and responsive to their electorate (McNair, 1993; 1998).

- *Postmodernism and cultural criminology:* Postmodernism is a notoriously difficult subject to grasp. As far as we can state that there are 'defining characteristics' of postmodernism, they include: the end of any belief in an overarching scientific rationality; the abandonment of empiricist theories of truth; and an emphasis on the fragmentation of experience and the diversification of viewpoints. The postmodernist rejection of claims to truth proposed by the 'grand theories' of the past, challenges us to accept that we live in a world of contradictions and inconsistencies which are not amenable to objective modes of thought. Within criminology, postmodernism implies an abandonment of the concept of crime and the construction of a new language and mode of thought to define processes of criminalization and censure. It is often suggested that, for postmodernists, there are *no* valid questions worth asking, and Henry and Milovanovic (1996) insist that crime will only stop being a problem once the justice system, media and criminologists stop focussing attention on it.

  Media and culture are central to a postmodern analysis; style is substance and meaning resides in representation. Consequently, crime and crime control can only be understood as an ongoing spiral of inter-textual, image-driven, media loops (Ferrell, 2001). Cultural criminology embraces these postmodern ideas and underpins them with some more 'radical' yet established concerns, borrowing especially from the work of British scholars in the 1970s on subcultures and mediated forms of social control. And, in a decisive break with traditional, 'positivist' criminologies which have been unconcerned with 'feeling' and 'pleasure', cultural criminology also draws attention to the fact that crime can have a carnivalesque quality; it is exhilarating, performative and dangerous.

STUDY QUESTIONS

1 Choose one of the theories discussed in this chapter and discuss the contribution it has made to our understanding of the relationship between media and crime.

2 As the *War of the Worlds* radio broadcast demonstrates, concerns about media effects frequently reflect or crystallise deeper anxieties in periods of social upheaval. What examples of contemporary concerns about the effects of the media can you think of, and in what ways might they be attributed to wider anxieties about social change?

3 Conduct a content analysis of a week's news. What evidence can you find for the proposition that news is ideology and that the mass media are effectively assimilated into the goals of government policy on crime, law and order?

4 In a challenge to Marxist-inspired critiques, some cultural theorists (for example, Fiske, 1989) argue that all popular culture is the 'people's culture' and emerges from 'below' rather than being imposed from 'above'. It is thus seen to be independent of, and resistant to, the dominant hegemonic norms. What implications does this have for those who hold deviant or oppositional viewpoints? Can 'popular' culture really be described as non-hierarchical when it celebrates power and violence for men, and sexual availability and victimization among women and children?

5 At the heart of postmodern analyses lies the thorny question of why crime is threatening and frightening, yet at the same time popular and 'entertaining'. How would you attempt to answer this question?

FURTHER READING

There are now numerous good introductions to criminological theory. Among the best and most accessible are: Walklate, S. (1998) *Understanding Criminology: Current Theoretical Debates*, (Open University Press); Hopkins-Burke, R. (2001) *An Introduction to Criminological Theory* (Willan); and Tierney, J. (1996) *Criminology: Theory and Context* (Longman). McLaughlin, E. and Muncie, J. (2001) *The Sage Dictionary of Criminology* (Sage) provides useful definitions and good, basic introductions to many of the theories discussed in this chapter. Similarly, there are several fairly comprehensive introductions to media theory, for example, McQuail, D. (2000) *Mass Communication Theory: An Introduction* (Sage), which is now in its fourth edition. The new Sage journal, *Crime, Media, Culture: An International Journal* is devoted to cross-disciplinary work that promotes understanding of the relationship between crime, criminal justice, media and culture.

2

The Construction of Crime News

Chapter Contents

OVERVIEW

Chapter 2 provides:

- An analysis of how crime news is 'manufactured' along ideological lines.
- An understanding of the ways in which the demands and constraints of news production inter-twine with the perceived interests of the target audience to produce a set of organizational 'news values'.
- An overview of 12 key news values that are prominent in the construction of crime news at the beginning of the 21st century.
- A discussion of the ways in which the construction of news sets the agenda for public and political debate.

KEY TERMS

agenda-setting	crime news	public appeal
audience	ideology	public interest
binary oppositions	moral majority	social constructionism
celebrity	newsworthiness	
crime	news values	

The diversity of theoretical approaches discussed in the previous chapter will have alerted you to the fact that the influence of the media – the ways in which media shape our ideas, values, opinions and behaviour – can be conceptualized both negatively and positively, depending on the perspective adopted. Those who have attempted to demonstrate a link between media content and crime or deviance have employed numerous theoretical models in order to establish alter-native, and frequently oppositional, views, ranging from the idea that the media industry is responsible for much of the crime that blights our society, to the idea that media perform a public service in educating us about crime and thus aid crime prevention. Some have even argued that media are redefining and mak-ing obsolete traditional notions of crime and deviance altogether. It is clear from these divergent viewpoints that the media's role in representing reality is highly contested and subject to interpretation. Although fictional accounts of crime (in film, television drama, music lyrics and so on) are arguably of greatest salience in discussions of media influence, the reporting of crime news is also of importance and is no less shaped by the mission to entertain. Indeed, while it might be expected that the news simply reports the 'facts' of an event and is an accurate representation of the overall picture of crime, this is not the case. Even the most cursory investigation of crime reporting demonstrates that crime news follows markedly different patterns to both the 'reality' of crime and its representation in official statistics. Thus, despite often being described as a 'window on the world' or a mirror reflecting 'real life', the media might be more accurately thought of as a prism, subtly bending and distorting the view of the world it projects.

Whether we adhere to the 'effects' theory of media influence, the hegemonic understanding of media power as an expression of élite interests, the pluralist idea of an open media marketplace, or notions of a postmodernist mediascape, we have to conclude that media images are *not* reality; they are a *version* of reality that is culturally determined and dependent on two related factors. First, the mediated picture of 'reality' is shaped by the production processes of news organizations and the structural determinants of news-making, any or all of which may influence the image of crime, criminals and the criminal justice system in the minds of the public. These factors include the over-reporting of crimes that have been 'solved' and resulted in a conviction; the deployment of reporters at institutional settings, such as courts, where they are likely to come across interesting stories; the need to produce stories which fit the time schedules of news production; the concentration on specific crimes at the expense of causal explanations, the consideration of personal safety, which results in camera operators covering incidents of public disorder from behind police lines; and an over-reliance on 'official', accredited sources for information. The second factor that shapes news production concerns the assumptions media professionals make about their **audience**. They sift and select news items, prioritize some stories over others, edit words, choose the tone that will be adopted (some stories will be treated seriously, others might get a humorous or ironic treatment) and decide on the visual images that will accompany the story. It is through this process – known as **agenda-setting** – that those who work in the mass media select a handful of events from the unfathomable number of possibilities that occur around the world every day, and turn them into stories that convey meanings, offer solutions, associate certain groups of people with particular kinds of behaviour, and provide 'pictures of the world' which may help to structure our frames of reference. Far from being a random or personal process, editors and journalists will select, produce and present news according to a range of professional criteria that are used as benchmarks to determine a story's **'newsworthiness'**. This is not to say that alternative definitions do not exist or that other non-mediated influences are at least as important. But if a story does not contain at least some of the characteristics deemed newsworthy, it will not appear on the news agenda.

News values, then, are the value judgements that journalists and editors make about the **public appeal** of a story and also whether it is in the **public interest**. The former can be measured quantitatively: put simply, lack of public appeal will be reflected in poor sales figures or ratings and is frequently used to justify the growing dependence on stories with a dramatic, sensationalist or celebrity component. The issue of public interest is rather more complicated and may involve external interference, such as corporate or, more commonly, political pressures. Although the press are hampered by very few limitations regarding what they may print, broadcasting is subject to a range of restrictions which are framed by notions of 'impartiality' (McQueen, 1998). The BBC is especially vulnerable to political leverage (the Hutton inquiry into the suicide of government weapons advisor, Dr David Kelly, and attempts by senior police officers and Home Secretary, David Blunkett, to ban a BBC documentary uncovering racism among police recruits are two recent examples from 2003 that serve to make the point). Intervention may be coercive, ranging from the control of information to an outright ban on publication or broadcast of material on the grounds that it is not in the public interest – often a euphemism for disclosure of information that is not in the government's interest (cf. Hillyard and Percy-Smith, 1988, for examples). Alternatively, pressure might be so abstrusely exerted as to appear as self-censorship on the part of editors and producers. But as Fowler (1991) notes, the news values that set the media agenda rarely amount to a journalistic conspiracy – they are much more subtle than that. Nowhere in a newsroom will you find a list pinned to the wall reminding reporters and editors what their 'angle' on a story should be. Rather, the commercial, legislative and technical pressures that characterize journalism, together with a range of occupational conventions – which are often expressed in terms of 'having a good nose for a story', but which are actually more to do with journalists sharing the same *ideological* values as the majority of their audience – results in a normalization of particular interests and values (Wykes, 2001). This shared ethos enables those who work in news organizations to systematically sort, grade and select potential news stories, and discard those which are of no perceived interest or relevance to the audience.

The first people to attempt to systematically identify and categorize the news values that commonly determine and structure reported events were Galtung and Ruge (1965/1973). Their concern was with news reporting generally, rather than crime news *per se*, but their view that incidents and events were more likely to be reported if they were, for example, unexpected, close to home, of a significant threshold in terms of dramatic impact, and negative in essence, clearly made them relevant to crime reporting. Following their classic analysis, another influential study was published in 1977 by Steve Chibnall. Despite it being nearly 30 years old, and being concerned with journalistic priorities in the post-War period from 1945 to 1975, *Law and Order News* arguably remains the most influential study of news values relating to crime reporting and has led to numerous applications of the concept of news values in a myriad of different contexts (including Hall et al., 1978; Hartley, 1982; Hetherington, 1985; Ericson et al., 1987, 1989, 1991; Cavender and Mulcahy, 1998; Surette, 1998; Manning, 2001; Greer, 2003a).

However, Britain is a very different place now than it was half a century ago. The prison population has soared from just over 40,000 in 1977 to 73,850 in April 2003 (expected to rise to in excess of 99,300 by June 2009), and contemporary news reports contain references to crimes – road rage, joyriding, car-jacking, ecstasy dealing, identity theft – not heard of 30 years ago. Conversely, non-violent crimes such as property offences which, in the post-War period constituted nearly a quarter of stories in *The Times* (Reiner, 2001; Reiner et al., 2001) are now so commonplace that they are rarely mentioned in the national media. The media landscape has itself changed almost beyond recognition. In 1977 there were just three television channels, a fraction of the newspaper and magazine titles, and although e-mail had just been developed it was the preserve of a handful of academics sitting in computer labs on either side of the Atlantic. The structures of ownership and control have altered and news, like all other media output, is significantly more market-driven and dictated by ever-looming deadlines than it was previously. Politics is not as polarized as it was in the 1970s when the ideological battlefield was fiercely contested between capitalists and socialists. At the same time, contemporary audiences are arguably more knowledgeable, more sophisticated and more sceptical than at any time previously, and are certainly sufficiently media-savvy to know when they are on the receiving end of political 'spin' (Manning, 2001). What is more, some critics argue that the pressure on media professionals to produce the ordinary as extraordinary shades into the postmodern, and that what was historically described as news gathering has, in the new millennium, begun to take on the same '"constructed-for-television" quality that postmodernists refer to as "simulation"' (Osborne, 2002: 131). The time seems right, then, for a reassessment of the criteria that structure the news that we read, hear, watch and download at the beginning of the 21st century. So what constitutes 'newsworthiness' in 2004?

Of course, some of the criteria identified by Galtung and Ruge in 1965 and Chibnall in 1977 still broadly hold true and will be drawn on in the analysis that follows. It is also important to remember that different values may determine the selection and presentation of events by different news media (and, for that matter, by different or competing organizations), and that the broadcast media tend to follow the news agenda of the press in deciding which stories are newsworthy. Not surprisingly, the news values of the *Sun* are likely to be somewhat different from those of the *Independent* and different again from those of the BBC. Even among news organizations which appear to be very similar, such as the British tabloid press, there may be differences in news reporting which are largely accounted for by the house style of the title in question. For example, some stress the 'human interest' angle of a crime story (with first-hand accounts from victims and witnesses, an emphasis on tragedy, sentimentality and so on) and may be primarily designed to appeal to a female readership, while others sensationalize crime news, emphasizing sex and sleaze, but simultaneously adopting a scandalized and prurient tone.

News values are also subject to subtle changes over time, and a story does not have to conform to all the criteria in order to make the news – although events that score highly on the newsworthiness scale (that is, conform to several of the news values) are more likely to be reported. Newsworthiness criteria vary across different countries and cultures, and it should be noted that the list that follows has been devised with the UK media in mind. It is, therefore, by no means exhaustive, but it considers a total of 12 features that are evident in the output of most contemporary media institutions, and are of particular significance when examining the reporting of crime. One other point that should be borne in mind is that while 'crime' could in itself be classified as a news value, it goes without saying that in a study of crime news, all the news values outlined in this chapter pertain explicitly to *crime*. It is also taken for granted that the vast majority of crime stories are *negative* in essence, and that news must contain an element of 'newness' or *novelty*; the news has to tell us things we did not already know (McNair, 1998). Crime, negativity and novelty do not therefore appear in the list below as discrete news values, but are themes that underpin all the criteria discussed. It is understood that *any* crime has the potential to be a news story, that it will contain negative features (even if the outcome is positive and it is presented as an essentially 'good news' story), and that it will contain new or novel elements (even if it has been composed with other, similar stories to reinforce a particular agenda or to create the impression of a 'crime wave'). This list of news values is concerned, therefore, with how previously unreported, negative stories about crime – already potentially of interest – are determined even more newsworthy by their interplay with other features of news reporting.

News values for a new millennium

The 12 news structures and news values that shape crime news listed below are discussed in the rest of this chapter:

- Threshold
- Predictability
- Simplification
- Individualism
- Risk
- Sex
- Celebrity or high-status persons
- Proximity
- Violence
- Spectacle or graphic imagery
- Children
- Conservative ideology and political diversion

Threshold

Events have to meet a certain level of perceived importance or drama in order to be considered newsworthy. The threshold of a potential story varies according to whether the news reporters and editors in question work within a local, national or global medium. In other words, petty crimes such as vandalism and street robberies are likely to feature in the local press (and will probably be front page news in rural or low-crime areas) but it takes offences of a greater magnitude to meet the threshold of national or international media. In addition, once a story has reached the required threshold to make the news, it may then have to meet further criteria in order to stay on the news agenda, and the media frequently keep a crime wave or particular crime story alive by creating new thresholds. For example, a perennial staple of crime news reporting is attacks on the elderly in their homes. Such stories are often used as 'fillers' during quiet news periods and tend to be reported in waves, suggesting a widespread social problem rapidly approaching crisis point (see, for example, the *Mirror*'s 'shock issue', 12 July 2002). But although serious assaults on elderly people might in themselves initially be deemed newsworthy, journalists will soon look for a new angle to keep the story 'fresh' and give it a novelty factor. This might simply involve an escalation of the level of drama attached to the story, or it might require the implementation of other news structures and news values in order to sustain the 'news life' of the story (Hall et al., 1978: 72). In 2002 the British news media introduced several supplementary thresholds to give new angles to stories about assaults on the elderly. They included the thresholds of *escalating drama* and *risk* ('Attacker of elderly "could kill" next time', *BBC News Online*: 1 August 2002); *celebrity* ('Robbers raid [Bruce] Forsyth's home', *Observer*: 21 July 2002); a *sexual* component ('A 93-year-old woman has spoken of her bewilderment after a man conned his way into her home and raped her elderly daughter', *BBC News Online*: 9 May 2002); the *macabre* ('A teenager obsessed with vampires stabbed to death an elderly neighbour before cutting out her heart and drinking her blood', *Guardian*: 3 August 2002); an *ironic* angle ('Pensioners fight off bogus callers with poker and walking stick', *BBC News Online*: 9 November 2002); and the *counter-story* ('Man, 76, stabs 21-year-old neighbour to death for singing too loudly', *BBC News Online*: 12 November 2002). These additional thresholds may, then, take many forms (we might add to the above list any number of other factors including the 'whimsical', the 'humorous', the 'bizarre', the 'grotesque', the 'nostalgic', the 'sentimental' and so on; see Hall et al., 1978; Roshier, 1973). After several months of press hysteria over the entry into the UK of political refugees and illegal immigrants, the *Daily Star* (21 August 2003) filled their front page on a quiet news day in midsummer with the headline 'Asylum seekers eat our donkeys'. This illustrates the point well: the addition of new thresholds introduce a novel element to a familiar theme and may revive a flagging news story.

Predictability

As the introduction to this chapter suggested, it goes without saying that an event that is rare, extraordinary or unexpected will be considered newsworthy. Like the thresholds outlined above, unpredictability gives a story novelty value. In particular the media's 'discovery' of a 'new' crime is often sufficient to give it prominence. Hall et al. (1978: 71) demonstrate how mugging was characterized as a 'frightening new strain of crime' by the British press in the 1970s, and since that time the appearance of crimes such as ram-raiding, car-jacking and steaming on our shores (all of which have been imported from the US, according to the British press) has been sufficiently unexpected and novel to guarantee their newsworthiness.

But equally, a story that is *predictable* may be deemed newsworthy because news organizations can plan their coverage in advance and deploy their resources accordingly (for example, reporters and photographers). This results in a reliance on official sources such as the police, politicians, and spokes-persons from high-profile organizations who are regularly used and deemed 'reliable' by news reporters. Crime itself is frequently spontaneous and sporadic, but news media will know in advance if, for example, the Home Secretary is announcing a new initiative to combat crime or the Home Office is due to release its annual crime statistics and will plan their coverage before the event has actually occurred. This is also true of criminal trials, which can contain an element of predictability. Media organizations can estimate the time that a criminal case will remain in court and, having deployed personnel and equipment, they are likely to retain them there until the end of the trial. Hence a degree of continuity of coverage is also assured.

Another aspect of predictability is that, for the most part, the media agenda is structured in an ordered and predictable fashion. Having set the moral framework of a debate, those who work in the media will rarely do a U-turn and refashion it according to a different set of principles. Put simply, if the media expect something to happen it will happen, and journalists will usually have decided on the angle they are going to report a story from before they even arrive at the scene. One of the most frequently cited examples of this tendency was the media coverage of anti-Vietnam demonstrations in London in 1968 (Halloran et al., 1970). The media anticipated violence and were going to report the event as a violent occasion, whatever the reality on the day. Consequently, one isolated incident of anti-police violence dominated coverage of the demonstration and deflected attention from its general peacefulness and, indeed, its anti-war message. In recent years, anti-capitalism demonstrations around the world have received similar treatment, leading many to conclude that the mass media tend to report events in the ways they have previously reported them. Another regular event that illustrates this tendency is the annual Notting Hill

Carnival held in London over the August Bank Holiday weekend. Since riots marred the carnival in 1976 and occurred less seriously in 1977, the media has consistently reported the event within a framework which emphasizes racism, crime and violence, often overshadowing the many positive and joyous aspects of the parade. This is despite the fact that crime rates remain relatively low compared with those at other musical events attended by far fewer people (the event currently attracts in excess of 1.5 million people each year). The imposing police presence that accompanied the carnival for many years engendered a feeling of hostility on both sides which the media were eager to exploit. As Gary Younge explains:

> Thanks largely to the press, carnival moved from being a story about culture to one about crime and race. For years after, carnival stories would come with a picture of policemen either in hospital after being attacked or in an awkward embrace with a black, female reveller in full costume ... [In 1977] riot police were briefly deployed. The next day, the Express's front page read: 'War Cry! The unprecedented scenes in the darkness of London streets looked and sounded like something out of the film classic *Zulu*'. Calls for carnival's banning came from all quarters. Tory shadow home secretary Willie Whitelaw said, 'The risk in holding it now seems to outweigh the enjoyment it gives' ... The Telegraph blamed black people for being in Britain in the first place, declaring: 'Many observers warned from the outset that mass immigration from poor countries of substantially different culture would generate anomie, alienation, delinquency and worse' ... As recently as 1991, following a stabbing, *Daily Mail* columnist Lynda Lee-Potter described the carnival as 'a sordid, sleazy nightmare that has become synonymous with death'. (Younge, 2002: unpaginated)

Even today, the British media emphasize trouble or potential trouble when reporting on the carnival, and the broadsheets are as culpable as the tabloids in this respect. For example, under the headline 'Police cameras ring Notting Hill' the *Guardian* reports that 'more than 70 closed circuit television cameras were deployed by police at Notting Hill carnival yesterday to help cut crime' but somewhat contradictorily goes on to say that 'the first day of Europe's biggest street party saw just six arrests for minor offences' (*Guardian*, 30 August 1999).

Simplification

Events do not have to be simple in order to make the news (although it helps), but they must be reducible to a minimum number of parts or themes. This process of simplification has several aspects. First, news reporting is marked by brevity in order that it should not strain the attention span of the audience. Second, the range of possible meanings inherent in the story must be restricted.

Unlike other textual discourses – novels, poems, films and so on – where the capacity of a story to generate multiple and diverse meanings is celebrated, news discourse is generally not open to interpretation and audiences are invited to come to consensual conclusions about a story (Galtung and Ruge, 1965/1973). Thus, not only does news reporting privilege brevity, clarity and unambiguity in its presentation, but it encourages the reader, viewer and listener to suspend their skills of critical interpretation and respond in unanimous accord. As far as crime news is concerned, this usually amounts to moral indignation and censure directed at anyone who transgresses the legal or moral codes of society. In the aftermath of high-profile cases (for example: the murders of Lin and Megan Russell by Michael Stone, who was classified as suffering from a Dangerous Severe Personality Disorder; the terrorist attacks in New York on 11 September 2001; the massacre of children in their Dunblane school by Thomas Hamilton; the murder of a toddler by two schoolboys from Liverpool), notions of potential 'dangerousness' have come to be applied indiscriminately to whole sections of society. In this oversimplified world-view of popular journalism, sufferers of mental illness can be portrayed as potential murderers; asylum seekers as potential terrorists; gun club members become potential spree killers and, most insidiously, children come to be seen as 'evil monsters' with no hope of rehabilitation (Greer, 2003c). Such reproach is particularly evident in the tabloid press, who have arguably taken to heart the words of former Prime Minister John Major, said in the context of the Bulger case, that we should seek to 'condemn a little more and understand a little less'.

A further feature of the simplification of crime news is that immediate or sudden events, such as the discovery of a body or an armed robbery, are likely to be reported because their 'meaning' can be arrived at very quickly, but crime trends, which are more complex and may take a long time to unfold, are difficult to report unless they can be marked by means of devices such as the release of a report or official statistics. In other words, a 'hook' is required on which to hang such stories in order that they fit with the daily or hourly time-span of most media.

Personalization is another aspect of the process of news simplification, which simply means that stories about people are favoured over those concerning abstract concepts or institutions, the result of which is that events are frequently simplistically viewed as the actions and reactions of individuals (see 'Individualism' below). This is one element of a wider trend in which the British press in particular are unwilling to take up valuable column inches in explaining the background to an event. Sectarian violence in Northern Ireland and acts of terror and genocide the world over are thus frequently presented as spontaneous acts, with little or no attempt at contextualization.

Furthermore, the trend towards graphic and spectacular imagery (which is explored in more detail below) and – in broadcast media – audience participation, leaves little room for informed commentary or expert analysis. The absence of criminologists' voices from crime news discourse is a concern of many in our field (Barak, 1994b). Neil Postman comments that as each new media technology develops it creates:

> [A] peek-a-boo world, where now this event, now that, pops into view for a moment, then vanishes again. It is a world without much coherence or sense; a world that does not permit us to do anything ... [yet] is also end-lessly entertaining. (Postman, 1985: 78–9)

A final aspect of the simplification of news reporting is that the mass media are inclined to deal in **binary oppositions**; a tendency that is as true of crime report-ing as any other form of reportage. Thus, stories involving crime and criminals are frequently presented within a context that emphasizes good versus evil, folk heroes and folk devils, black against white, guilty or innocent, 'normal' as opposed to 'sick', 'deviant' or 'dangerous' and so on. Such polarized frameworks of under-standing result in the construction of mutually exclusive categories; for example, parents cannot also be paedophiles. All these processes of simplification add up to a mediated vision of crime in which shades of grey are absent and a complex real-ity is substituted for a simple, incontestable and preferably bite-sized message.

Individualism

The news value *individualism* connects *simplification* and *risk* (see p. 47). Individual definitions of crime, and rationalizations which highlight individual responses to crime, are preferred to more complex cultural and political explanations. As described above, the media engage in a process of personalization in order to simplify stories and give them a 'human interest' appeal, which results in events being viewed as the actions and reactions of people. Consequently, social, polit-ical and economic issues tend only to be reported as the conflict of interests between individuals (the Prime Minister and the Leader of the Opposition, for example), while the complex interrelationship between political ideology and policy may be embodied in a single figure, such as the 'Drug Tsar'. As Fiske notes, the effect of this is that 'the social origins of events are lost, and individ-ual motivation is assumed to be the origin of all action' (Fiske, 1987: 294).

Both offenders and those who are *potentially offended against* are constructed within an individualist framework. Put simply, the criminal is usually described as being 'impulsive, a loner, maladjusted, irrational, animal-like, aggressive and violent' (Blackman and Walkerdine, 2001: 6) – all qualities which allude to the offender's autonomous status and lack of normative social ties (see Chapter 6 on the construction of offenders in the television programme *Crimewatch UK*). Most offenders are viewed as exhibiting signs of individual pathology, but one study that examines what most people would consider to be the 'worst' type of crime explains serial killing as the consequence of a culture which glorifies violence as 'an appropriate and manly response to frustration' and which stresses individualism and the freedom to explore one's self and one's impulses (Leyton, 1989: 364, cited in Coleman and Norris, 2000: 109).

Furthermore, news reporting frequently encourages the public to see themselves as vigilantes and positions those who are offended against (or who fear being the victims of crime) as vulnerable and isolated, let down by an ineffective social system (Norfolk farmer, Tony Martin, who killed a 16-year-old intruder, being a prime example). In other words, immediate, micro-solutions to crime are sought with little time for reflection or critical analysis. Consequently, the mediated image of crime is dominated by the figure of the dangerous predator or psychopath, and those who try and protect themselves from being the victims of crime are frequently portrayed as 'have a go heroes' (although it should be noted that the Tony Martin case divided press and public alike). Such representations are in contrast to victims who are killed in the commission of an offence. Victims who can be constructed as 'tragic innocents' are usually firmly located within familial and social contexts, thus enhancing even more strongly the impression of the offending 'outsider' acting alone (see Chapter 6). Meanwhile, as discussed in the previous chapter, institutions, corporations and governments may be literally getting away with murder. Media reports of crime may encourage us to fit security locks, take out expensive insurance policies and avoid going out alone at night, but they do not cause us to cancel our holiday plans or avoid travelling by train (Slapper and Tombs, 1999). Even when an offence that occurs within a large organization actually makes the news, it may once again be explained by recourse to individual pathology. The collapse of the British merchant bank Barings in 1995 was one such complicated, technical case which might have seemed somewhat abstract to the general public. To avoid complex explanations, the media constructed the story around the figure of Barings employee, Nick Leeson, the 'rogue trader' who was single-handedly held responsible for the loss of £869 million (cf. Tomlinson, 1997).

For Reiner et al. (2001) individualism is a consequence of the increasing tendency to view society as being obsessed with 'risk' and all its attendant notions, including risk assessment, risk management and risk avoidance (see 'Risk' below). The new vocabulary surrounding this 'foxy but evocative term' (Leacock and Sparks, 2002: 199) highlights a shift in perceptions of how risk should best be dealt with. As social problems have come to be seen as the product of chance or of individual action, and solutions are sought at the level of individual self-help strategies – such as insurance or personal protection – a 'winner–loser' casino culture is created (Reiner et al., 2001: 177; cf. James, 1995; Taylor, 1999). Individuals are held responsible for their fates and the media devalue any styles of life other than spectacular consumerism (Reiner et al., 2001: 178). The outcome of individualism in criminal justice is that deviants are defined in terms of their 'difference' and isolated via policies of containment, incapacitation and surveillance. Popularly conceived as a 'breed apart', many offenders are judged within a moral framework which constructs them as morally deficient malcontents who must be dealt with punitively and taught the lesson of individual responsibility (Surette, 1994).

Risk

Given that the notion of modern life being characterized by **risk** has become such a widespread and taken-for-granted assumption, it is surprising to find that the media devote little attention to crime avoidance, crime prevention or personal safety. The exception to this is if a message about prevention can be incorporated into an ongoing narrative about a serious offender 'at large', in which case the story will be imbued with a sense of urgency and drama (Greer, 2003a). The vast majority of serious offences, including murder, rape and sexual assault, are committed by people known to the victim. There are also clearly discernible patterns of victimization in certain socio-economic groups and geographical locations. Yet the media persist in presenting a picture of serious crime as random, meaningless, unpredictable and ready to strike anyone at any time (Chermak, 1994: 125). Such discourse as exists in the media (particularly the popular press) regarding prevention and personal safety invariably relates to offences committed by strangers, thus implicitly promoting stereotypes of dangerous criminals prepared to strike indiscriminately (Soothill and Walby, 1991; Greer, 2003a; see also Chapter 6 of this volume).

The idea that we are all potential victims is a relatively new phenomenon. After the Second World War, news stories encouraged compassion for offenders by providing details designed to elicit sympathy for their circumstances, thus endorsing the rehabilitative ideal that dominated penal policy at that time (Reiner, 2001). In today's more risk-obsessed and retributive times, crime stories have become increasingly victim-centred. Perceived vulnerability is emphasized over actual victimization so that fear of crime might be more accurately conceived as a fear for personal safety (Bazelon, 1978). Sometimes, the media exploit public concerns by exaggerating potential risks in order to play into people's wider fears and anxieties. Following the September 11th terrorist attacks in America, the British media fuelled a vision of apocalyptic meltdown with a series of stories ranging from terrorist plots to target the UK, to warnings about falling meteorites heading for earth. Yet it must be remembered that audiences are not passive or undiscriminating. Many crime scares and moral panics simply never get off the ground, and while it might be argued that the media fail to provide the public with the resources to independently construct alternative definitions and frameworks (Potter and Kappeler, 1998), people's sense of personal risk will usually correspond to their past personal experiences and a realistic assessment of the likelihood of future victimization above and beyond anything they see or hear in the media (see Chapter 6 of this volume).

Sex

One of the most salient news values – especially in the tabloid press, but also to a significant degree in the broadsheets and other media – is that of sex. Studies of the press by Ditton and Duffy (1983) in Strathclyde, by Smith (1984) in Birmingham, and by Greer (2003a) in Northern Ireland, reveal that newspapers over-report crimes of a sexual nature, thus distorting the overall picture of crime that the public receives, and instilling exaggerated fears among women regarding their likelihood of being victims of such crimes (see also Cameron and Frazer, 1987; Soothill and Walby, 1991; Carter, 1998; Naylor, 2001). Ditton and Duffy found that when reporting assaults against women, the press frequently relate sex and violence, so that the two become virtually indistinguishable. Furthermore, the over-reporting of such crimes was so significant that in Strathclyde in March 1981, crimes involving sex and violence accounted for only 2.4 per cent of recorded incidents, yet occupied 45.8 per cent of newspaper coverage (Ditton and Duffy, 1983). So interlinked are the themes of sex and violence, and so powerfully do they combine to illustrate the value of 'risk', that the prime example of newsworthiness is arguably the figure of the compulsive male lone hunter, driven by a sexual desire which finds its outlet in the murder of 'innocent' victims (Cameron and Frazer, 1987). As such, sexually motivated murders by someone unknown to the victim invariably receive substantial, often sensational, attention. On the other hand, sexual crimes against women where violence is not an overriding component of the story (bluntly, sex crimes that are non-fatal) and sexual assaults by someone known or related to the victim are generally regarded as routine and 'pedestrian' and may contain only limited analysis (Carter, 1998; Naylor, 2001). Moreover, the sexually motivated murder of prostitutes – who do not conform to media constructions of 'innocent' victims – also invariably receive considerably less coverage than those of other women.

Bronwyn Naylor (2001) argues that the frequency with which articles appear about apparently random stranger violence against 'ordinary' women and girls not only indicates that such stories fulfil key news values, but also that they permit highly sexualized, even pornographic representations of women. At the same time, these narratives tend to be highly individualized so that offences involving females – whether as victims or perpetrators – are rarely reported by the popular media without reference, often sustained and explicit, to their sexualities and sexual histories. Victims are frequently eroticized: for example, the conviction of Stuart Campbell in December 2002 for the sexually-motivated murder of his 15-year-old niece, Danielle Jones, was accompanied by media reports of their 'inappropriate', that is, abusive, sexual relationship, and photographs of a pair of blood-stained, white lace-topped stockings belonging to the girl found at Campbell's home. Meanwhile, female offenders are often portrayed as sexual predators – even if their crimes have no sexual element (see Chapter 5). This narrative is so widely used that it leads Naylor to question the purpose of such stories and how readers consume them:

> These stories draw on narratives about particular kinds of masculinity and about violent pornography, reiterating a discourse about masculine vio-lence as a 'natural force', both random and inevitable. They normalize this violence, drawing on and repeating the narrative that all men are poten-tially violent and that all women are potentially and 'naturally' victims of male violence (2001: 186).

She goes on to suggest that not only does the media's obsession with 'stranger-danger' give a (statistically false) impression that the public sphere is unsafe and the private sphere is safe, but also that it influences government decisions about the prioritization of resources, resulting in the allocation of funding towards very visible preventative measures (such as street lighting and CCTV cameras) and away from refuges, 'or indeed from any broader structural analysis of violence' (Naylor, 2001: 186).

Celebrity or high-status persons

The obsession with *celebrity* is evident everywhere in the media and a story is always more likely to make the news if it has a well-known name attached to it. Put simply, the level of deviance required to attract media attention is significantly lower than for offences committed by 'ordinary' citizens because a certain threshold of meaningfulness has already been achieved (Greer, 2003a). As such, a 'personality' will frequently be the recipient of media attention even if involved in a fairly mundane or routine crime that would not be deemed newsworthy if it concerned an 'ordinary' member of the public. Whether they are the victims of crime (for example, the mugging of actress, Liz Hurley, or the burglary of pop star Geri Halliwell's Notting Hill flat), perpetrators of crime (such as Gary Glitter and Jonathan King, both bastions of the British music industry, who have each been charged with offences relating to the sexual exploitation of children), or personal-ities who are simply famous for their endorsement of criminalized activities (for example, Brigitte Bardot, the French actress who has brought the activities of animal rights protesters to a much wider audience than they might have achieved otherwise), celebrities, their lives, and their experiences of crime are deemed intrinsically interesting to the audience. Even otherwise under-represented cate-gories of crime such as libel, perjury and embezzlement are guaranteed wide-spread media attention if they have a 'name' associated with them.

However, it is sexual deviance that dominates the news agenda of the tabloids, and a celebrity or high-status person who unexpectedly takes personal and professional risks by engaging in a sexually deviant act is an enduring feature of news in the postmodern mediascape. The conviction and imprisonment of Jeffrey Archer in 2001 thus represented a cardinal news story for the British media, as it involved a protagonist who was both a high-status person (a peer of the realm, no less) and a media celebrity, convicted of perjury after lying about money he had paid for the services of a prostitute. The extended period of *schadenfreude* enjoyed by the press is partially explained by their delight at exacting revenge on Lord Archer, who had previously successfully sued a tabloid newspaper for libel (and after the trial had to pay back the damages he had won). But it also illustrates the extent to which those who work in the media news industries are especially drawn to stories that unite celebrity or elevated status with sexual deviance and crime because they provide a titillating juxtaposition of high life and low life for an audience who, it is assumed, lead conventional and law-abiding 'mid lives' (Barak, 1994b).

Convicted criminals can also become media 'celebrities' by virtue of the notoriety of their crimes. Sometimes criminals are cast as **'folk devils'** by the media, and they are deemed newsworthy long after their convictions because the mass media take a moral stance on public distaste and revulsion towards their crimes. One such example is Peter Sutcliffe, known as the Yorkshire Ripper who, in 1981, was convicted of the murders of 13 women in the north of England. After two decades of confinement in a high-security hospital, he remains something of a media celebrity, with endless newspaper column inches and frequent television documentaries devoted to his crimes and his life since arrest. However, the fact that he will never be released into the community means that the media are able to treat Sutcliffe as a side-show, an entertaining if somewhat macabre diversion to fill media space when there is little else of importance to report. There are a handful of other criminals who occupy a particular symbolic space in the collective conscience of the British public (the Kray twins, the Great Train Robbers, Denis Nielsen, Fred and Rosemary West, the young killers of James Bulger), but arguably the most notorious figure in the history of the British criminal justice system is Myra Hindley (the 'Moors murderess') who, with her partner, Ian Brady, was convicted in 1966 of her part in the abduction, torture and murders of two children. Until her death in November 2002, Hindley was Britain's longest-serving prisoner and was a regular figure in the pages of the popular press, who waged a systematic and profoundly retributive campaign that culminated with front page copy on the day after her death announcing that the 'devil' had gone to hell 'where she belonged' (see Chapter 5). So successful was this campaign to keep her in prison that it became all but impossible for any Home Secretary – relying on public mandate as they do – to authorize the release of Hindley.

However, it is not just those who represent show-business and notorious crime who are elevated to visibility in the news. High-status individuals in 'ordinary' life (business people, politicians, professionals, the clergy and so on) are also deemed newsworthy and are frequently used to give a 'personal' angle to stories that otherwise might not make the news. This is especially germane when such individuals are defined as deviants: the more clearly and unambiguously the deviant personality can be defined (thus reducing uncertainty and reflecting the underlying news judgement of 'simplification'), the more intrinsically newsworthy the story is assumed to be, especially if it intersects with other news values. This is equally true of local media who report the deviant activities of people from the community they serve. Here, the value of 'proximity' comes into play (see below), but the recipient of news attention will normally be of high-status within the community; for example, a teacher, priest or doctor (Greer, 2003a). Paradoxically, then, despite the media's general tendency to portray crime as a menace wrought by a disaffected underclass on ordinary, respectable folk, it is the middle-class, high-status or celebrity offender who is deemed most newsworthy and will have the greatest number of column inches or hours of airtime devoted to their deviant activities.

Proximity

Proximity has both spatial and cultural dynamics. Spatial proximity refers to the geographical 'nearness' of an event, while cultural proximity refers to the 'relevance' of an event to an audience. These factors often intertwine so that it is those news stories which are perceived to reflect the recipient's existing framework of values, beliefs and interests and occur within geographical proximity to them that are most likely to be reported. Proximity obviously varies between local and national news. For example, a relatively 'ordinary' crime like mugging or arson may be reported in local media but might not make the national news agenda unless it conforms to other news values, for example, it was especially violent or spectacular or involved a celebrity. The converse of this trend is that events that occur in regions which are remote from the centralized bases of news organization or in countries that are not explicitly linked (in alliance or in opposition) to the UK or US rarely make the news. For example, the extended global coverage of two hijacked passenger jets ploughing into the twin towers of the New York World Trade Centre on 11 September 2001, like earlier footage taken in Dallas in October 1965 of the assassination of President John F. Kennedy, illustrates the degree to which America is regarded a world superpower. Their news is our news in a truly global sense, and both these crimes cast a long shadow in the collective memory of people with no connection, however tenuous, with the events of those days. But as others have pointed out, for those not of the 'First World', there have been other 'September 11ths' which have received little, if any, media coverage in the West (Brown, 2002; Hogg, 2002; Jefferson, 2002).

Cultural proximity also changes according to the political climate and cultural mood of the times. There was little media coverage of the Iran–Iraq war in the 1980s, but more recently Iraq has rarely been out of the news. In short, there may be a domestication of foreign news whereby events in other areas of the world will receive media attention if they are perceived to impinge on the home culture of the reporter and his or her audience. If there is no discernible relevance to the target audience, a story has to be commensurately bigger and more dramatic in order to be regarded as newsworthy. Novelist Michael Frayn comments facetiously:

> The crash survey showed that people were not interested in reading about road crashes unless there were at least 10 dead. A road crash with 10 dead, the majority felt, was slightly less interesting than a rail crash with one dead ... Even a rail crash on the Continent made the grade provided there were at least 5 dead. If it was in the United States the minimum number of dead rose to 20; in South America 100; in Africa 200; in China 500. But people really preferred an air crash ... backed up with a story about a middle-aged housewife who had been booked to fly aboard the plane but who had changed her mind at the last moment. (Frayn, 1965: 60)

Cultural proximity also pertains to perpetrators and victims of crime within the UK. When an individual goes missing (whether or not foul play is immediately suspected) the likelihood of the national media lending their weight behind a campaign to find the missing person depends on several inter-related factors. If the individual in question is young, female, white, middle-class and conventionally attractive, the media are more likely to cover the case than if the missing person is, say, a working-class boy or an older woman. Even in cases where abduction and/or murder is immediately suspected, the likelihood of media interest will vary in accordance with the background of the victim. If the victim is male, working class, of African Caribbean or Asian descent, a persistent runaway, has been in care, has drug problems, or is a prostitute (or any combination of these factors), reporters perceive that their audience is less likely to relate to, or empathize with, the victim, and the case gets commensurately lower publicity. The compliance of the victim's family in giving repeated press conferences and making themselves a central part of the story is also a crucial factor in determining its newsworthiness, as is their willingness to part with photographs and home video footage of their missing child. Hence, the disappearances of Sarah Payne, Milly Dowler and the 'Soham girls', Holly Wells and Jessica Chapman, were all eminently newsworthy stories: attractive, photogenic girls from 'respectable', middle-class homes with parents who quickly became media-savvy and were prepared to make repeated pleas for help on behalf of the police (and in the case of the Paynes and the Dowlers have continued to court the media, even after the story would normally be 'closed', in order to publicize public safety campaigns established in the names of their murdered children). Even the relatively high-profile case of the murder of 10–year-old Damilola Taylor in Peckham, South London was, initially at least, constructed very differently to the murders of the girls mentioned above. For over a week the victim remained virtually invisible as media reports concentrated almost exclusively on issues of community policing and the levels of violent crime on the streets. It was not until Damilola's father flew into the UK from Nigeria (and made press statements and television appearances) and CCTV footage was released to the media that this little boy became a person in his own right – a person worthy of media attention and public mourning and remembrance. Nevertheless, the public grieving for Damilola failed to reach the near hysterical outpourings of anger and sadness that accompanied the deaths of Sarah, Milly, Holly and Jessica.

To further illustrate this hierarchy of media interest in such cases, it is instructive to analyse similar stories from the same time period and compare the level and tone of coverage accorded to them. For example, a short time after the disappearance of 14-year-old Milly Dowler from Surrey in March 2002, the body of a teenage girl was recovered from a disused quarry near Tilbury Docks. Before the body had even been identified, sections of the tabloid press were carrying headlines announcing that Milly had been found. But it turned out to be the corpse of another 14-year-old girl, Hannah Williams, who had disappeared a year earlier. Yet it was the hunt for Milly that continued to dominate the news for the weeks and months to follow. Almost as soon as she was found, Hannah was forgotten. Quite simply, unlike Milly who was portrayed as the 'ideal' middle class teenager, Hannah's background made it difficult to build a campaign around her. She was working class and had run away before. Furthermore, her mother – a single parent on a low income – 'wasn't really press-conference material' according to a police spokeswoman (Bright, 2002: 23).

Violence

The news value which is arguably most common to all media is that of 'violence'. Violence fulfils the media's desire to present dramatic events in the most graphic possible fashion, and even the most regulated media institutions are constantly pushing back the boundaries of acceptable reportage when it comes to depicting acts of violence. In *Policing the Crisis: Mugging, the State and Law and Order*, Hall et al. comment:

> Any crime can be lifted into news visibility if violence becomes associated with it, since violence is perhaps the supreme example of … 'negative

consequences'. Violence represents a basic violation of the person; the greatest personal crime is 'murder', bettered only by the murder of a law-enforcement agent, a policeman. Violence is also the ultimate crime against property and against the State. It thus represents a fundamental rupture in the social order. The use of violence marks the distinction between those who are *of* society and those who are *outside* it ... The State, and the State only has the monopoly of legitimate violence, and this 'violence' is used to safeguard society against 'illegitimate' uses. Violence thus constitutes a critical threshold in society; all acts, especially criminal ones, which transgress that boundary are, by definition, worthy of news attention. It is often complained that 'the news' is too full of violence; an item can escalate to the top of the news agenda simply because it contains a 'Big Bang'. Those who so complain do not understand what 'the news' is about. It is impossible to define 'news values' in ways which would not rank 'violence' at or near the summit of news attention. (Hall et al., 1978: 68)

Despite its 'big bang' potential, in the years since Hall and his colleagues made this assertion, violence has become so ubiquitous that – although still considered newsworthy – it is frequently reported in a routine, mundane manner with little follow-up or analysis. Unless a story involving violence conforms to several other news values or provides a suitable threshold to keep alive an existing set of stories, even the most serious acts of violence may be used as 'fillers' and consigned to the inside pages of a newspaper (Naylor, 2001). Yet whether treated sensationally or unsensationally, violence – including violent death – remains a staple of media reporting. According to research, the British press devote an average of 65 per cent of their crime reporting to stories involving interpersonal violence, although police statistics indicate that only around 6 per cent of recorded crime involves interpersonal violence (Williams and Dickinson, 1993).

Postmodernists might argue that one of the reasons for the expansion in depictions of violence to gain audience attention in crime news is that real life has become increasingly saturated with images of violence, humiliation and cruelty. For cultural criminologists like Presdee (2000), crime and violence have become objectified and commodified, and thus desired, to the extent where they are widely distributed through all forms of media to be pleasurably consumed. Presdee offers numerous examples of the commodification of violence, humiliation and cruelty which, he claims, are evidence of the consumer's need for privately enjoyed, carnivalesque transgression. From 'sports' that, having all but disappeared, are now enjoying a dramatic upturn in popularity (albeit underground), such as bare-knuckle fighting, badger-baiting and dog-fighting, to 'Reality TV' and gangsta rap, the evidence of our lust for pain and humiliation is all around us:

> The mass of society bare their souls to the media who, in turn, transform them into the commodity of entertainment. Confidentialities are turned against the

subject, transforming them into the object of hurt and humiliation as their social being is commodified ready for consumption. (Presdee, 2000: 75)

Little wonder then, that news has followed a similarly dramatic and vicarious path. With an increasing imperative to bring drama and immediacy to news production, the caveat 'You may find some of the pictures that follow distressing' seems to preface an increasing number of television news reports. This leads us to consider the spectacle of violence as portrayed through graphic imagery.

Spectacle and graphic imagery

Television news is generally given greater credence by the public than newspapers, partly because it is perceived to be less partisan than the press, but also because it offers higher quality pictures which are frequently held to demonstrate the 'truth' of a story or to verify the particular angle from which the news team has chosen to cover it. As described above, violence is a primary component of news selection. But there are many different types of violence and it tends to be acts of violence that have a strong visual impact and can be graphically presented that are most likely to receive extensive media coverage. In his study of the professional codes governing popular news reporting, Chibnall (1977) suggests that the violence most likely to receive media attention is that which involves sudden injury to 'innocent others', especially in public places. Emotive language such as 'brutal thugs', 'rampaging hooligans' and 'anarchy' frequently accompany the reporting of crimes and disorder and serve to whip up public hysteria about the 'enemy' within. But such definitions serve to impose severe limitations on public discourses and debates about crime, so that it is 'spectacular' crimes (joyriding, rioting, arson, clashes between police and citizens and so on) that get most attention. They make good copy and are visually arresting on television. But those crimes which occur in private spheres, or which are not subject to public scrutiny, become even more marginalized, even more invisible. Hence, crimes like domestic violence, child abuse, elder abuse, accidents at work, pollution of the environment, much white collar crime, corporate corruption, state violence and governments' denial or abuse of human rights, all receive comparatively little media attention, despite their arguably greater cost to individuals and society. Similarly, long-term developments, which may be more important than immediate, dramatic incidents in terms of their effects, may not be covered because they cannot be accompanied by dramatic visual imagery.

The 'spectacle' of news reporting has arguably blurred the lines between 'real' and 'fake' and made it increasingly difficult to distinguish between 'fact' and 'fiction', especially in television programming. This is the age of 'fake TV'; a 'relentless and grotesque' drive towards infotainment (Osborne, 2002: 131). Channel 4 caused controversy in 2001 when it broadcast *Brass Eye*, a spoof current affairs programme in which celebrities were duped into condemning paedophilia in the most ludicrous terms, and the same station was prosecuted for passing off actors as 'real' participants in a documentary about male prostitution. Furthermore, not only do programmes like *Big Brother* blur the line between entertainment and reality and call into question the extent to which people behave 'normally' while being watched on television, but televised court trials in the US have made celebrities out of lawyers and judges, and led to accusations that they, too, are not immune to playing up for the cameras. In addition, 'real' footage of the kind captured on CCTV or on video cameras by witnesses and bystanders as a criminal event unfolds, is increasingly used in news broadcasts to visually highlight the event's immediacy and 'authenticity'. Such images have graphically and poignantly contributed to the spectacle of crime and violence in the postmodern era. Many of the most shocking events that occurred in the last few years of the 20th century entered the collective consciousness with such horrifying impact precisely because news reports were accompanied by images of the victim at the time of, immediately prior to, or soon after, a serious violent incident. The video footage of black motorist Rodney King being beaten up by four white LA police officers, and the live broadcast of O.J. Simpson being chased for miles down the freeway by police following the brutal murder of his wife, are examples from the US of graphic imagery being used to heighten the drama of already newsworthy stories. In this country, the last moments of the lives of Diana, Princess of Wales leaving the Ritz Hotel in Paris, James Bulger being led out of a Bootle shopping centre, Jill Dando shopping in Hammersmith, and Damilola Taylor skipping down a Peckham street, are all forcefully etched on the British psyche. Combining the mundane ordinariness of everyday life with the grim inevitability of what is about to unfold, CCTV footage – played out by the media on a seemingly endless loop appeals to the voyeuristic elements in all of us, while at the same time reinforcing our sense of horror, revulsion and powerlessness (see Chapters 6 and 7 for further discussion of CCTV and surveillance). In 2001 the Oklahoma bomber, Timothy McVeigh, exploited these conflicting emotions by urging Americans to watch him die at the hands of the State. Victims, relatives and witnesses were allocated tickets for a CCTV showing of his execution (McCahill, 2003); an event which many predict will soon lead to executions routinely being broadcast on US television networks.

Children

Writing in 1978, Stuart Hall and his colleagues argued that any crime can be lifted into news visibility if violence becomes associated with it, but three decades later it might be said that any crime can be lifted into news visibility if children are associated with it. In fact, Philip Jenkins (1992) argues precisely this, suggesting that *any* offence, particularly those that deviate from the *moral consensus*, are made eminently more newsworthy if children are involved. This is true whether the children at the centre of the story are victims or offenders, although Jenkins concentrates on child victims who, he says, not only guarantee the newsworthiness of a story, but can ensure the media's commitment to what might be called 'morality campaigns'. This amounts to what Jenkins describes as the 'politics of substitution'. In the 1970s, those who wished to denounce and stigmatize homosexuality, the sale of pornography or religious deviation (for example, satanism) found little support in the prevailing moral climate. But the inclusion of children in stories about these activities makes it impossible to condone them within any conventional moral or legal framework. Thus we have witnessed over the last 30 years a process of escalation whereby morality campaigns are now directed 'not against homosexuality but at paedophilia, not pornography but child pornography, not satanism but ritual child abuse' (Jenkins, 1992: 11). The focus on children means that deviant behaviour automatically crosses a higher threshold of victimization than would have been possible if adults alone had been involved (1992: 11). Nevertheless, despite Jenkins's assertion that the involvement of children guarantees news coverage of a story, this is not necessarily the case. Sexual abuse within the family remains so low down on the media's agenda as to render it virtually invisible, and as we shall see in later chapters, the mass media persist in preserving the image of the ideal family and underplaying or ignoring the fact that sexual violence exists – indeed, is endemic – in *all* communities, and that sexual abuse of children is more likely to occur within the family than at the hands of an 'evil stranger'.

Children who commit crimes have arguably become especially newsworthy since the murder of two-year-old James Bulger by two 10-year-olds in 1993, which was the first case for at least a generation in which the media constructed pre-teenage children as 'demons' rather than as 'innocents' (Muncie, 1999a: 3). The case also proved a watershed in terms of criminal justice and crime prevention. The 10-year-olds were tried in adult court and the case was the impetus for a massive expansion of CCTV equipment in public spaces throughout the country (Norris and Armstrong, 1999; McCahill, 2003). But at a more fundamental level, it presented a dilemma for the mass media. Childhood is a *social construction*; in other words, it is subject to a continuous process of (re)invention and (re)definition and, even in the modern period, has gone through numerous incarnations from 18th-century romantic portrayals of childhood as a time of innocence, to more recent conceptions of childhood as a potential site of psychological and psychiatric problems (Muncie, 1999a). But with the exception of a brief period in the early 19th century when children were viewed as inherently corrupt and in need of overt control and moral guidance (which coincided with a period when child labour was the norm among the working classes, before legislation took children out of factories, mills and mines and relocated them in schools and reformatories), the notion of children being 'evil' has not been prominent. By and large, childhood has been seen as fundamentally separate from adulthood, and children regarded as requiring nurture and protection, whether by philanthropic reformers, educators, parents, welfare agencies, the medical profession or the law. But with the murder of James Bulger by two older children, the notion of childhood innocence gave way to themes of childhood horror and evil. Public outrage was fuelled, in part, by sensational and vindictive press reporting which variously described the 10-year-olds as 'brutes', 'monsters', 'animals' and 'the spawn of Satan' (1999a). As far as the British media were concerned, these children were not 'innocents'. Yet neither were they uniquely deviant. While the Bulger case provided 'the strongest possible evidence to an already worried public that there was something new and terrifying about juvenile crime' (Newburn, 1996: 70), it was merely the apex of a wave of hysteria that, in the early 1990s, incorporated young joyriders, truants, drug users, burglars, gang members and, memorably, 'Ratboy'; a child of 14 with a string of offences to his name who had absconded from local authority care and was reportedly living in a sewer (1996: 70). The reasons why children and young people are the usual subjects of such moral panics will be explored in Chapters 3 and 4, but suffice it to say here that the young are frequently used as a kind of measuring stick or social barometer with which to test the health of society more generally. Children and adolescents represent the future, and if they engage in deviant behaviour it is often viewed as symptomatic of a society that is declining ever further into a moral morass. For the media, then, deviant youth is used as a shorthand ascription for a range of gloomy and fatalistic predictions about spiralling levels of crime and amoral behaviour in society at large.

Conservative ideology and political diversion

What all the news values discussed so far have in common is their reliance on a broadly right-wing consensus which, in many news channels (especially the tabloid press), is justified as encapsulating the 'British way of life'. In matters of crime and deviance, this agenda emphasizes deterrence and repression and voices support for more police, more prisons and a tougher criminal justice system. In addition, it appears that we now live in a society where political process and media discourse are indistinguishable and mutually constitutive. The symbiotic relationship between the mass media and politicians is illustrated by the support given by the former to the latter in matters of law and order. For two decades a version of 'populist punitiveness' has characterized British governments' attitudes to penal policy, a stance which is replicated in the US and in many other countries around the world. There seems little opposition from any political party in the UK to proposals to incarcerate ever younger children, to introduce curfews, to bring in legislation to prevent large 'unauthorized' gatherings, and to introduce new and harsher measures against immigrants, protesters, demonstrators, the homeless and the young unemployed. All these issues are most directly conveyed to the public at large by the mass media.

Of course, the 'British way of life' that is defended most vehemently by newspapers such as the *Sun* and the *Daily Mail* is fiercely nostalgic and may now only be applicable to a minority (ironically usually termed the *'moral majority'*) of British citizens. Despite claiming to be the voice of the people, the criminalization of certain individuals and activities by these newspapers highlights the general perceived intolerance towards anyone or anything that transgresses an essentially conservative agenda. It is also partial explanation for the vigorous policing and punishment of so-called 'victimless crimes': recreational use of drugs, sexual permissiveness, especially among young people, public displays of homosexuality and lesbianism, anti-establishment demonstrators exercising their democratic right to protest, and spectacular youth cultures. All are activities which are subject to continuous, and sometimes overblown, repression. At times the generalized climate of hostility to marginal groups and 'unconventional' norms (to the dominant culture of journalists, at least) spills over into racism and xenophobia. The moral concerns over mugging in the 1970s was focused on young men of African Caribbean descent; the inner-city riots of the 1980s were frequently attributed entirely to black youths; and recent media coverage of the immigration into Britain of people from other countries frequently demonstrates a shocking disregard for others' human rights, and the media's inability (or unwillingness) to differentiate between political refugees and illegal immigrants. Even people from ethnic and/or religious minorities born and raised in this country may be subjected to overwhelmingly negative press. For example, British-born Muslims first became newsworthy when a *fatwah*, or death threat, was issued against author Salman Rushdie in 1989, resulting in a great deal of unfavourable coverage portraying all Muslims as fanatics and fundamentalists. Since then, Muslims in the UK have continued to be identified in negative contexts, even when cast as victims (Barak, 1994b; cf. Hartman and Husband, 1974).

The concentration of news media on the criminal and deviant activities of people from the working classes and from religious, ethnic and cultural minorities serves to perpetuate a sense of a stratified, deeply divided and mutually hostile population. Some politicians have been quick to galvanize the support of an anxious and fearful public, and have undoubtedly contributed to negative reporting which has agitated social tensions. By simultaneously focussing attention on hapless victims of serious crime and calling for tougher, more retributive punishment, politicians not only promote an essentially conservative agenda, but also deflect attention from other serious social problems. Indeed, it could be argued that much of what makes up our newspapers is in fact a mere side-show, a diversionary tactic which removes attention from more serious problems in society, particularly those of a political nature. The media hysteria which has, in recent years, accompanied victims of HIV and AIDS, lone/unmarried parents, teenage and pre-teenage mothers, child abusers, satanic ritual abusers, video nasties, juvenile delinquents, joyriders, ravers, users of cannabis, ecstasy and other recreational drugs, paedophiles, homosexual members of parliament (indeed, homosexuals generally), adulterous celebrities, and girl gangs, might all be reasonably argued to constitute part of the overtly sanctimonious moral discourse directed at the institution of the family, which has characterized the media and political agendas since the 1980s. From John Major's ill-fated 'Back to Basics' campaign, to Tony Blair's promotion of a 'new moral order' (prompted by studies showing that Britain has the highest rate of teenage pregnancies in Europe), successive British leaders have harnessed the mass media to criminalize certain groups of people and divert attention from the systemic social problems of their making; poverty, patriarchy, and an education system that is failing its pupils, among them.

News values and crime news production: some concluding thoughts

While the possibility of a direct causal relationship between media consumption and behavioural response (for example, between violent screen images and real-life violence) is downplayed by most media academics in the UK, it is nonetheless widely accepted that those who work in the media do have some degree of influence in terms of what potential stories they select and how they then organize them, defining or amplifying some issues over others. The time and space available for news is not infinite and journalism is, of necessity, a selective account of reality (McNair, 1993, 1998). No story can be told without judgements being made about the viability of sending costly resources to film, photograph and report it, or without implicit suppositions being made about the beliefs and values of the people who will be reading, viewing or listening to it.

The desire to accommodate public tastes and interests has prompted some critics to accuse the British media of pandering to what the first Director General of the BBC, Lord Reith, used to call the 'lowest common denominator' of the audience. Since the British media went through a process of deregulation in the late 1980s and early 1990s criticism has intensified, and both broadcast and print media have been accused of 'dumbing down' their news coverage and measuring newsworthiness by the degree of amusement or revulsion a story provokes in the audience. The news values that have been discussed in this chapter seem to support this view. They illustrate that the news media do not cover systemically all forms and expressions of crime and victimization, and that they pander to the most voyeuristic desires of the audience by exaggerating and dramatizing relatively unusual crimes, while ignoring or downplaying the crimes that are most likely to happen to the 'average' person. At the same time, they sympathize with some victims while blaming others. Nevertheless, the tabloidization of news (on television and radio as well as in print) is arguably a cultural expression of democratic development, giving voice to new forms of political engagement with issues such as environmentalism, health and sexuality (McNair, 1998; Manning, 2001). And while the interests and priorities of the contemporary audience may be regarded as populist and trivial, the fact is that more people consume news today than have at any time previously. Furthermore, there is a valuable investigative tradition in journalism which continues to play an important role, not least in the spheres of crime control, crime prevention and uncovering police corruption and miscarriages of justice.

Summary

- News values are the combined outcome of two different but interrelated factors which together determine the selection and presentation of news. First, news values are shaped by a range of technological, political and economic forces that structure and constrain the form and content of any reported event at the point of newsgathering. Second, news values cater for the perceived interests of the audience and they capture the public mood; a factor usually summed up by news editors as 'giving the public what it wants'.
- Drawing on 'classic' studies by Galtung and Ruge (1965/1973) and Chibnall (1977), which analysed news production in the mid-20th century, this chapter has developed a set of 12 news values appropriate to the new millennium. While faithful to certain news fundamentals that were highlighted in these works, the chapter has suggested that as society has evolved, so too do the cultural and psychological triggers which condition audience responses and, correspondingly, influence the construction of media narratives.
- In addition to the news values discussed in detail, it is taken for granted that crime is inherently highly newsworthy and is usually 'novel' and 'negative' in essence. News values not only shape the production of crime news in the 21st century, but they also aid our understanding of why public perceptions about crime are frequently inaccurate, despite media audiences being more sophisticated and better equipped to see through 'spin' than ever before.
- The 12 news values discussed in this chapter will be drawn on throughout the remainder of this book in order to demonstrate how types of crime and specific criminal cases are selected and presented according to prevailing cultural assumptions and ideologies.

STUDY QUESTIONS

1   How have news values changed over the last 50 years? Which of the news values identified in this chapter would you say have become most prominent recently? What do these variations tell us about the changing nature of society?

2   This chapter has focused mainly on the news values used to set the *national* news agenda. What news values are most evident in crime reports in your local newspaper, or on your local radio or television news programme? How do they differ from the national and international media?

3   Using international news services accessed via 'new' media technologies, conduct a content analysis of the major crime news stories covered, and draw up a list of the news values prioritized. As global news outlets expand and develop, what changes do you foresee in the news values used to shape the reporting of crime news in the future?

4   How would each of the theoretical perspectives reviewed in Chapter 1 view the production of crime news?

FURTHER READING

It is still worth returning to the seminal study of press news values produced by Galtung, J. and Ruge, M., originally published in 1965, but most easily accessed in S. Cohen and J. Young (eds) (1973) *The Manufacture of News* (Constable). Chibnall, S. (1977) *Law and Order News* (Tavistock) also still deserves close attention. Greer, C. (2003) *Sex Crime and the Media* (Willan) considers the extent to which news values shape the reporting of sex crime in Northern Ireland, and highlights the news value 'proximity' as being especially important in this context. Wykes, M. (2001) *News, Crime and Culture* (Pluto) discusses news values in relation to crime and deviance and includes several fascinating case studies. Manning, P. (2001) *News and News Sources: A Critical Introduction* (Sage) is a useful introduction to news production more generally. Finally, two websites that offer free archive searches for news stories are those provided by the *Guardian* newspaper and the BBC. They can be found at www.guardian.co.uk and www.news.bbc.co.uk respectively.

3

Media and Moral Panics

Chapter Contents

OVERVIEW

Chapter 3 provides:

- An overview of the well-known but often misinterpreted and misrepresented concept of 'moral panics'.
- An analysis of the pros and cons of the moral panic model as a conceptual tool for understanding public responses to mediated crime and deviance.
- An examination of the five defining features that identify moral panics, as they have traditionally been conceived.
- A discussion of 'deviancy amplification' and the extent to which attempts by authorities to control deviant behaviour actually lead to its increase.

KEY TERMS

consensus	folk devils	social reaction
demonization	labelling	stigmatizing
deviance	moral panic	subculture
deviancy amplification spiral	risk	youth

'Moral panic' is a familiar term in academic studies of crime, **deviance** and the media. It refers to public and political reactions to minority or marginalized individuals and groups who appear to be some kind of threat to consensual values and interests. The **social reaction** is predominantly media-fuelled. The mass media – usually led by the press – will define a group or act as 'deviant' and focus on it to the exclusion of almost everything else. The concept of **moral panic** originated in British sociology in the 1970s with the publication of Stanley Cohen's (1972/2002) *Folk Devils and Moral Panics: The Creation of the Mods and Rockers*. Although not the first scholar to explore the role of the mass media in labelling non-conformist groups and manufacturing crime waves (that was Jock Young in 1971), Cohen has been credited as providing the first *systematic* empirical study of the media amplification of deviancy and subsequent public responses (Muncie, 1987; 1999a). Since then, the concept of moral panics has been applied, developed, lauded and criticized in equal measure (Hall et al., 1978; Waddington, 1986; Watney, 1987; Jenkins, 1992; Goode and Ben-Yehuda, 1994; Thompson, 1998; Jewkes, 1999; Critcher, 2003). In fact, so enshrined is the notion of the 'moral panic' that it is not only found in criminology textbooks, but has also entered the public consciousness and is regularly referred to within the popular media, who have uncritically employed it to describe public reactions to numerous social phenomena from child abusers to flu epidemics. Yet the field out of which the moral panic thesis emerged and was made famous – sociology – all but abandoned the term within 10 years of its inception (for example, it warrants only the briefest of mentions in the 4th edition of Giddens' best-selling *Sociology* textbook, 2001, and in Abercrombie et al.'s 4th edition of the *Penguin Dictionary of Sociology*, 2000). Moreover, despite the fact that an understanding of moral panics relies on a working knowledge of the production practices of the mass media, few university degree courses in media studies pay more than a glancing acknowledgement of the media's alleged power to define and amplify deviance to the level where society experiences a sense of collective panic akin to a disaster mentality.

This chapter aims to account for these omissions and to consider the pros and cons of the moral panic thesis as a conceptual tool. It is beyond the scope of this book to speculate in detail about why the notion of moral panics remains central to most criminological accounts of deviant youth subcultures, despite its decline in popularity among scholars from sociology and media studies. However, it can justifiably be claimed that, in its early formation, the concept clearly lent itself to amalgamation with American criminology, which was highly influential in the UK. It is relatively easy to comprehend how the conceptualization of moral panics by Stanley Cohen, Jock Young, Stuart Hall and others found intellectual and empirical compatibility with Lemert's (1951) study of social pathology, Becker's (1963) analysis of the labelling of 'outsiders', and Matza's (1964) study of delinquency and drift. Moreover, it is no coincidence that the emergence of a distinctive British school of subcultural theory accompanied a succession of youth subcultures in the UK, starting with the Teddy boys in the 1950s, followed by mods and rockers and hippies in the 1960s, and skinheads, punks and African–Caribbean groups such as rude boys and Rastafarians in the 1970s. Since that time, British criminologists have continued to test the validity of the moral panic model and it has recently enjoyed a particularly strong revival in relation to the media reporting of child abusers and paedophiles (Jenkins, 1992, 2001; Silverman and Wilson, 2002; Critcher, 2003; see also Chapter 4).

With this evolution in mind, this chapter considers the background and defining features of the moral panic model as it has traditionally been conceived. The discussion pays particularly close attention to moral panics directed at deviant youth; a theme which will be developed in the following chapter, which explores the confusion and paradoxes that surround contemporary attitudes to children.

The background to the moral panic model

Cohen opens his book with the much quoted passage:

> Societies appear to be subject, every now and then, to periods of moral panic. A condition, episode, person or group of persons emerges to become defined as a threat to societal values and interests; its nature is presented in a stylised and stereotypical fashion by the mass media; the moral barricades are manned by editors, bishops, politicians and other right-thinking people; socially accredited experts pronounce their diagnoses and solutions; ways of coping are evolved or (more often) resorted to; the condition then disappears, submerges or deteriorates and becomes more visible. Sometimes the object of the panic is quite novel and at other times it is something which has been in existence long enough, but suddenly appears in the limelight. Sometimes the panic passes over and is forgotten, except in folklore and collective memory; at other times it has more serious and long-lasting repercussions and might produce such changes as those in legal and social policy or even in the way the society conceives itself. (1972/2000: 9)

As Cohen intimates in this extract, threats to societal values and interests are not *always* personalized (in cases of food scares, health epidemics, NHS patients dying because of inadequate treatment, environmental concerns and so on). However, when we are thinking of **subculture** membership there are, broadly speaking, four types of people who may be the targets of moral outrage: those who commit serious criminal acts, from muggers and rioters (invariably young, working-class men who can be characterized as 'yobs') to individuals who commit sexual offences and murder; those whose behaviour strays from organizational procedures or who break conventional codes of conduct in the workplace, such as strikers and picketers; those who adopt patterns of behaviour, styles of dress or ways of presenting themselves which are different to the 'norm', such as mods, rockers, punks, hippies, skinheads and urban gang members; and, finally, the miscellaneous groups of people who fail to conform to consensual, conservative ideals, especially concerning the traditional institution of the family. These might include people with Aids (which, throughout the early 1980s, was coined the 'gay plague' by sections of the popular press), lone mothers, welfare cheats and those who download child pornography from the Internet. However, 'moral panics', as they were initially conceived by Stan Cohen and Jock Young, were explicitly concerned with the symbolic nature of youth cultures. Indeed, since Cohen propelled the moral panic model into the gaze of academics and laypersons alike with his study of the clashes between mods and rockers on British beaches in the mid-1960s, moral panics have been created about numerous youth subcultures including juvenile muggers, children viewing violent videos, 'new age travellers', ravers and ecstasy users. As we will see in the next chapter, moral panics have also been generated about children's safety, especially in relation to the risks posed to them by adult sex offenders.

Although all these groups – and many others who have not been mentioned – are immensely diverse, five distinct but interconnected factors have conventionally been identified in most moral panics (listed below and then discussed in greater detail). However, this chapter will argue that the five defining features of moral panics highlighted in traditional conceptualizations are inadequately theorized and that the relationship between them is more complex than is often suggested. Integral to the discussion, then, will be a consideration of the deficiencies of the moral panic model, and the problems with its application, which have caused some to argue that it has no validity. Dismissed as a 'polemical rather than an analytic concept' directing concern to issues 'without substance or justification', Waddington is one such critic. He argues that the notion of moral panics is riddled with value-laden terminology and has gone so far as to suggest that the concept should be abandoned altogether (Waddington, 1986: 258). The discussion that follows will attempt to represent both pros and cons of the moral panic model as a conceptual tool, and will assess the extent to which it aids our understanding of public responses to mediated events.

The five defining features of moral panics in traditional formulations of the model are:

1   Moral panics occur when the mass media take a reasonably ordinary event and present it as an extraordinary occurrence.
2   The media set in motion a 'deviancy amplification spiral' in which a moral discourse is established by journalists and various other authorities, opinion leaders and moral entrepreneurs, who collectively demonize the perceived wrong-doers as a source of moral decline and social disintegration.
3   Moral panics clarify the moral boundaries of the society in which they occur, creating consensus and concern.
4   Moral panics occur during periods of rapid social change, and can be said to locate and crystallize wider social anxieties about risk.
5   It is usually young people who are targeted, as they are a metaphor for the future and their behaviour is regarded as a barometer with which to test the health or sickness of a society.

How the mass media turn the ordinary into the extraordinary

The mundanity and sheer 'ordinariness' of the events which gave rise to a moral panic in the seaside town of Clacton in 1964 are beautifully captured by Cohen:

Easter 1964 was worse than usual. It was cold and wet, and in fact Easter Sunday was the coldest for eighty years. The shopkeepers and stall owners were irritated by the lack of business and the young people had their own boredom and irritation fanned by rumours of café owners and barmen refusing to serve some of them. A few groups started scuffling on the pavements and throwing stones at each other. The Mods and Rockers factions – a division initially based on clothing and life styles, later rigidified, but at that time not fully established – started separating out. Those on bikes and scooters roared up and down, windows were broken, some beach huts were wrecked and one boy fired a starting pistol in the air. (1972/2002: 29)

Although Cohen admits that these two days were 'unpleasant, oppressive and sometimes frightening' (1972/2002: 29), the levels of actual intimidation, conflict and violence in Clacton (and in Brighton where similar incidents occurred during the same period) were relatively low. The media, however, carried headlines such as 'Day of Terror by Scooter Gangs' (*Daily Telegraph*) and 'Youngsters Beat Up Town' (*Daily Express*), and they routinely used phrases such as 'riot', 'orgy of destruction', 'battle', 'siege' and 'screaming mob' to convey an impression of an embattled town from which innocent holidaymakers were fleeing from a rampaging mob. Indeed, the term 'riot' has since become a stock phrase used by journalists to cover *any* emotionally-charged incident involving three or more people (Knopf, 1970).

Like any other newsworthy event, the media construct moral panics according to their criteria of 'news values' (see Chapter 2). Exaggeration and distortion are thus key elements in the meeting of the required *threshold* to turn a potential news event into an actual story. Moral panics will also frequently involve the news value *predictability*, in the sense of media prognoses that what has happened will inevitably happen again. Even when it does not, a story will still be constructed to that effect, through the reporting of non-events which appear to confirm their predictions (Halloran et al., 1970; Cohen, 1972/2002). *Simplification* occurs through a process of symbolization whereby names can be made to signify complex ideas and emotions. A word ('mod') becomes symbolic of a status ('deviant') and objects (a particular hairstyle or form of clothing) come to signify that status and the negative emotions attached to it (Cohen, 1972/2002). The cumulative effect is that the term 'mod' becomes disassociated with any previously neutral connotations it had (such as the denotation of a particular consumer style) and acquires wholly negative meanings (1972/2002). When it comes to political and public responses to these processes, one of Cohen's key findings was that, while the media frequently associate certain minority groups with deviance and condemn their use of *violence*, they nonetheless accept that violence is a legitimate way for the police to deal with problems, and is sometimes a necessary form of retaliation. Perceptions derived from these presentations may also influence 'official' attitudes so that they come to match the stereotypes. The media-constructed definitions of the situation are therefore reinforced and all sides behave as 'expected' (Cohen and Young, 1973). The problem is that violence and the language of conflict are so commonplace that audiences may arguably become desensitized to coverage of confrontation and there is a perception among many journalists that the public demand entertainment (albeit voyeuristically), thus creating an increasingly sensationalized style of reporting.

The role of the authorities in the deviancy amplification process

It has been suggested that moral panics have their origins in moral crusades such as the American Prohibition Movement of 1900–1920 and, before that, the European witch hunts of the 16th and 17th centuries (Goode and Ben-Yehuda, 1994). The moral crusaders of contemporary society are journalists, newspaper editors, politicians, the police and pressure groups, who combine to set in motion a spiral of events in which the attention given to the deviants leads to their criminalization and marginalization. One version of the moral panic model thus suggests that it is those with vested interests who use the media as a conduit to make a moral statement about a particular individual, group or behaviour (although question of source is by no means straightforward or universally agreed upon, as we shall see shortly). It is argued that those in power label minority groups as subversive with a view to exploiting public fears, and then step in to provide a 'popular' solution to the problem which, in the current rhetoric of populist punitiveness, usually amounts to getting tougher on crime. But not only does increased attention appear to validate the media's initial concern, it may also result in the target group feeling increasingly alienated, particularly when as – often happens – politicians and other 'opinion leaders' enter the fray, demanding tougher action to control and punish the 'deviants' and warning of the possible dangers to society if their activities are not held in check. Such widespread condemnation may lead the group to feel more persecuted and marginalized, resulting in an increase in their deviant activity, so that they appear to become more like the creatures originally created by the media. The continuing deviancy results in greater police attention, more arrests and further media coverage. Thus a *'deviancy amplification spiral'* (Wilkins, 1964) is set in motion (see Figure 3.1). Although a conservative analysis would posit that the spiral demonstrates the media's justification in responding to public interest and rising crime, a more radical account would argue that the hysteria generated in this process is an effective way for governments to control their citizens, dissuade people from adopting unconventional lifestyles and coerce them into conforming to society's mores.

The deviancy amplification spiral thus describes what happens when a society outlaws a particular group. As negative social reaction escalates and the 'deviants' become increasingly isolated, they become more and more criminally oriented. The spiral of deviancy may go on for weeks or even months, but it never spirals

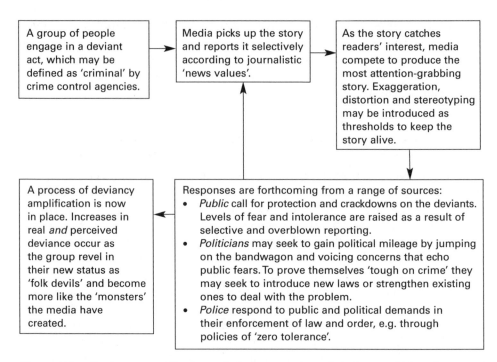

| A group of people engage in a deviant act, which may be defined as 'criminal' by crime control agencies. | Media picks up the story and reports it selectively according to journalistic 'news values'. | As the story catches readers' interest, media compete to produce the most attention-grabbing story. Exaggeration, distortion and stereotyping may be introduced as thresholds to keep the story alive. |

| A process of deviancy amplification is now in place. Increases in real *and* perceived deviance occur as the group revel in their new status as 'folk devils' and become more like the 'monsters' the media have created. | Responses are forthcoming from a range of sources:
• *Public* call for protection and crackdowns on the deviants. Levels of fear and intolerance are raised as a result of selective and overblown reporting.
• *Politicians* may seek to gain political mileage by jumping on the bandwagon and voicing concerns that echo public fears. To prove themselves 'tough on crime' they may seek to introduce new laws or strengthen existing ones to deal with the problem.
• *Police* respond to public and political demands in their enforcement of law and order, e.g. through policies of 'zero tolerance'. |

Figure 3.1 *Deviancy amplification spiral: the reporting of deviance within a framework of exaggeration, distortion, prediction and symbolization sets into motion a series of interrelated responses*
Source: developed from Wilkins, 1964

out of control for a number of reasons. Media interest will eventually wane and move on to other issues and, after a period of time, the *'folk devil'* becomes familiar and therefore is perceived as being less of a threat. Ways of coping with the perceived threat are evolved, either as a result of new legislation introduced to minimize or eliminate the problem, or more mundane strategies evolved by the people most affected. Finally, in the case of youth subcultures, the deviant may eventually stop being deviant, grow up and move on.

Defining moral boundaries and creating consensus

In the identification of a group responsible for a perceived threat, a division quickly becomes apparent between 'us' – decent, respectable and moral – and 'them' – deviant, undesirable outsiders. The perception that the threat is real, serious and caused by an identifiable minority does not have to constitute a universal belief, or even be held by a majority, but the national press will report it in such a way as to imply that their condemnation of the threatening behaviour represents a consensus. In addressing an imagined national community, newspapers will frequently appeal to a nostalgic conservative ideology, a desire for retribution, and to a much vaunted opinion that 'common sense' should prevail. What these three combined factors amount to is a popular ideological perception that 'thing's aren't what they used to be'. In an echo of mass society theory a century ago (see Chapter 1), many have argued that society is rapidly and inexorably deteriorating due to a decline in religious morality, a growing lack of respect for authority, the disintegration of the traditional nuclear family, the media as provider of role models for the nation's children and – in very recent years – the existence of perverts who prey on our children via the Internet. Moreover, there is a widespread acceptance among politicians and the media that the appropriate response to this sorry state of affairs is to call for tougher action on the part of the police, the courts and the prisons. Take this letter written in the 1950s by a 'family doctor':

> Teddy boys ... are all of unsound mind in the sense that they are all suffering from a form of psychosis. Apart from the birch or the rope, depending on the gravity of their crimes, what they need is rehabilitation in a psychopathic institution. (Brake, 1980: 11)

In the ensuing half century it arguably is not the sentiment that has changed, but the age at which young people are pathologized which has diminished to the level where it is frequently primary school-aged youngsters who are seen to be at risk of turning 'bad'. In addition, the notion of 'troublesome youth' has been emphatically enshrined in political rhetoric and law with a range of policies that *demonize* and criminalize children. The Crime and Disorder Act of 1998 introduced three different types of curfew on children, including 'anti-social behaviour orders' and 'child safety orders', which allow the police and local authorities to act on any child considered to be 'at risk' of behaving in an anti-social manner (Muncie, 1999a). The impression conveyed is that children behaving in ways disapproved of by adults is an entirely new phenomenon – a perception that is surely open to challenge from anyone who can remember their own childhood! With the introduction of more and more legislation which seeks to privatize childhood, clearing the streets of young people and criminalizing behaviour that once seemed 'normal' experiences in adolescence (everything from mild sexual experimentation to playing with fireworks), it is no wonder that childhood appears to be in crisis. These moves seem to indicate what Scraton calls the 'sharp end of a continuum of child rejection; a sharp end most accurately described as child-hate, in the same vein as race-hate, misogyny or homophobia' (Scraton, 2002: 15).

However, as we can see from the deviancy amplification spiral in Figure 3.1, it may be that some politicians and opinion leaders are simply seeking to gain political favour from voicing opposition to those whom the media has *labelled* 'deviant'. With politicians competing to come up with the best soundbite on morality ('moral vacuum', 'moral chaos', 'moral crisis' and so on) a moral *panic* is virtually guaranteed, and in condemning the actions of a minority, and being seen to be 'tough on crime', politicians are assured of favourable coverage in the majority of the British press. As one commentator bluntly puts it in relation to the death of James Bulger, Prime Minister Tony Blair 'employed a dead toddler to shift Labour to a hard line on law and order' (N. Cohen, 1999: 84). Within days of James' death there were authoritative calls from politicians, self-proclaimed 'experts' and the press for the greater use of imprisonment for children and young people (Scraton, 2002). The combined assault of law-makers, law-enforcers and the newspapers which purport to reflect the views of their readership serves to widen the chasm between the activities of a few, isolated deviants and the rest of society, and in marginalizing those who are already on the periphery, they give an inner strength to the core. Thus, it might be suggested that not only do moral panics draw together communities in a sense of collective outrage, but they actually make the core feel more complacent in the affirmation of their own morality; when we have defined what is 'evil', we know by implication what is 'good'. Consequently, conventional accounts of moral panics emphasize that they demonstrate that there are limits to how much diversity can be tolerated in a society and they confirm the authority of those who make such judgements (Durkheim, 1895/1964).

Rapid social change – risk

As we saw in our discussion of news values in the previous chapter, over recent years a number of commentators have characterized contemporary Western society as a *'risk'* society in which awareness of potential dangers to individual, group and global concerns has overshadowed traditional, more mundane matters (Douglas, 1966; Giddens, 1991; Beck, 1992; Ericson and Haggerty, 1997). For advocates of the moral panic thesis, they constitute one of the most salient examples of a culture attuned to the possibility of disaster, and the overriding features of a moral panic concerning a deviant group are, in many cases, said to be strikingly similar to those which characterize a natural disaster such as an earthquake or hurricane, or a man-made disaster such as a bombing (Cohen, 1972/2002). In addition to following a sequence of warning–impact–reaction, the concept of moral panics might be said to have further parallels with disaster models in its capacity to expose to the public domain behaviour, attitudes and emotions which are usually confined to the private sphere. But the moral panic thesis has been criticized for its apparent inability to establish a link between the scale of the disaster and the scale of response to it. Not only does it fail to accurately determine public levels of concern, and whether people are motivated by the media to the exclusion of all other influences, but it also makes it impossible to gauge whether the problem is a real one or not. For Goode and Ben-Yehuda (1994) this problem of proportionality is easily solved. Quite simply, problems become the subject of moral panics when they are familiar, close at hand and appear to directly impinge on individuals' lives. Accordingly, future-oriented threats such as the potentially catastrophic effects of the shrinking ozone layer, a rogue meteorite hitting earth, or the risk of nuclear war are unlikely to become the subjects of moral panic. But even this seems too simplistic. Few folk devils have had a direct impact on the lives of more than a handful of people and, as we saw in Chapter 1, in times of political and social turbulence, even an invasion by Martians can seem a plausible occurrence.

The reasons why a society appears especially susceptible at certain times is debatable. A number of writers have pointed to the transition from a period of modernity to one of postmodernity as explanation for the apparent destabilization of many established aspects of social life. The 'unfreezing' of traditional features of modernity has opened up new structural possibilities which have been described as 'beyond modernity' (Hall et al., 1992). But as with any transition from one kind of social order to another, traditional processes and values have been weakened and displaced. Liberal ideologies emphasizing individual choice have combined with advances in technology to produce a greater cultural pluralism, and an increasing awareness of the possibilities of constructing new identities. At the same time, however, the blurring of public and private boundaries has extended to society's institutions, which have sought to regulate social life in ways previously unimaginable (see Chapter 7). Alternative visions and conflicting points of identification have been formed, which have led to what is often referred to as a 'crisis of identity' whereby media-inspired and consumer-driven aspirations have started to merge and collide with traditional identifications (such as those based on class, race, gender, nationality), resulting in a decentring of the subject or, to put it another way, an 'unstable amalgam of self' (Hall et al., 1992). The ambivalent and paradoxical nature of this period of late modernity is summed up by Berman:

> To be modern is to find ourselves in an environment that promises us adventure, power, joy, growth, transformation of ourselves and the world – and, at the same time, that threatens to destroy everything we have, everything we know, everything we are. Modern environments and experiences cut across all boundaries of geography and ethnicity, of class and nationality, of religion and ideology: in this sense, modernity can be said to unite all mankind. But it is a paradoxical unity, a unity of disunity: it pours us all into a maelstrom of perpetual disintegration and renewal, of struggle and contradiction, of ambiguity and anguish. To be modern is to be part of a universe in which, as Marx said, 'all that is solid melts into air'. (Berman, 1983: 1)

As described in Chapter 1, America was experiencing such a maelstrom of disintegration and renewal at the time of the 1938 *War of the Worlds* broadcast. But these processes can similarly be detected in the Britain of the mid-1950s: the time of the first modern, media-led moral panic in this country, which was directed at Teddy boys. At this time a number of social trends were converging to challenge and de-centre traditional norms and values. The 'feel good factor' still hung over the nation after victory against Hitler, but for many the celebrations were tempered by the trauma of the quarter of a million British deaths and the destruction of homes and workplaces. The war had left the country in a state of economic crisis, yet by the late 1950s a new spirit of optimism emerged and the 1960s became a time of full employment. New social patterns were also radically altering the face of Britain: family relationships changed as legislation was introduced to make divorce easier and more socially acceptable for women; new technologies and the emergence of the service and leisure industries were challenging traditional industrial practices, with semi-professional and professional jobs being created at roughly the same pace as the number of manual workers declined; and migration of British citizens from New Commonwealth countries was taking place. All these factors combined to make many people feel very uncertain and anxious about their lives, and concerns about change, instability and the displacement of what went before became consolidated in the group identities of the new youth subcultures.

Youth

The social construction of **youth** as a problem that had bubbled just beneath the surface of British social and political life for many years (Pearson, 1983) exploded into the public consciousness in the late 1950s and almost immediately became the subject of sociological inquiry (for example, Abrams, 1959). It is often said that 'youth' came into its own in the post-War era. Before the Second World War, young people tended to model themselves on their parents, or those of their parents' generation, and their clothes, manners, aspirations and expectations were all characteristic of a previous era. But in the 1950s, young people became seen as a specific social category, distinct from other age groups, and the word 'teenager' was coined for the first time. They rejected their parents' values and interests, and became powerful citizens and consumers in their own right. Traditional class boundaries were also broken down as the media and leisure industries homogenized teenagers into a vibrant, consumer group. Cafés, milk bars and dance halls sprang up, and a range of cultural products were explicitly aimed at a young audience. Hollywood film stars such as Marlon Brando and James Dean, rock-and-roll artists like Buddy Holly and Elvis, pirate radio stations such as Caroline and Luxembourg, and television programmes including *Ready, Steady, Go* and *Juke Box Jury* all heightened the sense of excitement and freedom that was associated with being a teenager in the 1950s and 1960s. Teenagers were more affluent than they had ever been before, and formed a larger section of society than other age groups because of the post-War 'baby boom' years.

They had significant purchasing power, and they represented vitality and social mobility to a degree which marked them out from other generations. More than at any time previously, youth represented the future and became a powerful metaphor for 'New Britain' in all its vibrant, urban modernity.

However, the combination of rapid social change with distinctive, unconventional and often spectacular styles of physical appearance and behaviour was a heady mixture. If 'youth' represents the future, a future in the hands of these unconventional and unpredictable young people who seemed to be actively resisting authority and rejecting everything that was traditional or conventional, was simply too frightening for many to contemplate. For all the unfettered fun attached to being a teenager in the late 1950s and early 1960s, there was a darker edge; a flip side to the apparently positive traits of youth. Modern life, the growth of the city, and increased opportunities for leisure were the focus of growing disquiet. Young people represented vitality and social mobility to a degree which marked them out from previous generations, but 'modern' equated to 'brash', being cosmopolitan and classless were inextricably linked to having too much wealth and too little morality, and the homogeneity brought to young people by the growth in consumer industries aimed specifically at them made them thoughtless and selfish in the eyes of many older people. Cohen suggests that this first generation of teenagers symbolized the confused and paradoxical feelings that many held in this period of rapid social transformation:

> They touched the delicate and ambivalent nerves through which post-War social change in Britain was experienced. No one wanted depressions or austerity, but messages about 'never having it so good' were ambivalent in that some people were having it too good and too quickly. (Cohen, 1972/2002: 192)

Young people were thus seen as both a catalyst for change and the guardians of future morality; they personified the desire to move forward, to innovate, to experiment, but were simultaneously the conduits of all the fears in society about change and the unknown. At one and the same time they represented all that was new, shiny and modern, and everything that was transitory, disposable and tacky.

Problems with the moral panic model

The concept of 'moral panics' has been widely criticized for its perceived limitations, yet it is a theory that just refuses to go away. A fundamental difficulty with moral panics is not the concept itself, but the way that it has been embraced by the generations of writers, researchers, journalists and students who have been applying it uncritically ever since its inception in 1971. As Kidd-Hewitt and Osborne (1995) point out, the criminological study of crime and the media has become fixed within a pattern of inquiry which frequently relies on 'ritualistic reproductions' or misrepresentations of Cohen's original conceptualization of the term, and *Folk Devils and Moral Panics* left 'such significant and substantial foundation stones that they are constantly mistaken for the final edifice, instead of notable developments to be built upon' (Kidd-Hewitt and Osborne, 1995: 2). Indeed, so much has been written about the original analysis of mods and rockers since its publication in 1972, that it comes as a surprise to find that few writers have gone beyond a faithful re-write of the original text and a somewhat fawning adherence to its theoretical premises. So what *are* the shortcomings of the moral panic thesis? Several points of possible ambiguity or contention have already been discussed and it should already be clear that some aspects of the moral panic model are open to several different interpretations. But there remain some fundamental flaws in the idea of moral panics that have yet to be satisfactorily addressed, and it is to these that we now turn.

A problem with 'deviance'

The deviancy amplification spiral is problematic on a number of counts. First, not all folk devils can be said to be vulnerable or unfairly maligned (paedophiles provide one such example), and the accelerating loss of credibility that is implied in the amplification process is not applicable to all groups. Furthermore, there has never been universal agreement about the length of time that public outrage has to be expressed in order to qualify as a moral panic. If we return to Cohen's formulation of the concept we are bound to infer that moral panics are, by their very nature, short-term, sporadic episodes which explode with some volatility on the collective consciousness only to disappear a few weeks or months later. But the origins of some concerns – for example, juvenile delinquency – may go back a considerable length of time and current anxieties about deviant youth have been well rehearsed in this country over several hundred years (Pearson, 1983). Even the current state of heightened anxiety over paedophiles appears to have been sustained for the best part of a decade (see Chapter 4). The deviancy amplification spiral has also been criticized for being too rigid and deterministic, grossly oversimplifying the notion of deviancy. There are different levels of what we call 'deviancy', and a theory which accounts for public reactions to cannabis users may not be appropriate in accounting for public outrage over date rapists. Furthermore, the aetiology of deviancy is rarely given the same consideration as the deviant action or behaviour itself. Muncie, echoing Durkheim, comments:

> Moral Panics ... form part of a sensitizing and legitimizing process for solidifying moral boundaries, identifying 'enemies within', strengthening the powers of state control and enabling law and order to be promoted *without cognisance of the social divisions and conflicts which produce deviance and political dissent.* (Muncie, 2001: 55–6, emphasis added)

In other words, moral panics define for society the moral parameters within which it is acceptable to behave, and marginalize and punish those groups who step outside those parameters, but rarely do they encourage examination of the reasons *why* the group is behaving in that way in the first place. All too often, 'deviance' is simply used as a byword for 'irrationality' (implying mental instability or even animality), 'manipulability' (implying that those involved are passive dupes) or 'unconventionality' (implying that they are weird, alien, uncontrollable). Thus the causes of 'deviance', which in some cases may be entirely legitimate, are seldom considered and are frequently overshadowed by scornful commentaries about the appearance and lifestyle of the groups involved. In addition, the media may resort to conjecture and exaggeration concerning violence or predictions of future violence, or by reference to any sporadic incidents of conflict that occur. As Hall says, 'the tendency is ... to deal with any problem, first by simplifying its causes, second by **stigmatizing** those involved, third by whipping up public feeling and fourth by stamping hard on it from above' (Hall, 1978: 34). This comment is made about football hooliganism, but could equally be said about any other moral panic, from spectacular youth subcultures to the problem of paedophiles.

A problem with 'morality'

A related difficulty with definition is that the 'moral' element in moral panics has either been accepted unproblematically, or otherwise glossed over with little concern for a particular episode's place within a wider structure of morality and in relation to changing forms of moral regulation (Thompson, 1998). In the following chapter we will consider 'morality' as it pertains to the sexualization of children and the age at which young people become sexually active. In brief, we might consider it somewhat hypocritical of society to impose legal sanctions on 'under age' sex (which in a new Sexual Offences Bill will criminalize 15-year-olds for all forms of sexual conduct), while at the same time tolerating the overt sexualization of much younger children in other cultural realms – fashion, music, advertising and so on. The age of consent was set at 16 in an attempt to thwart the use of children as prostitutes in Victorian England. Prior to 1875, it had been 12. However, in the wake of several cases where 13–15-year-old girls have run away from home with their boyfriends, the debate about the age at which young people become sexually mature has been re-ignited (*Observer*, 2 November

2003). It is, however, a debate that is likely to become hijacked by moral crusaders if prior experience is an indicator (a campaign in the 1980s led by Victoria Gillick to stop doctors prescribing contraception to under-16s has been held partially responsible for a simultaneous rise in teenage pregnancies) and it may prove impossible to discuss reasonably and rationally in a culture in which romanticized images of childhood as a time of winsome innocence prevail over a reality that includes child abuse, neglect, exploitation and the highest teenage pregnancy rate in Europe.

Jock Young (1971, 1974) highlights a further aspect of the ambiguity inherent in definitions of morality, suggesting that many of the people who think of themselves as 'moral' and take exception to the *im*morality of deviants, actually have a grudging admiration – envy, even – for those who are seen to be 'breaking the rules'. According to Young (1971), if a person lives by a strict code of conduct which forbids certain pleasures and involves the deferring of gratification in certain areas, it is hardly surprising that they will react strongly against those whom they see to be taking 'short cuts'. For Young, this ambivalence is partial explanation of the vigorous repression against what might be termed 'crimes without victims'; homosexuality, prostitution, drug-taking and – in the new moral climate – consensual sex among those under 16. But in many instances, moral panics appear to contain little or no moral element at all and the term has become a shorthand description for *any* widespread concern including, most prominently in recent years, health scares, especially those linking health problems to food and diet.

Problems with 'youth' and 'style'

In much of the moral panic literature, there is a presupposed assumption that the youth groups or other deviants involved are inevitably economically marginalized and turn to crime and deviance as an anomic means of combating the boredom and financial hardship associated with being out of work (see Chapter 1). Certainly, Cohen suggests that the mods and rockers were driven to violence as a result of feeling marginalized from the mass consumer culture directed at young people in the early 1960s. Yet an alternative reading might argue that the mods and rockers were the products of rising affluence and optimism, and far from being peripheral to the economic health of the country, they were largely responsible for making the 1960s swing! Since that time youth fashions and subcultural affiliations have spawned multi-million pound industries, and today's young people have on offer a vast range of concurrent subcultures which may in some cases present the solutions to their subjective socio-economic problems (Burke and Sunley, 1996), but actually in most cases do little more than provide a temporary sense of 'belonging', a statement of being independent of the parent culture and a form of conspicuous consumption.

Group identity is thus at least as likely to be a statement of style and status as it is to be an act of resistance through ritual. All youth cultures require a relatively high level of financial input, whether they are based on music, fashion, football or some other 'fanship', and as Cohen remarks in his introduction to the revised second edition of *Folk Devils and Moral Panics*, the delinquent quickly changed from 'frustrated social climber' to 'cultural innovator and critic' (Cohen, 1980: iv). Even the punks of the 1970s, who are frequently characterized as a product of dole-queue despondency (Hebdige, 1979), were by no means all out of work and lacking economic means. Commitment to the punk movement was based on political disaffection, rebellion against the parent culture, enjoyment of the music, resistance to conventional codes of dress and many other varied factors. But it was orchestrated by a music producer (Malcolm McLaren) and a fashion designer (Vivienne Westwood) and was essentially a commercial enterprise. Entry into any youth subculture represents a part of the normal transition from childhood to adulthood that most young people in Western society pass through. But there are few, if any, youth cultures and styles which are not manufactured by one or more elements of the consumerist culture industry. Even the gang cultures of the impoverished inner-city ghettos of America and Britain have strong affiliations to particular designer labels.

Furthermore, 'spectacular' youth subcultures – the stock in trade of moral panic promoters – are, arguably, not as evident as they once were. Moral panic theory tends to suggest that young people have restricted choices in their statements of style, personality and consumption. But for postmodernist critics, the subject has no fixed or permanent identity, but assumes different identities at different times in an endless act of self-creation. Indeed, a postmodern critique would posit that identity is an 'open slate ... on which persons may inscribe, erase and rewrite' their histories and personalities at will (Gergen, 1991: 228), a phenomenon that has become positively celebrated with the inception and expansion of the Internet. Even sexual identity is seen by some commentators as a reflexively organized endeavour involving an increasing number of choices and possibilities (Giddens, 1991; Jewkes and Sharp, 2003). Thus, in today's multimedia society, young people are able to make the transition from childhood to adulthood via a vast and diverse range of coexistent subcultures, which they may move in and out of at will, thus making their attachments to particular groups only marginal and fleeting. As such, it might be suggested that the notion that moral panics define the limits of how much diversity a society can tolerate is simply not as compelling as it once was, although this is a contested issue. Some would argue that clothing and appearance can still be utilized as symbols of class conflict and social division, and that there remain subcultural styles which are not appropriated by mainstream consumer culture and which are adopted by individuals and groups with the intention of making others feel ill-at-ease. Others would counter that in today's postmodern, technologically advanced, culturally fragmented, pastiche culture, diversity is not only tolerated but is celebrated to the extent where 'street' styles (that is, those emerging from the 'bottom' or margins of society) are often very quickly absorbed into the mainstream fashion industry, a trend that makes the 'deviant' cues of any one group appear less visible and less important in the wider context.

A further difficulty with the construction of youth as a social problem is that it might be suggested that youth now only exists in discourses about crime and deviance. Youth arguably no longer describes a generational category, but instead encapsulates an attitude, a lifestyle not determined by age (Frith, 1983). The generation gap is shrinking, and unlike 50 years ago when young people were more or less miniature versions of their parents, in contemporary society it is now very often adults who look to their children for style codes. Not only is it more likely that adolescents and their parents will share the same tastes in clothing, music, literature and leisure pursuits than in any previous generation – a trend exemplified by the Harry Potter phenomenon – but increasingly young people (indeed, from primary school age) are influencing the political agenda, especially in relation to issues such as animal rights and environmentalism. Collective concerns such as these not only transcend traditional class and ethnic distinctions, but they demonstrate a 'morality' and code of ethics which seem conservative in comparison with the youth subcultures of their parents' and grandparents' generations.

A problem with 'risk'

Another weakness with the moral panic model is that it seems not only to suggest that young people have limited life choices and that is why they form distinctive subcultures, but that the overstated reaction to these cultures on the part of the 'moral majority' is precipitated by a creeping sense of disorientation and bewilderment at the pace of change in modern life. This argument is evident in many parents' fears about their children's exposure to new and alternative media, including violent computer games and the Internet. But modernity has been a long project and it seems inconceivable that the pace of change was (relatively) any more rapid or confusing in the mid-20th century when Cohen observed the events involving mods and rockers – or is, for that matter, at the beginning of the 21st century as fears prevail about paedophiles prowling Internet chat rooms – than it was one 100 or 200 years previously. Was there ever a generation which did not feel that it was poised at the edge of something bigger, more exciting and – for some – potentially more frightening? And even though contemporary life is increasingly being labelled a 'risk' society (Giddens, 1991; Beck, 1992), is it really accurate to characterize this period of late modernity as a universal, endlessly cyclical state of 'panickyness'? (Sparks, 1992: 65).

In the second, revised edition of *Folk Devils and Moral Panics*, Cohen himself surmizes that the level and intensity of media activity is sometimes exaggerated by researchers and writers in order to 'fit' their particular illustration of the moral panic thesis at work, and that the material selected as 'proof' of the slide into crisis (newspaper editorials, in the main) does not amount to such monumental proportions (Cohen, 1980).

A problem of 'source'

Although the panics over Teddy boys in the 1950s and mods and rockers in the 1960s meet the criteria of the moral panic thesis in terms of being discrete, transitory incidents that appear to have emerged suddenly and explosively and disappeared equally abruptly some time later, it has been left to later writers (for example, Muncie, 1987; Watney, 1987; McRobbie, 1994) to point out that concerns about deviance are much more diffuse and less political than is suggested in many accounts of panic. In other words, the disparate concerns over drugs, sexual permissiveness or perversion, liberal attitudes to marriage, the political re-emergence of the far right, and youth violence, are among the frequently conflicting issues which arise from a number of different sources and are dispersed throughout society. Meanwhile, specific moral panics such as the periodic scares about street crime (mugging in the 1970s; joyriding in the 1990s), black youth (again targeted in the mugging episode of the 1970s and the inner-city riots of the 1980s) or, currently, asylum seekers and paedophiles, represent a generalized climate of hostility to marginal groups and 'unconventional' or untraditional norms. Far from happening out of the blue, as is sometimes suggested, moral panics may be viewed accordingly as part of the longer-term ideological struggles which are waged right across society and within all fields of public representation (Watney, 1987). As such, the initial targeting of the deviants and the structured responses to them may be regarded as an integral part of the hegemonic function of the media, telling us far more about the nature of the media and their complex relationship with other social institutions than they do simply about the concerns of those in power.

The question of source also problematizes the idea that moral panics are the means by which élite interests become filtered down through society so that they appear to be to everyone's advantage. The term 'moral panic' implies that public reaction is unjustified and, in critical criminological accounts (for example, Hall et al., 1978), there is a suggestion that moral panics are essentially smokescreens put up by governments to cynically manipulate the media and public agendas. Some critics hang on to the belief that moral panics originate at a macro level and are engineered by a political and cultural élite as a deliberate and conscious effort to generate concern or fear which is actually misplaced. Others maintain that they originate at a more micro level with the general public, and that concerns expressed by the media, politicians, police and so on, are simply an expression or manifestation of wider, grassroots disquiet (a position more in line with Cohen's account and more credible in relation to the paedophile scare). A third model proposes that it is at a *meso* or middle level of society – with social agencies, pressure groups, lobbyists and moral crusaders – that moral panics start. This theory is given credence by those who claim that it is interest groups who stand to gain the most from moral panics. We have already seen this view rehearsed in relation to panics over children viewing violence, where it is often asserted that it is pressure group leaders, academics and politicians who seek to make a name for themselves by jumping on a populist bandwagon. A fourth view of the source of moral panics, and a variation on the meso-level explanation, is that it is journalists themselves who are primarily responsible for generating moral panics, simply as a way of increasing circulation or entertaining their audience (Young, 1974). Despite the fact that we can no longer talk of the 'mass' media in quite the same monolithic sense as we once did, campaigns such as the *News of the World*'s 'naming and shaming' crusade (a campaign originally started by local paper, the *Bournemouth Echo*) might be said to be a powerful means of gaining readers and satisfying the demands of the market, while paying scant regard for the political consequences of such action (Aldridge, 2003).

A problem with 'audience'

The overriding problem with traditional characterizations of the moral panic model is that they presuppose that in finding **consensus** on certain issues, audiences are gullible and that they privilege mediated knowledge over direct experience; an assumption that is clearly not viable. In fact, more than any other factor, recent cultural and media theorists have resisted the moral panic thesis's implicit supposition that the public are naively trusting of media reports and cannot tell when they are being manipulated by politicians. In contrast to this assumption, research concerning the relationship between the media agenda and the public agenda (that is, what the public take from the media and think about or discuss among themselves) stresses that there are many examples of public indifference or resistance to issues that constitute political and/or media crusades. Indeed, studies of advertising demonstrate that the least successful advertising campaigns are those commissioned by social agencies with the intention of changing people's behaviour – for example, anti-drugs campaigns and 'safe sex' messages – while the failure of the general public to take notice of issues which are deemed important by figures in power is evident in the falling numbers of couples in the UK who are marrying, despite the continuing efforts of political and church leaders. Furthermore, both the 1992 American Republican presidential campaign with its overt moral agenda and the British Prime Minister's 'Back to Basics' campaign of two years later spectacularly failed to interest the voters. Although John Major's agenda was slightly less right-wing than the American 'family values' crusade that openly attacked homosexuality, abortion and divorce, the difference was largely one of style rather than ideology, and both campaigns fizzled out in a tide of public indifference (Goode and Ben-Yehuda, 1994). More recently, New Labour's consistently high ratings in the opinion polls throughout their terms of office would seem largely as a result of their success in shedding their image of being 'soft on crime' and 'out-toughing' the Conservatives' stance on law and order (Downes and Morgan, 2002). Yet they are famous for being the 'party of spin', and it is arguable that the government is reflecting the public's genuine and valid concerns about crime and lawlessness, rather than creating media froth to divert public attention from other matters. Furthermore, the demonization of those whose lifestyle and beliefs exist outside the political, social or legal norm does not guarantee public – or even media – support. 'Official' attempts to castigate, demonize or ridicule 'deviants' are often resisted, calling into question the notion of a gullible and docile public yielding to the interests of those in power.

Above all, as mentioned in Chapter 1, contemporary media research is audience-centred, not media-centred and the emphasis is very much on what people do *with* the media as opposed to what the media do *to* people. Ironically, far from being a docile mass, mopping up the views and opinions of authorities and opinion leaders, the media audience have, in a number of cases, turned the tables on the professionals, casting journalists, editors, photographers and, in some cases, experts such as teachers and social workers, in the role of folk devils, rather than those who are their subject matter. For example, Jenkins's (1992) study of satanic ritual abuse claims in the 1980s found that while some factions did indeed view threats to women and children as a major cause for alarm, many others believed that exaggerated reactions to the supposed threats on the part of the social services and media reporters was the real cause for concern.

The longevity and legacy of the moral panic model: some concluding thoughts

Many of the criticisms levelled at moral panics in this chapter have been recently addressed by Stanley Cohen himself in a new Introduction to the third edition of his famous book (2002). Published to celebrate the 30th anniversary of *Folk Devils and Moral Panics,* Cohen addresses some of the problems associated with the concept he popularized (notably, the problems of proportionality, volatility and the value-laden aspect of the term). He also analyses several 'boundary marking' cases from the last 15 years (James Bulger, Stephen Lawrence, Leah Betts, the Columbine High School massacre and so on) and considers the extent to which they can be construed as 'successful' moral panics (2002: ix *ff*).

As indicated in the introduction to this chapter, it is difficult to explain why criminology – and its related fields – continue to place the moral panic thesis at the heart of studies of deviance and disorder (for example, it is interesting to note that the *Sage Dictionary of Criminology* devotes substantial entries to 'moral panic', 'folk devil' and 'deviancy amplification', as well as to related concepts such as 'demonization', 'labelling', 'scapegoating', 'social reaction', and 'stereotyping'; McLaughlin and Muncie, 2001) when both sociology and media studies have more or less ignored it for decades. Why the latter subject areas have neglected it for so long is perhaps easier to comprehend. British sociology moved from considerations of structural changes and class-based divisions in the 1970s to the rise of New Right economic policies and ideology in the 1980s. The moral panic thesis seemed less relevant because it appeared to focus on sporadic and discrete episodes making a sudden and dramatic impact, rather than the underlying political-economic trends and their relationship to discourse and ideology; a dilemma already apparent in Hall et al's (1978) study of the moral panic over mugging. Media studies, on the other hand, which had whole-heartedly embraced sociological concerns in the 1960s and 1970s had taken a cultural turn by the 1980s. New enquiries in the field emphasised the audience as active makers of meaning or postmodern critics who were well qualified to see through the ideological veils put up by journalists and reporters.

The moral panic thesis was thus regarded by the new vanguard as reactionary, paternalistic and media-centric and the fact that, to a large extent it has been the mediated version of deviance and not the phenomenon itself which has been the focus of attention, is highly problematic for many media researchers. The genuine, deep-seated anxieties at the root of reaction, and the 'outsiders' onto whom these anxieties are displaced, have become secondary concerns amidst all the rhetoric about the persuasive powers of the media. The desire to search for a single causal explanation for undesirable moral or social changes – television for the 'disappearance' of childhood; adolescents for a suspected decline in social morality; the Internet for facilitating the activities of paedophiles – almost certainly serves to deflect attention away from other possible causes. But whether the real causes of social problems are 'closer to home' or simply much too complicated to understand (as Connell, 1985, argues) the concentration on symptoms, rather than causes or long-term effects, leads to a somewhat superficial analysis of crime and deviance and frequently negates the fact that those who commit crimes are not 'others', they are 'us' and are of our making. Above all, the construction of crime and deviance as moral panic designed to sell newspapers, signifies a shift from 'hard' news towards the safe territory of sensationalized reporting and public entertainment. As Cohen himself notes, the increasingly desperate measures taken by media organizations to secure a significant audience share results in a hierarchy of newsworthiness whereby a footballer's ankle injury gains more media attention that a political massacre (2002: xxxiii). Moral panics may thus alert us to the shifting sands of audience responses, ranging from significant social reaction at one extreme to disinterest and non-intervention (or even denial) at the other. Ultimately, perhaps, moral panics should be regarded in the way that Cohen intended – as a means of conceptualizing the lines of power in society and the ways in which 'we are manipulated into taking some things too seriously and other things not seriously enough' (2002: xxxv). The longevity of the concept is not that difficult to comprehend – studying moral panics is, says Cohen, 'easy and a lot of fun' (Cohen, 2002: xxxv). But implicit in his reflections 30 years on is the caveat that a faithful adherence to the original moral panic thesis may make it impossible to arrive at a balanced and reasonable estimation of the real role of media in people's lives and the true impact of crime on society.

Summary

- Chapter 3 has interrogated the much used but frequently misinterpreted concept of moral panics made famous by Stanley Cohen in 1972. It has discussed both strengths and weaknesses of the term and briefly considered why 'moral panics' are at the heart of much criminological debate about political struggles and cultural reproduction yet, simultaneously, barely feature in contemporary sociology and media studies texts on the subject.
- The discussion has centred on the five defining features of moral panics: the presentation of the ordinary as extraordinary; the amplifying role of authorities; definitions of morality; notions of risk associated with social change; and the salience of youth.
- The chapter has also examined the problems that these five features raise in the context of 30 years of adaptation, adoption, expansion and criticism, some of which has come from Cohen himself (2002: vii ff).
- While it has been recognized that there are some fundamental flaws in the way that the term 'moral panic' has been uncritically applied to issues ranging from asylum seekers to dangerous dogs, and from health scares to the music of Marilyn Manson, it has not been suggested that the idea is invalid or unhelpful in conceptualizing social reactions to both immediate, short-term crises and to long-term general reflections on the 'state-of-our-times' (Cohen, 2002: vii). As Cohen (2002: x–xi) points out, if we accept that moral panics may reflect genuine public anxieties (for example, the anger directed at convicted paedophiles who are released into the community) rather than consisting only of media-generated froth, and that not all likely candidates for public outrage actually quite add up to a moral panic (Cohen highlights the example of the racist murder of Stephen Lawrence), then we have a sound conceptual basis for examining the ways that morality and risk are perceived in postmodern society.

STUDY QUESTIONS

1 How convincing is the 'moral panic' thesis in explaining media reporting of, and public responses to, minority and/or deviant groups, in your view?

2 Moral panics have almost exclusively been directed at male, working-class subcultures. Can you think of any examples where girls or young women have been the recipients of moral outrage? How successful or otherwise has criminological theory been in offering explanations for female subcultural crime?

3 What recent examples of criminal or deviant behaviour can you think of which might be described as 'moral panics'? What is the primary source of the labelling of 'demons' in your chosen cases?

4 What kinds of crime are *not* the subject of moral panics, and with what effect on public perceptions of crime?.

FURTHER READING

Although this chapter has focused on moral panics in the modern era, they are far from a new phenomenon. Pearson, G. (1983) *Hooligan: A History of Respectable Fears* (Macmillan) is the 'classic' work on the moral panics that have shaped public anxieties about crime and delinquency through the centuries, but other analyses are emerging including a chapter by Peter King on 'Moral panics and violent street crime 1750–2000' in Godfrey, B. et al. (2003) *Comparative Histories of Crime* (Willan). It is worth paying close attention to Cohen, S. (1972) *Folk Devils and Moral Panics* (MacGibbon and Kee), especially now it is in its 30th anniversary, third edition with a new, revised introduction (published in 2002 by Routledge). Of the recent books on moral panics, Critcher, C. (2003) *Moral Panics and the Media* (Open University Press) is the most up to date, but Goode, E. and Ben-Yehuda, N. (1994) *Moral Panics: The Social Construction of Deviance* remains one of the most interesting books on the subject. Jenkins, P. (1992) *Intimate Enemies: Moral Panics in Contemporary Great Britain* (Aldine de Gruyter) is also excellent, especially on moral panics over juveniles.

4

Media Constructions of Children: 'Evil Monsters' and 'Tragic Victims'

Chapter Contents

OVERVIEW

Chapter 4 provides:

- A discussion of the complex and frequently contradictory assumptions made about children in contemporary Britain.
- An analysis of public fears and anxieties surrounding childhood which reached a peak in 1993 with the murder of two-year-old James Bulger by two older children.
- A comparison of media representations of this crime, and other reported incidents that portrayed children as 'persistent offenders', 'evil monsters' and so on, with alternative media accounts representing children as vulnerable innocents who must be protected, not from other children, but from adults who seek to harm and exploit them.
- Evidence that suggests that children killed by strangers are much more likely to receive media attention than those who are killed by close relatives in the home.
- Support for the suggestion (which, in a somewhat crude formulation, underpins the moral panic thesis) that high-profile crimes involving child victims draw people together and mobilize their feelings of loss and guilt to produce a sense of 'imagined community'.

KEY TERMS

adultification	evil monsters	persistent offending
children	imagined community	risk
dangerousness	infantilization	social constructionism
doli incapax	paedophiles	tragic victims

In the last chapter it was noted that some aspects of the behaviour of contemporary British youth which might once have been conceived as normal, natural and an inevitable part of growing up are increasingly becoming subject to moral censure and opprobrium. Yet, alongside the manufacture of fears about young people and crime, there has been a homogenization of age brackets into aspirational lifestyle categories which has resulted in a blurring of the distinctions between youth and adulthood. It might be argued, then, that the hostility once directed at an age group who were fundamentally different in appearance and aspirations to their parents' generation has, more recently, transmuted into something more confused. *Children* and adolescents are still the subjects of moral panic and public outrage but, as we saw in our discussion of news values in Chapter 2, they are frequently also cast as *tragic victims*. In fact, never have society's attitudes towards young people been as polarized as they are at the turn of the new millennium. Alongside youth *as* folk devils, we now have children as *the victims of* folk devils (Critcher, 2003). It is precisely this confusion over the concept of childhood that will be discussed in this chapter. First we will explore changing **social constructions** of childhood, before developing a more detailed critique concerning the paradoxical attitudes to children and young people that emerged in the mid-1990s. In 1993 children became regarded as *evil monsters* capable of committing the most depraved of acts, but by 1996 the dominant construction of children was that of impressionable innocents who must be safeguarded, especially from the new number one demons – paedophiles.

1993 – Children as 'evil monsters'

Since the teenage rebellions of the 1950s and 1960s, the age at which young people may be designated *folk devils* has decreased, and since the early 1990s there have been regular reports about pre-teenage children committing increasingly serious offences ranging from burglary to rape. This trend has only served to reinforce the equivocal attitudes to *youth* noted by Cohen, to the extent where the precise boundaries of 'youth' and 'adolescence' are now unclear: 'no one seems to be sure exactly when childhood is left behind or when adulthood is achieved' (Muncie, 1999a: 3). This problem is compounded by the fact that ideas about the onset of adolescence and the age at which children are deemed to understand the difference between right and wrong are not fixed, but are subject to contestation and change over time. Prior to the mid-19th century when positivism emerged to challenge it, ideas about crime and punishment were dominated by a theoretical perspective known as 'classicism'. A central feature of this approach was that punishment should fit the crime, not the individual offender. As a result, children were seen as equally culpable as adults when they committed an offence and were liable to the same penalties, including incarceration in prisons and prison hulks, and transportation to penal colonies. However, in Victorian society a new conception of childhood emerged out of the dominant cultural, medical and psychological discourses of the time. For the first time in modern history, childhood was thought of as a separate stage of development prior to the independence and responsibility that come with adulthood. Children were seen as requiring nurturing and protection through legislation; it was during this period that compulsory schooling started to be introduced, and laws were passed limiting the number of hours children could work and prohibiting them from working in certain industries.

Since this time, messages about childhood have been somewhat mixed. For example, in contemporary Britain we have seen the emergence of the 'adultified'

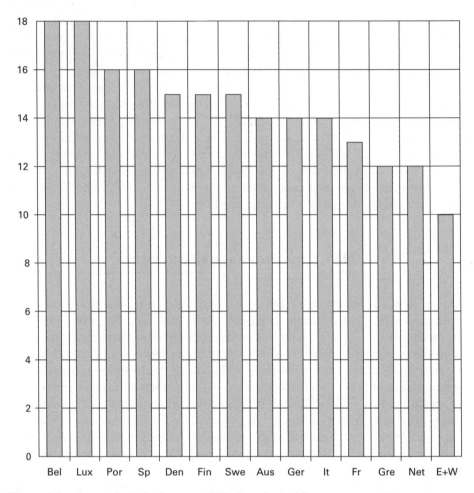

Figure 4.1 *Ages of criminal responsibility in selected European countries*
Source: Goldson, 2003

child, with rises in teenage pregnancies, children being tried in adult courts, children winning the right to 'divorce' their parents and so on. England and Wales not only criminalize children at a much earlier age (see Figure 4.1), but also are by far the most inclined to lock them up. Staggeringly, in England and Wales twice as many children are incarcerated as in Belgium, Portugal, Spain, Denmark, Sweden, Finland, Austria, France and The Netherlands combined (Goldson, 2003). Yet, simultaneously, children are subjected to a greater degree of protective control and regulation which has led to a 'major reorganization of the childhood experience ... [whereby] roaming about with friends or walking to and from school are becoming increasingly rare experiences' (Furedi, 1997: 115). Furthermore, a combination of social, political and economic forces that include a government target of 50 per cent of school leavers in university and a 300 per cent rise in house prices since the mid-1980s in many parts of the country, has resulted in many young people being forced to remain in a state of extended *infantilization*, living with their parents until they are well into their 20s or 30s.

Within criminal justice, the confusion in contemporary ideas about childhood are exemplified by the case of the two pre-teenage boys tried in an adult court for the murder of two-year-old James Bulger in 1993. As noted in Chapter 2, this case redefined the nature of childhood in almost exclusively negative terms and gave rise to numerous stories about delinquent and dangerous juvenile offenders. Previously held to be a relatively neutral ascription, the case of Jon Venables and Robert Thompson gave the word 'child' a range of emotive and troubling connotations previously reserved for ascriptions such as 'youth', 'juvenile' and 'adolescence' (Muncie, 1999a; Newburn, 2002). Together these terms encompass a series of Lombrosian inferences, ranging from notions of uncontrolled freedom, irresponsibility and dangerousness to those of moral emptiness and even innate evil. The murder of James Bulger occurred at a time of rising concern about 'persistent young offenders', but this single case has become something of a watershed in the history of youth justice and in our atti-tudes towards children. Above all, the conviction of two 10-year-olds for the murder of a toddler graphically illustrates how notions of childhood innocence and vulnerability coexist with images of mini-monsters, clearly delineating children as tragic victims and children as evil monsters. The *Daily Mail* of 25 November 1993 encapsulated this contradiction in its headline 'The evil and the innocent' and, while the characterization of blond-haired, blue-eyed James as the epitome of an ideal child needed little reinforcement, the moral decrepi-tude of the 10-year-old murderers was achieved through interconnecting polit-ical, legal and media discourses that sought to prove their guilt via a subtle process of *adultification*.

As others have pointed out, in most European countries evidence would have been heard that was deemed inadmissible in this case – evidence from the boys' 'family backgrounds, their relationships with teachers and peers, their psycho-socio-sexual make-up' and so on (Morrison, 1997: 94). In fact, as Figure 4.1 shows, in most European countries, Venables and Thompson would have been con-sidered too young to be tried at all, let alone tried in an adult court, and there would thus have been no question of guilt or innocence (Muncie, 1999b). In English law, however, children between the ages of 10 and 14 can be held accountable for a crime, providing it can be established that they knew they were committing it (the legal doctrine known as *doli incapax*, literally 'incapable of evil') and they will – as a rule – be tried in a 'youth court', which differs in style and approach to adult courts.

As Morrison (1997) notes, in the Bulger case, expert witnesses were called to a Crown Court to give evidence about intellectual maturity, not mental disturbance, and when Venables and Thompson were convicted, it was deemed that they were old enough to understand the difference between right and wrong. Meanwhile, one of the defending barristers showed the jury 247 press cuttings he had assembled which compared the boys to Myra Hindley and Saddam Hussein (1997), a move which probably only served to reinforce the judge's opinion that the murder was an act of 'unparalleled evil and barbarity'. Morrison contemplates the notion of Venables and Thompson being tried before a jury of 10-year-olds, since this would fulfil the role that juries are intended to serve – trial by one's peers. Of course, most people would regard such an idea as preposterous, not least because they would not trust the jurors' maturity, judgement and intelligence. But, as Morrison concludes, these were the very qualities said to be present in the two boys when they killed James Bulger. They are also the kind of qualities that the Prime Minister imbued them with when he appealed to the British public to condemn rather than understand, a sentiment echoed in his Home Secretary's blunt statement that no excuses could be made for 'a section of the population who are essentially nasty pieces of work' (*The Times*, 22 February 1993). Meanwhile, the *Daily Star* vented feelings of vengeance and rage on behalf of the British public with their headline 'How Do You Feel Now, You Little Bastards' (25 November 1993).

The hypocrisy of an adult society – given its own apparently insatiable appetite for violence, brutality and war (Scraton, 2002) – heaping such ugly sentiments on to the heads of two 10-year-old murderers is an interesting phenomenon. In the aftermath of the Bulger case, the focus of public discourse was not on how two fairly ordinary working-class families with many of the problems and difficulties that beset thousands of similar families across the country, could implode to the degree where two children murder another child. It remained resolutely fixed on the idea that they were a couple of malevolent misfits who came together and spurred each other on along a continuum of offences, starting with bunking off school and stealing from shops, and ending with the murder of a toddler they picked up in a Liverpool shopping centre. The unanimous cry from the British media was that these little boys should be locked up and the key thrown away. By contrast, a similar case in Norway elicited a very different response from the media, politicians and the public. There the murder of a five-year-old by three children aged six, the year after the Bulger case, was reported as a tragic accident and all four of the children involved were presented as victims. In a more recent case (July 2003), which had sad echoes of the Bulger murder, a 12-year-old boy in Japan was captured on CCTV leading a four-year-old to his death. The older child could not be prosecuted under Japan's Criminal Code, which designates 14 as the age of criminal responsibility and, instead, the boy was placed in a child welfare centre while his needs – and those of his family – were assessed (http://news.bbc.co.uk).

The political and media hysteria surrounding the killing of James Bulger already demonstrate some of the paradoxical sentiments with which we view children. Although seen as an aberration, the 'spawn of the devil', no less, according to several tabloid newspapers, Venables and Thompson were nonetheless portrayed as part of a more generalized moral decline:

> The British have sensed for some time that violent crime was gnawing at the edges of the country's social fabric and that those in authority seemed powerless to stop its relentless progress. But it has taken one particular murder to crystallise the country's fears, encapsulate the concern and encourage people to ask out loud what kind of nation we are becoming ... It is the world of the video nasty brought to reality. (*Sunday Times*, 21 February 1993)

As Morrison suggests, 'If child-killings are the worst killings, then a child child-killing must be worse than worst, a new superlative in horror' (1997: 21). Elizabeth Newson summed up the feelings of many in her much publicized report *Video Violence and the Protection of Children*:

> So here is a crime that we could all wish had been perpetrated by 'evil freaks'; but already the most cursory reading of news since then suggests that it is not a 'one-off'. Shortly after this trial, children of similar age in Paris were reported to have set upon a tramp ... kicked him and thrown him down a well. In England an adolescent girl [Suzanne Capper] was tortured by her 'friends' over days, using direct quotes from a horror video (*Child's Play 3*) as part of her torment, and eventually set on fire and thus killed; while ... two schoolboys were today expected to appear in court accused of torturing a six-year-old on a railway line [in Newcastle upon Tyne]. (1994: 273)

Newson goes on to note that 'we do not have the information to be able to comment on the full background of any of these crimes at present', but that does not stop her from linking them to the 'easy availability to children of gross images of violence on video' (1994: 273); a connection that has become part of the folklore of both the Bulger and Capper murders. As Petley points out, the strain of class dislike and disdain for 'others' is highly evident in such expressions. His ironic comment that violent films are 'fine for us middle-class intellectuals who will judge it on "aesthetic" grounds' but not for 'the plebs in case it gets them worked up' (1997: 90) is amply demonstrated by Brian Appleyard who, in an echo of the infamous comments made about women and servants at the obscene publications trial of D.H. Lawrence's *Lady Chatterley's Lover*, asks rhetorically: 'Would you allow an ill-educated, culturally deprived, unemployable underclass unlimited access to violent pornography?' (*Independent*, 1 December 1993). It is difficult to believe that Appleyard's further comment that he would not wish it 'to be seen by the criminal classes or the mentally unstable or by inadequately supervized children with little else in their lives' was made, not about some music hall production at the end of the 19th century, but about the Quentin Tarantino film *Reservoir Dogs* (cf. Petley, 1997).

Yet the fact that the murder of a two-year-old by two 10-year-olds was not viewed as a unique event, but simply the worst example of a much wider phenomenon, indicates a level of concern that statistical measurements of offending and victimization among children simply do not support. As Scraton (2002) observes, in the decade prior to James Bulger's death, just one child under five had been killed per year by a stranger, and none by another child. By contrast, over 70 children under five had been murdered each year by a parent or an adult known to them. Yet the fact that children are more likely to be murdered by their parents or by other family members than by strangers of any age is virtually absent from media and public discourse. Furthermore, it is important to note that, when it comes to the portrayal of children as victims, once again, some children are more 'ideal' victims than others. Consider, by way of example, the case of eight-year-old Victoria Climbié who was tortured and killed by her aunt, Marie Therese Kouao and her aunt's boyfriend, Carl Manning, in 2000. Although her death resulted in a high-profile inquiry by Lord Laming and new legislation designed to protect children (including the appointment of the first Government Minister for Children), the circumstances of Victoria's life and death, her family background and the motivations of her killers have received only a fraction of the media attention and public mourning extended to the some of the other cases discussed in this book. Like Damilola Taylor, Victoria had only been in England for a few months (she was sent by her parents from the Ivory Coast 'for a better life') and she was black. But to further ensure her non-newsworthiness, she met her death at the hands of a close relative (cf. Laming, 2003).

Their unwillingness to report the extent of child abuse and murder within the home is further evidence of the media's obsession with the randomness of *risk* and their overwhelming tendency to locate *dangerousness* exclusively in the public realm. The net result of this emphasis is that it is *paedophiles* who have come to be the recipients of moral outrage in the 21st century. And more specifically, it is paedophile strangers, not paedophiles within the family, who are the bogeymen of modern Britain.

1996 – Children as 'tragic victims'

So embedded is the notion that paedophilia is the most heinous crime of our age that many commentators have suggested that it is the most significant *moral panic* of the last two decades (Jenkins, 1992, 2001; Silverman and Wilson, 2002;

Critcher, 2003). Sex offences have always been newsworthy stories, but the term 'paedophile' first rose to prominence in 1996 when the theme of 'paedophiles in the community' swept across the UK, receiving extensive coverage in both regional and national media (Kitzinger, 1999: 209; cf. Soothill et al., 1998). There were several catalysts for this sudden eruption of coverage. In the UK there had been a significant increase in public awareness of cases being exposed which involved child sexual abuse in residential child care homes and other institutions where children were supposed to be protected. In Northern Ireland several cases of Catholic priests accused of sexual offences against children made headlines and fuelled accusations of high-level cover-ups within the church (Greer, 2003a). Anxiety escalated in the autumn of 1996 when a released paedophile was charged with a series of child murders in Belgium, and again there were accusations of a high-level cover-up, this time involving politicians, the police and civil servants (Critcher, 2003). In the UK, the sexually motivated crimes of Fred and Rose West were uncovered, and 1996 was also the year in which 'Megan's Law' was created in the US following the rape and murder two years earlier of seven-year-old Megan Kanka by a twice-convicted sex offender who lived in the same street in New Jersey. These cases all tapped into existing concerns in the UK where disquiet was already being expressed at the relatively lenient sentences being handed down to some convicted paedophiles and their early release from prison. With the introduction of community notification legislation in America (dubbed 'Megan's Law'), lobbyists in this country were given a powerful new focal point for their campaigns. In response to public pressure and with a general election looming, the Sex Offenders Act was hurriedly introduced in 1997, followed a year later by the Crime and Disorder Act. These acts legislated for a national UK register of convicted or cautioned sex offenders to be held by the police, and for the police to be able to apply to the Magistrates' courts for a sex offender order to prohibit an individual from doing anything which might be deemed to put the public at risk.

In other words, sex offender orders are future-oriented; they require the police to predict an individual's likely future behaviour and make 'an assessment in respect of the present risk he [sic] presents' (CDA, 1998). What is more, the usual civil liberties that would attend the treatment of suspected or past offenders are overridden in the case of sex offenders. In English law, those who have been convicted of a crime and have served a sentence then have their civil liberties restored but, in respect to sex offenders, the safety of the public is prioritized over the liberty of the individual (Ashenden, 2002). The individual does not have to have done anything to infringe the law in the present (or even to have a previous conviction for a sexual offence); he or she must simply give the police 'reasonable suspicion' that they might be a risk in the future (2002). For many commentators this is hugely problematic for three reasons (Cowburn and Dominelli, 2001). First, it raises expectations about protection of the vulnerable that cannot be fulfilled on the basis of professional knowledge about sex offenders as it presently stands, and puts faith in the notion that community safety can be achieved by more sophisticated risk assessment methodologies and greater diligence on the part of workers within the criminal justice system. These views are at odds with the opinions of some professionals, including the Association of Chief Officers of Probation (ACOP), who argue that putting the feelings of a community before the needs of individual offenders, or potential offenders, may result in community vigilantism and the driving of offenders underground (Kitzinger, 1999). Second, future-oriented risk assessments pay little credence to the notion of rehabilitation for sex offenders, especially given the prevailing view that, where children are concerned, there is no risk worth taking. Third, it ignores yet again the much larger problem of women and children who are sexually abused within the private domain and perpetuates the myth of the home as a place of safety. According to the charity Childline, of the 9,857 children who phoned their helplines in 2001/02, 95 per cent knew their abuser (www.childline. org.uk). Meanwhile, it is estimated that between 5–20 per cent of women and 2–7 per cent of men have experienced sexual abuse in the home (Kitzinger, 1999). Yet the invisibility of children abused or killed by members of their family is in sharp contrast to the outrage and near-hysteria that accompanies cases of children murdered by other children, by adult strangers or, especially in the last five years, by sexually motivated adult strangers.

As Kitzinger notes, the second half of the 1990s witnessed a confluence of events which heightened public awareness of the problems associated with releasing convicted sex offenders into communities, and put the popular press and their reading public on 'paedophile alert' (1999: 213). However, it was not until the summer of 2000 that the hysteria over paedophilia reached its zenith with the *News of the World*'s 'naming and shaming' campaign which, itself, was a response to the abduction and murder of eight-year-old Sarah Payne (cf. Ashenden, 2002, for a review of this episode). It is difficult to assess precisely the extent of the media's influence in political-legal discourse and decision making, but certainly the media's prolonged coverage of the disappearance of Sarah Payne cemented the relationship between 'dangerousness' and 'risk'. Furthermore, the presentation to the British public of an identifiable hate-figure – the 'paedophile' – allowed the popular media to reduce the pervasive problem of sexual violence to a few men whose names and photographs could be printed in the newspapers.

An additional consequence of the media's construction of the problem is that the overriding image of the paedophile is still of a rather grubby, inadequate loner; a misfit who is not 'one of us'. But this image (the inaccuracy of which is self-evident in the reality of sophisticated networks of traders in abusive images of children on the Internet) is not confined to our popular media. The government further entrenches this characterization in its guidance notes to the application of sex offender orders. The Home Office fall back on a well-worn stereotype of the paedophile to illustrate how the orders might work, citing a man with a previous caution for indecent conduct toward a child 'hanging around' outside a school, approaching departing children and offering them sweets (Home Office, 1998). As Ashenden notes, the presentation of an archetype of the paedophile has dual outcomes. First, it makes the topic less uncomfortable as it feeds into a familiar stereotype and enables the public to disassociate themselves from the individual described, and second, it simultaneously maintains the horror of the unknown predator (Ashenden, 2002). At one and the same time, then, the moral panic over paedophilia has perpetuated the notion that sexual dangerousness resides in strangers and that those strangers are not like 'us'. While 'we' are 'normal', morally decent, law-abiding citizens, 'they' lurk at school gates and in playgrounds, preying on innocents in the pursuit of fulfilling their sexual depravities.

As a 'moral panic', paedophilia certainly fits several of the criteria. While it cannot be characterized as an 'ordinary' crime, paedophilia is far from extraordinary and the murder of children by strangers has remained remarkably consistent over the last 30 years, with about six such deaths annually. Yet the media persist in portraying it as a growing threat; a risk that could strike at random. Fears over paedophiles using the Internet to stalk or groom their victims may well be partially borne out of their parents' distrust of new computer and information technologies, and their anxieties about the further fragmentation of the family. Other media technologies, notably CCTV, have made cases of child abduction by strangers especially fascinating, providing graphic imagery of the last movements of victims to a voyeuristic viewing public who already know their fate. Moreover, like all moral panics paedophilia has acquired a remarkable degree of consensus. There are few issues that have galvanized public reaction more fiercely than that of adults who have a sexual preference for children, and in response to those who act on their desires, procuring children in playgrounds and Internet chat rooms, there is striking unanimity in the condemnation expressed by the media, the Home Office and local communities. It is easy to see, then, why the paedophile has been characterized as the folk devil *par excellence* in contemporary Britain. He (the kind of language and imagery used in popular discourses about paedophiles reinforce the presumption that sex offenders are male) is '*absolute* other' (Greer, 2003a: 40); an individual without *any* redeeming qualities, nearly always reduced to a set of sub-human, even bestial, thoughts and urges that are totally alien to right-minded people.

However, like many of the examples mentioned in the previous chapter, the paedophile crisis does not fit all the criteria traditionally associated with the moral panic model, the weaknesses of which should by now be clear. As discussed in the previous chapter, one of the fundamental discrepancies in accounts of moral panics is in explanations of their origins. In the case of paedophilia, the general view is that the process of demonization did not emanate from government (although it might be said that the new sex offender legislation and concomitant public debate had the effect of stigmatizing a large number of men, including those who had actually committed no offence). But most critics would argue on this point that the sex offender legislation was introduced in response to public fears rather than as a means of manufacturing them. Similarly, while it has been argued that public anxieties concerning youth crime generally, and the Bulger case in particular, were a manipulation on the part of the government to construct a 'demonology of deviance' and advance a particular political agenda (Freeman, 1997), most commentators support the theory that the invocation of evil in this case was led by the judiciary and the media (Stokes, 2000). Having said that, we should not overlook the fact that a government does not have to manufacture a crisis in order to benefit from it, and that the construction of social problems as matters of individual wickedness rather than as failures of collective responsibility or social policy, can work to the advantage of governments seeking to diffuse political responsibility (Lacey, 1995; Freeman, 1997; Stokes, 2000).

The 'outing' and persecution of known paedophiles might therefore best be viewed as a meso-level concern. Kitzinger argues that neighbourhood pressure groups, disillusioned by the failure of authorities to prevent child abuse, were already taking direct action as early as the 1990s. These protest groups, consisting mostly of mothers who were outraged at official impotence and scared for their children's safety, provided the impetus for extensive media reports about paedophiles long before the 'watershed' case of Sarah Payne's abduction and murder. Jenkins's (1992) study of the moral panic over satanic child abuse also supports the 'meso' theory of source, albeit from a rather more cynical standpoint. He suggests that the 'exposure' by social workers of a vast and unsuspected prevalence of child abuse fulfilled a number of ideological and professional needs, including providing much needed extra funding for an under-resourced service, and much sought-after credibility – initially, at least – for a relatively low-status profession.

Guilt, collusion and voyeurism

The factors highlighted above reinforce the notion, proposed by left realists, that crime must be taken seriously and not regarded as mediated artifice (Young, 1987), but there is another pertinent point to be made, and it is one that is rarely discussed. By reducing serious crimes to moral panics, the media succeed in masking the collective sense of guilt that underpins traumatic events, while at the same time pandering to the voyeur in all of us. In the case of James Bulger a sense of shame and guilt extended beyond the immediate community (primarily the 'Liverpool 38' as the press dubbed them; the people who saw James being dragged to the railway line where he met his death, but who failed to intervene) and seeped into the conscience of the nation as a whole. Subsequent cases such as the abduction and murder of Sarah Payne and Holly Wells and Jessica Chapman, have further shocked a society that effortlessly falls back on notions of 'evil within our midst' while denying its own flaws and colluding in the demonization of offenders as 'others'. In his analysis of the Bulger trial, Morrison (1997) candidly reminds us that most of us experienced events in our youth of which we are now embarrassed or ashamed; after all, children can be cruel, selfish and unconstrained. His own tainted memory is of the rape of a girl at her 14th birthday party by a group of 15- and 16-year-old boys. He did not have sexual intercourse with her, but he assaulted her, and failed to intervene when he knew that others were raping her, or report what he knew was happening. But at the same time as we recall, and recoil from, our own memories of ourselves as youths, we hang on to the ideal of children as precious innocents who must be protected from the sordid and the spoiled. No wonder that out of such incongruity, when children commit serious crimes, a deep and pervasive cultural unease is borne.

Our failure to protect youngsters from the 'perverts' and 'monsters' in our midst provokes a similar sense of collective anxiety and cultural unease. Yet, again, there are clear paradoxes in our cultural attitudes and legal responses to the sexualization and sexual victimization of young people. One legal anomaly is that the maximum sentence that can be imposed for unlawful sexual intercourse with a girl under the age of 13 is life, yet the maximum sentence for unlawful sex with a girl aged 13 or over is two years. The opportunity for paedophiles to exploit this legal distinction was brought home to the public in June 2003 when a paedophile was given a three-year sentence (subsequently raised to four-and-a-half years when the offender appealed against his sentence in October of that year) for unlawful sex with two girls aged 13. According to prosecutors, he had made contact with one of the girls via a chat room when she was 11 and had 'groomed' her for two years before abusing her shortly after her 13th birthday. Not only does it seem curious that the sexual abuse of a girl a few days before her 13th birthday can carry such a divergent sentence to that which can be imposed for the same crime a week later, but both seem incongruous in the context of an age of consent that is set at 16.

A further illustration of the anomalies that cause confusion over young people's sexuality is evident in the sustained, and frequently salacious, media reporting of teenage 'runaways'. In the aftermath of an intense period of anxiety surrounding the safety of young girls following the disappearances of Sarah Payne, Millie Dowler, Holly Wells and Jessica Chapman, the media spun out the panic through the summer of 2003 by reporting numerous incidents in which girls went missing with male acquaintances. There were several stories involving girls who had been targeted by men on the Internet, including the case of the 12-year-old who disappeared to Europe with a 31-year-old American marine (which will be further discussed in Chapter 7) and the 14-year-old who went on holiday with a 46-year-old 'family friend'. In addition, throughout August and September 2003, much media coverage was devoted to cases involving 14- and 15-year-old girls who went missing with their 16- or 17-year-old boyfriends. While the fact that these young women were all under the age of consent makes the media construction of them as victims somewhat understandable, there was little discussion of the fact that they were all willing partners who left their families under no coercion. The complex issues of morality underpinning these cases (what did the boys and, in some cases, much older men, offer these girls that was otherwise missing from their lives? How would these cases be treated in countries where the age of consent for girls is lower?) was elided in favour of the simple explanation that the girls were the passive victims of male manipulators who tricked them into leaving the safety of their loving families. A similar process is evident in media reports of young people and drugs. Periodic panics that have occurred when young people (for example, 18-year-old Leah Betts in 1995 and 10-year-old Jade Slack in 2003) have died as a result of taking drugs, have been presented as potent images of innocence corrupted by a dangerous and malevolent subculture (Osgerby, 1998). As we have seen previously in Chapter 2, the contemporary mediated landscape results in reality being reduced to a set of binary oppositions. While very young children like Jon Venables and Robert Thompson may be constructed as 'adults', there is simply no place for any discussion of 'adult' behaviour among children who are constructed as victims. For them, childhood innocence is a blank canvas, devoid of sexuality and sexual fantasy, and vulnerable to corruption by the peddlers of drugs and perverse pleasures – invariably sick, older males (Coward, 1990).

Confusing messages about the sexual maturity of children is also evident within popular culture. It might reasonably be argued that sexual attraction to children is not extraordinary in a society where youth is revered, and that the distinction between childhood and adulthood has become increasingly blurred, especially for girls. In particular, the music, fashion and cosmetics industries must all take their share of the blame for the confusing messages they propagate about child sexuality. As Silverman and Wilson (2002: 42) state, the vogue for small girls to dress as adult women and adult women to dress as small girls suggests that children 'have a broad appeal to many adults who are not paedophiles, and would frankly be offended by the suggestion'. Silverman and Wilson pose two questions that hint at the cultural discomfort provoked by this issue: Why does our society collectively collude with the idea of 'stranger danger' when we are all too aware that most children will be abused by someone they know? And why is it that our society 'discovered' the paedophile at exactly the same time as this process of sexualizing our children seemed to gain pace? (2002: 182). The suggestion that sexual attraction to children may not be the preserve of a few grubby, inadequate loners, but is actually pervasive in society, was graphically illustrated by 'Operation Ore' launched in May 2002 (cf. Jewkes, 2003b, 2003c). Throughout the police investigation of 7,272 British subscribers to a Texas-based subscription website called Landslide, the archetype of the grubby, socially inadequate, middle-aged man has not been very evident: instead, those that have been investigated have included high-profile celebrities, teachers, MPs, a prison governor, teenagers and women. The British subscribers represent a small fraction of the 390,000 individuals in 60 countries who subscribed to this one portal, but it has been suggested that as many as 250,000 Britons are still using child pornography sites (Cullen, 2003).

While concerns over children's safety have escalated, the agenda on child protection is still largely dominated by a concept laden with very specific ideas and assumptions – the paedophile. In diverting attention to 'stranger danger', and characterizing the paedophile as the personification of evil, the media have reinforced the belief that paedophiles are a separate species, a breed apart (Kitzinger, 1999). They have thus colluded in preserving the image of the ideal family that is at the heart of conservative ideology, and underplayed or ignored the fact that sexual violence exists – indeed, is endemic – in *all* communities, and that sexual abuse of children and infanticide are more likely to occur within the family than at the hands of an 'evil stranger'. Even though the scale of abuse perpetrated by priests, teachers, local authority employed carers, police officers and other 'upstanding' members of the community has, in recent years, had to be acknowledged by the media and other social institutions, it is muted in comparison to the coverage given to individuals who fit the archetype of the 'dirty old man' (and even more subject to moral censorship is any acknowledgement of abuse carried out by women, as we shall see in Chapter 5). The reluctance on the part of journalists, and the wider public for whom they write, to acknowledge the reality of abuse by men or women within the family – which accounts for more incidents and is arguably more damaging in the long-term than assaults by strangers – reflects a powerful emotional and intellectual block. Incest is, quite simply, 'a crime too far' (Greer, 2003a: 188).

In summary, the fervent, voyeuristic media coverage devoted to cases such as those of James, Sarah, Holly and Jessica, gives them a superordinancy that lifts them above other, equally horrible, crimes. The decisions of those who work within media organizations to select certain stories and present them according to their professional codes and institutional news values can thus secure a powerful symbolic place in the public psyche, while at the same time repressing the

collective sense of guilt and denial that such cases provoke. They are directed at events that have sufficient cultural resonance to threaten the fundamental basis of the social order. Yet, in constructing an indefensible, demonized 'other' against a backdrop of taken-for-granted normality, moral panics over children who kill and are killed avoid any real risk to the essential structures of society. Those who look for alternative explanations are silenced or condemned as 'do-gooders' seeking to make excuses for the worst examples of human depravity (Stokes, 2003). Not only does this close down further aetiological inquiry, but it also allows the community to remain emotionally and physically intact (cf. Barak, 1994b; Aldridge, 2003).

Moral panics and the revival of 'community': some concluding thoughts

In the previous chapter, we reveiwed the concept of moral panics which has traditionally united politics, media and everyday life and in this chapter we have focused on the fear and loathing that is directed at two modern folk devils, offending children and paedophiles, both of whom have been characterized as the 'evil monsters in our midst'. In Chapter 3 it was suggested that the moral panic model is unhelpful and, certainly, it is problematic when applied to pae-dophilia because it suggests that genuine public fears about the sexual abuse and exploitation of children are unfounded or overstated. Quite simply, Cohen's thesis – or rather, its application by countless acolytes – is open to the criticisms that it reduces serious problems to overblown media reporting, distorts the reality of crime which usually involves victims and often entails human suffer-ing, and can only account for public, spectacular crimes, not the serious offences that take place in private, hidden from the gaze of the media. The reduction of a widespread if largely hidden social problem to 'accessible proportions' (Cowburn and Dominelli, 2001: 403) arguably makes the issues reviewed in this chapter something *other than* or *beyond* moral panic, a term that diminishes inci-dents such as the murder or sexual abuse of a child to mere media-generated hysteria, negating the very real and rational responses that such crimes provoke (Kitzinger, 1999).

However, there are elements of the moral panic thesis that are interesting to explore further in this context, not least the emphasis it places on the notion of 'community'. As noted in Chapter 3, the tendency to fall back on notions of 'pure evil' are not that surprising; after all, once 'evil' has been defined, the public knows by implication what 'good' is. The labelling of paedophiles as 'enemies within' thus gives the hub of the group (often referred to euphemistically as the *'moral majority'*) a sense of their own cultural identity. This is especially apparent in the actions taken by communities in response to the releasing of convicted paedophiles in their towns. Echoing 19th-century fears concerning the elemental power of the crowd (reviewed briefly in Chapter 1), the view that it is the psychological predispositions, rather than the spatial arrangements of individuals, which forms the essential concept of the crowd finds forceful and compelling expression in the confession of a woman who was part of a vigilante group targeting paedophiles during the press 'outing' campaign in July 2000:

> [I] enjoyed walking up the street with a gang of women, all shouting to get the paedophiles out. I can't help it but this is how I felt. Walking the streets with all the noise, I got a buzz out of it. I know it sounds really childish. But when I came back here and thought 'what have I done' ... Now, I think if we have been to innocent people's homes, then I am ashamed. I do think it has got a bit hysterical. And because of what's happened we have been made to look like riff-raff. (*Observer*, 13 August 2000: 4)

Recall the writings of Gustave Le Bon (1895/1960), who argued that crowds were the beast within, the absolute antithesis of rational citizens. Writing in the same era, Charles MacKay (1841) declared that people 'go mad in herds, while they only recover their sense slowly, and one by one' (MacKay, 1841, reprinted 1956: xx). Yet is this coming together in unanimous condemnation of a perceived threat an act of madness or is it, as Pratt (2002) suggests, a rational response to the state's failure to deal with paedophiles in ways that such groups think appropriate; a movement that speaks of resistance and empowerment? As society becomes more fragmented and entire groups of people are excluded on the basis of their look, their style, their behaviour, and even on predictions concerning their potential behaviour (see Chapter 7), people tend to congregate around those issues that offer them a sense of unity, some semblance of community (Greer, 2003b). Through the perception of an identity held in common, each individual member of a group or crowd is able unconsciously to deny his or her feelings of powerlessness in a shared sense of power.

Despite their rarity, then, high-profile criminal cases involving child victims are used in much the same way as other cultural events – coronations, royal weddings, state funerals and assassinations – which become part of a collective memory through mass media. Although late modernity is frequently said to be characterized by fragmentation, surveillance, regulation, dangerousness and risk – all of which are said to mitigate against, if not make redundant the notion of community – individual life histories are structured, shaped and made sense of within frames of reference provided by the mass media (Jewkes, 2002). In fact, it may be precisely those 'negative' characteristics of late modernity that fuel people's need for unity and, in a context of uncertainty and insecurity, one of the primary means by which people are afforded a sense of social cohesion and connection with their communities may be via the media. It is therefore no longer only media personalities and celebrities who offer the illusion of intimacy (a phenomenon known in media studies as 'para-social interaction'; Horton and Wohl, 1956), but the victims of violent crimes, and their families, whose circumstances guarantee sufficient 'human interest' to bring people together in public outrage and mourning. It is, however, a climate of public mourning which – while instrumental to the creation and maintenance of an *imagined community* in otherwise fragmented and anonymous circumstances – is on 'our' terms. People want contact and some form of interaction, but *not too much* (Greer, 2003b), and that is why mediated experience can be so much more satisfying than lived experience. The common tendency to stigmatize offenders and sentimentalize or even sanctify victims and bereaved relatives of victims is thus symptomatic of a life lived vicariously via the media. Public responses to crimes involving child victims (which range from 'passive' responses such as floral tributes, roadside shrines and books of condolence, to 'active' expressions of violence and vigilantism) are a way of touching a stranger's life without having to endure one's own life being touched back by strangers in any palpable way – save from the fact that we feel better for having taken the time to send the message, sign the book, take part in 'direct action' (2003b). These expressions of grief and anger thus correspond with a particular imagination of proximity and closeness (the intimacy of a personal tribute, the primal pleasure of being part of a crowd bent on revenge), but it is an imagination which is largely faceless. Media-orchestrated, publicly articulated responses to serious and violent crime are thus basic components of imagined community, but it is a community that remains tangential and anonymous. Mediated expressions of fear and loathing are thus fundamentally in keeping with the nature of society in late modernity.

Summary

- *Confused attitudes to children*: Part of the reason for the elasticity of 'youth' as a concept is that adult society holds contradictory and conflicting views regarding the nature of youth. Views of childhood are paradoxically captured in notions of 'innocence' and 'evil' and are frequently enshrined in law and upheld daily by the popular media. One example of constructions of childhood 'innocence' is encapsulated in the age at which individuals can legally consent to sexual intercourse. The age of consent in this country is 16, and stories involving the sexualization or sexuality of children below that age are invariably reported in tones of outrage and hysteria. When it comes to sex, children are children until they reach 16. Yet, when it comes to youth justice, the Crime and Disorder Act (1998) abolished the presumption of *doli incapax* and structurally reconfigured youth justice in terms of moral under-standing and culpability from the age of 10. The inconsistencies that lie at the heart of differing ages of criminal responsibility within the justice system is thus key to the confusing ideas surrounding childhood in contemporary Britain. Moreover, such paradoxes play into the hands of a media which constructs events in terms of binary oppositions and stock stereotypes. The media can position child offenders and vic-tims of crime along a continuum from 'innocence' to 'evil', individualizing their pathol-ogy or vulnerability, in order that deeper questions about social structures – the family, education, political institutions and the media industries themselves – need never be asked.

- *Children as 'evil monsters'*: The murder of James Bulger was a watershed in public perceptions of childhood, as well as in English law. As Scraton (2003) argues, James Bulger's death was exploited to the full, first by the Conservatives who, at their party conference in 1993, whipped up fervour with demands for execution, castration and flogging, and then by a new Labour government which rushed through its wide rang-ing Crime and Disorder Act and set about appearing tougher on crime than its Conservative predecessors. And throughout it all, the figures of Robert Thompson and Jon Venables, whose photographs were printed in every paper as soon as the guilty verdicts were reached, were a gift to a media which had squeezed every last drop out of stories about 'persistent young offenders' and the 'yob society', and were now given a new motif for evil with which to provoke respectable fears in the shape of two 10-year-old boys.

- *Children as 'tragic victims'*: The media-orchestrated panic over sex offending focuses attention on the 'paedophile', a social construction which reinforces pub-lic fear of 'stranger-danger' and provides the community with an identifiable hate-figure on to whom they can project their anxiety and loathing. At the same time it has brought back to the fore notions of childhood innocence and vulnerability and emphasized the need to manage the threat posed by paedophiles via various 'risk assessment' strategies, while ignoring the reality of danger in the family and home. Mediated constructions of paedophiles and the public responses they shape thus not only present a partial image of the abuse and exploitation of chil-dren, but also let the community, in its broadest sense, 'off the hook' (Cowburn and Dominelli, 2001: 404). The impression of random danger is perpetuated, but it is a risk that can be accommodated provided that it is contained within terms which emphasize community. Crimes involving young victims of older or adult offenders are therefore a primary vehicle for expressions of community 'togeth-erness', ranging from vigilance to vigilantism, and from public sorrow to public vengeance.

STUDY QUESTIONS

1   Why are children and young people frequently perceived to be *the* crime problem in the UK? What are the problems with this characterization?

2   How do the different theoretical perspectives reviewed in Chapter 1 view young people who commit crime?

3   To what extent, and in what ways, has recent media coverage of paedophilia skewed the picture of sexual abuse in Britain? How do media constructions of the 'paedophile' differ from those of the 'rapist' in an earlier age?

FURTHER READING

The subject of youth and crime is thoroughly explored by Muncie, J. (1999a) *Youth and Crime: A Critical Introduction* (Sage), and by Newburn, T. in his chapter 'Young people, crime and youth justice' in M. Maguire, R. Morgan and R. Reiner (eds) (2002) *The Oxford Handbook of Criminology* (Oxford University Press). There are also several useful chapters in J. Muncie et al.'s *Youth Justice: Critical Readings* (Sage). The murder of James Bulger has been reviewed so extensively in both media studies and criminology that it is virtually impossible to single out any one study. Julian Petley has written much on the subject, including Franklin, B. and Petley, J. (1996) 'Killing the age of innocence: newspaper reporting of the death of James Bulger', in J. Pilcher and S. Wagg (eds) *Thatcher's Children? Politics, Childhood and Society in the 1980s and 1990s* (Falmer). Morrison, B. (1997) *As If* (Granta) is a semi-autobiographical analysis of the case by a journalist who attended the trial of Thompson and Venables and employed the case to reflect on his own experiences both as a child and as a parent. Finally, Scraton, P. (ed.) (1997) *'Childhood' in 'Crisis'?* (UCL Press) is an interesting collection and explores many of the issues covered in this chapter.

5

Media Misogyny: Monstrous Women

Chapter Contents

OVERVIEW

Chapter 5 provides:

- An exploration - underpinned by psychosocial and feminist approaches - of mediated responses to very serious offending by women, concentrating mainly on women who kill and rape.
- A consideration of whether women are treated more harshly or more leniently by the courts.
- A discussion of whether women who commit violent crimes in partnership with a man are passive victims or active partners who kill through choice.
- An analysis of the standard stories, stereotypes and stock motifs employed by the media to convey deviant women's 'evilness'.
- A consideration of women's 'otherness' and why women who commit very serious crimes are much more newsworthy than men who similarly offend.

KEY TERMS

agency	feminism	psychoanalysis
deviance	filicide	psychosocial
difference	heteropatriarchy	explanations
essentialism	infanticide	scopophilia
familicide/family	news values	spousal homicide
annihilation	otherness	unconscious

This chapter will consider the public's mediated responses to women who kill and commit other serious (for example, sexual) offences, and the discussion will attempt to tease out some of the explanations, derived in part from *psychoanalytical* readings, for the particularly virulent form of vilification that is directed at female offenders. As we have already seen, the modern media are highly selective in their constructions of offences, offenders and victims. For a crime to be reported at all, let alone be the subject of the kind of persistent, pervasive coverage which can result in the construction of offenders as folk devils, the prevailing ideological climate must be especially hostile to the offence that has been committed. Something about the juxtaposition of time and place will result in a case standing out as extraordinary or exceptional even in a society where the most horrific of crimes may be presented, if at all, as run-of-the-mill episodes. As we saw in the previous chapter, guilt, collusion and voyeurism are common themes that underpin some of the most newsworthy crimes of our age. Often, it is the existence of some kind of mediated representation – usually, these days, CCTV footage – of the crime, victim, and/or offender that jolts us out of our cosy stupor and forces us to recognize the reality of serious crime in places we least expect to see it. At the same time, the criminal act, its perpetrator(s) and/or its victim(s) must conform to some of the key journalistic **news values** described in Chapter 2. The synthesis of these two contexts – ideological climate and journalistic assumptions – are instrumental in creating public consensus and in shaping the process by which some individuals are designated 'others' – monsters in our midst. They also determine why some offences (for example, the part played by Myra Hindley in the murders of five children) cast a much longer shadow than others (for example, the murder of at least 150, and possibly as many as 350, adults by Harold Shipman). Following the line taken by many **feminist** critics, it will be argued in this chapter that the media tap into, and magnify, deep-seated public fears about deviant women, while paying much less attention to equally serious male offenders whose profile does not meet the **psychosocial** criteria of '**otherness**'. While many generalized points will be made about women's involvement in certain categories of offending (murder, manslaughter, infanticide and filicide, sexual assault, and rape) specific and, of necessity, selective, cases will be referred to throughout the chapter as illustrations of media misogyny. Those cases will, however, concern some of the most newsworthy and notorious female offenders in recent history from the UK and elsewhere.

Psychoanalytic perspectives

Contemporary media reflect other socio-political institutions in their attitudes to marriage and the family, which remain curiously embedded in the Victorian age. Notions of the feminine as passive, maternal, married and monogamous co-exist with sentimental ideas about childhood innocence, resulting in any 'other' identities – for example, single mothers and lesbian parents – being subjected to hostile censure (Wykes, 1998). When it comes to constructions of female offending (or, for that matter, female victimization), **difference** is readily constructed as **deviance** by causal association with crime (1998). Despite the fact that women rarely stalk, kill strangers or commit serial murder – in fact they are seldom violent, accounting for only around 10 per cent of convicted violent offenders – those who do so are highly newsworthy because of their novelty. The media, then, are happy to acknowledge that violent women are relatively uncommon, but concede that they are all the more fascinating and diabolical as a result.

In a psychoanalytic interpretation, 'difference' involves the denial of large parts of ourselves, or the projection of those parts of ourselves which make us feel vulnerable, onto others. Stemming from Freud's conceptualization of the Oedipal conflict which arises when an infant begins to have sexual feelings and desires towards the opposite-sex parent, and at the same time has accompanying feelings of resentment and jealousy towards the same-sex parent, this perspective helps to explain the persecution of the 'other' throughout history. Put simply, in the case of the male child, he has previously seen himself as sharing an identity with his mother, but is suddenly confronted with the reality of her sexual difference. This induces a fear of castration and a masculine identification with the father, not only physically, but also as a source of cultural power and moral authority. In the context of this discovery, culture (that is, the Law of the Father) wins over individual desire, and the child 'succumbs to a destructive unconscious solution' (Minsky, 1998: 83) in which he expels or externalizes the part of himself that he finds intolerable – in other words, the painful 'victim' feelings of humiliation and vulnerability – and projects them onto his newly discovered 'other', his mother. In this way he is able to disown the harmful feelings that interfere with his newly discovered sense of power and project them onto 'woman', who is now defined as 'different and therefore bad' (1998: 84). 'Subsequently, women, femininity or passivity wherever it exists may be deemed contemptible and feared because it represents a despised, castrated part of the self' (1998). Symbolic cultural representations (for example, those which reduce, repress, objectify, silence, humiliate, ridicule or otherwise marginalize women and other 'minorities') are intuitively 'picked up' by individuals, identified with at a psychic level and then played out within social relations, thus reinforcing and reproducing divisions and inequalities (Messerschmidt, 1986; Giddens, 1991; Minsky, 1996, 1998; Craib, 1998).

It is, then, the interplay between **unconscious** fears and culturally reinforced prejudices that defines who, at any given time, is designated 'the scapegoat "other"' against whom we bolster our own individual sense of identity, (Minsky, 1998: 2) and the victimization of feminized 'others' goes beyond gendered relationships and helps to explain not only sexism, but racism, nationalism, tribalism, terrorism, homophobia and religious persecution. Implicit in all these forms of intolerance is the notion of a despised 'other' as the means to maintaining an idealized self. An understanding of 'otherness' helps to explain why identities are often characterized by polarization and by the discursive marking of inclusion and exclusion within oppositional classificatory systems: 'insiders' and 'outsiders'; 'us' and 'them'; men and women; black and white; 'normal' and 'deviant' and so on. Not surprisingly, then, notions of difference and otherness have been put forward as a theory of crime and victimization. As previously noted, media representations of immigrants, political refugees and British-born black and Asian people are frequently underpinned by powerful psychic notions of otherness which frequently find expression in a tendency to see crime perpetrated by non-white people as a product of their ethnicity, while crimes against non-whites are all too frequently constructed in ways that are tantamount to blaming the victims.

The subject of this chapter, however, is the extent to which the relationship between unconscious fears and culturally constructed scapegoats can help to explain mediated responses to women who commit very serious crimes. Psychosocial and feminist theories will underpin the discussion and aid our understanding of the legal, criminological and media discourses surrounding women who seriously offend. Unsurprisingly, given the parameters of this book, it is media rather than legal discourses that will be our focus. However, as Belinda Morrissey argues, the close relationship between legal and media institutions has meant that 'the two function together and their representations ... mostly lend themselves to a single analysis, with dominant media depictions mirroring courtroom portrayals' (2003: 4). Both institutions have a vital role in maintaining notions of feminine wickedness in cases where women offend, just as they preserve ideas of feminine oppression in cases where women are portrayed as victims (2003: 4).

Feminist perspectives

In brief, feminist criminological perspectives emerged in the 1970s to challenge the androcentrism (or male-centredness) of traditional criminology. The first feminist text to make a profound and sustained impact on criminology was Carol Smart's *Women, Crime and Criminology* (1977), which exposed the culturally biased assumptions about women that had underpinned traditional ideas about female criminality since the days of Lombroso over a century before. Smart's pioneering approach led to a number of other influential feminist studies (among them: Heidensohn, 1985; Gelsthorpe and Morris, 1990; Howe, 1994; Lloyd, 1995; Lees, 1997) which argued that essentialist assumptions about women's psychological make-up and biological purpose condemned them to differential treatment within law. Women who commit serious offences are judged to have transgressed two sets of laws: criminal laws and the laws of nature. In Ann Lloyd's (1995) memorable phrase, such women are 'doubly deviant and doubly damned'.

There is no single 'feminist criminology', but rather a diverse set of approaches that make different, and often diverging, claims about the intersections of gender, race and class within crime, the criminal justice system and criminology (cf. Gelsthorpe, 2002). In their early manifestations, feminist perspectives centred largely on socialization theories and were applied most frequently to constructions of gender in studies of victimization, especially men's violence toward women. However, contemporary interest has broadened to include women as offenders and many feminist theorists have sought to understand unconscious as well as conscious processes in the formation of gendered identities. These critiques have addressed why it is that some women fail to conform to cultural stereotypes of 'femininity' despite their socialization and, of particular interest in the current context, how and why legal and media discourses both construct and reflect negative public emotions (ranging from antipathy to downright hostility) toward female offenders. Underpinning the discussion that follows, then, are three issues that have been addressed by feminist scholars in recent years. First is the question of whether women are treated more harshly or more leniently when they come before the courts accused of a serious offence. Second is the question of whether women who commit violent crimes in partnership with a man, or in self-defence against a man, are passive victims of male oppression or active law-breakers acting out of choice and desire. And third, in the light of answers to the previous two questions, how are women who kill and abuse represented in the media?

The question of whether women who offend are treated more harshly or more leniently than men has been hotly debated within feminist criminology, with many critics keen to debunk the so-called 'chivalry hypothesis' which presupposes that women 'get off lightly' in criminal cases because judges and juries extend to them the same kind of gallantry that they would to their female relatives. With regard to 'ordinary' offences, there is still striking disagreement about whether women are treated more or less severely than their male counterparts. Helena Kennedy QC surmizes that women who fulfil society's expectations of the good wife and mother, with all the attendant notions of demure sexuality that these labels imply, are more likely to secure judicial clemency (the 'fragrancy test' as she puts it, in reference to Mr Justice Caulfield's comments about Mary Archer during the trial of her husband, Jeffrey) than women who challenge these stereotypes (Kennedy, in preface to Lloyd, 1995: x). Lloyd further argues that conforming to the stereotype of helpless victim (for example, of an abusive partner) when in the dock 'can work for a woman' (1995: 19), although others have concluded that, while *most* women receive relatively light sentences, *some* female defendants are treated more severely due, not only to the woman's perceived conformity to the kind of gender stereotypes already mentioned (marital status, family circumstances and so on), but to other factors such as their class, ethnicity and age (Morris, 1987; Daly, 1994).

But whatever the fate of 'ordinary' female offenders within the criminal justice system, most feminist commentators assert that when women commit very serious crimes, including murder, they attract more media and public attention, the image created of them is more powerful, and they leave a more long-lasting impression (Heidensohn, 1985; Worrall, 1990; Lloyd, 1995). From Lizzie Borden, who was tried and acquitted of murdering her father and stepmother in Fall River, USA in 1893, to Maxine Carr accused of perverting the course of justice in the 'Soham schoolgirls' murder trial in 2003, women who are implicated or involved in very serious crimes provide the media with some of their most compelling images of crime and deviance (Heidensohn, 1985). No wonder that in popular discourse the female of the species is said to be more deadly than the male.

In fact, women who commit serious crimes are portrayed in terms very similar to those used to represent children who seriously offend (see Chapter 4). In the absence of any alternative discourse to explain the existence of violence and cruelty in those whom society views as essentially 'good', journalists fall back on stock notions of 'pure evil', which they illustrate with standard stories, motifs and stereotypes (listed below). As we shall see through the course of this chapter, these tried-and-tested narratives often keep aspects of the woman's involvement in the crime hidden, or only partially represented, allowing the public to dip into the cultural reservoir of symbolic representations and fill in the gaps as they see fit. Moreover, they combine to render women passive and unstable, lacking in moral agency and somehow not able to act as fully formed, adult, human beings.

The standard narratives used by the media to construct women who commit very serious crimes are:

- *sexuality and sexual deviance*
- *(absence of) physical attractiveness*
- *bad wives*
- *bad mothers*
- *mythical monsters*
- *mad cows*
- *evil manipulators*
- *non-agents.*

Sexuality and sexual deviance

In Chapter 2's exploration of journalistic news values, it was noted that the media concentrate on crimes of violence that involve the 'right sort of victims' (those who lend themselves to constructions of innocence and vulnerability), while those from more marginal groups, who cannot so easily be portrayed as blameless or pure, receive significantly less (and certainly less sympathetic) coverage. This preference for particular sorts of victims also extends to offenders, but conversely it is offenders who can be constructed as, in some sense, 'marginal' who are deemed most newsworthy. This makes women who commit serious offences already of news value by virtue of their relative rarity. However, women offenders become even more newsworthy when they can be further marginalized by reference to their sexuality. In line with the binary classification systems within which children are constructed as either tragic victims or evil monsters, women, their behaviour and their crimes are similarly polarized, often via antithetical constructions of their sexuality and sexual histories. In its simplest form, women are categorized as either sexually promiscuous or sexually inexperienced/frigid, a dichotomy highlighted in the title of a book on the subject, *Virgin or Vamp* (Benedict, 1992).

It is often suggested that, in their general reporting of women in public life, the press are at their happiest and most sanctimonious when they can portray a saintly madonna image of a woman either as devoted mother or in faithful support of a man. But real women invariably fail to live up to this impossible ideal and, across the whole range of offences, women are sexualized by those who work in the criminal justice system. As a result, women are frequently punished – and further punished symbolically by the media – more harshly. For example, behaviour which would be deemed 'normal' patterns of delinquency in young men is reinterpreted as wayward and amoral in young women, the consequence of which is that the 'offence' is frequently over-dramatized. In fact, non-criminal behaviour such as perceived sexual misconduct is more likely to result in girls being placed in care or through juvenile justice systems, while the courts are excessively punitive toward adult women who deviate from the maternal, monogamous, heterosexual 'norm' (Sarri, 1983; Wilczynski, 1997; cf. Heidensohn, 1985: 47 ff.). Meanwhile, cases which could be used by the media to raise questions about the potential dangerousness and culpability of institutions in which we trust (the family, the education system, social services, the police and so on) may be reduced to scintillating titbits reminiscent of a soft porn magazine. During Rose West's trial in October and November 1995, just about every denigratory term applicable to women was thrown at her by journalists:

> She was described variously in the news as: depraved, lesbian, aggressive, violent, menacing, bisexual, likes black men, likes oral sex, kinky, seductive, a prostitute, over-sexed, a child abuser, nymphomaniac, sordid, monster, she had a four-poster bed with the word c**t (*sic*) carved on the headboard, posed topless, exhibitionist, never wore any knickers, liked sex toys, incestuous, who shed tears in silence, no sobs, no sound at all. At puberty she developed, allegedly, an obsession for sex and 'Fred confided, "When Rose was pregnant her lesbian tendencies were at their strongest. I had to go out and get her a girl. She gets urges that have to be satisfied"' (*Sun* 3.11.95). (Wykes, 2001)

Quite simply, when it comes to the reporting of women who commit serious crimes, constructions of deviant sexuality are almost a given. From Myra Hindley and Rose West to Tracie Andrews and Claire Marsh (the youngest woman convicted of rape in the UK), women whose sexual deviance can be alluded to, if not covered by the tabloid press in salacious and slavering detail, represent cardinal *folk devils*, a contemporary incarnation of criminological positivism's 'born female criminal' (Lombroso and Ferrero, 1895). However, it is not just female offenders who are denigrated by a media with lofty expectations about appropriate behaviour for women; female victims are also subjected to reproach if they fail to comply with conventional and rigidly imposed feminine stereotypes. For example, Maggie Wykes highlights the prurient tone that was also adopted by the popular media regarding the victims of Fred and Rose West. The predictability of their fate was suggested by smug assessments of what happens to feckless girls who leave home young and/or accept lifts from strangers. Far from being humanized with details of their lives, family backgrounds and ambitions, they were portrayed as being 'from children's homes; lesbian; illegitimate; runaways; fostered; students; picked up on the "streets" or hitchhikers' (1998: 238–9). By contrast, there was virtually nothing in the reporting of the West case about the male clients who bought sex (from Fred's 12-year-old daughter, among others) at 25 Cromwell Street, nor about the many policemen who were familiar with the house and its occupants (1998).

Similarly derogatory ascriptions served to dehumanize the victims of 'Yorkshire Ripper' Peter Sutcliffe, the overriding impression of whom remains that they were prostitutes (not only untrue of many of his victims, but suggestive of low-life squalor that elicits little sympathy), with hardly any attention paid to their identities as mothers, daughters, partners, students and so forth. Consider this quote from the Assistant Chief Constable of West Yorkshire Police:

> [The Yorkshire Ripper] has made it clear that he hates prostitutes. Many people do. We as a police force will continue to arrest prostitutes. But the Ripper is now killing innocent girls ... You have made your point. Give yourself up before another innocent woman dies. (Cited in Chadwick and Little, 1987: 267)

The popular press also managed to blame Sutcliffe's wife, Sonia, for his crimes. The *Daily Mirror* (23 May 1981) ran the following quote from a police detective who investigated the case: 'I think that when Sutcliffe attacked his 20 victims he was attacking his wife 20 times in his mind'. According to the article, Sutcliffe worshipped his wife, and she dominated and belittled him. Barrister John Upton comments:

> This was just one of many pieces that put forward Sonia Sutcliffe's failings as a wife – her inadequacies as a sexual partner, her wish not to have children, her mental health difficulties – as the direct cause of his butchery. A woman was expected in the eyes of a prurient, disapproving public not just to stand by her serial killer man but to stand in place of him. (Upton, 2000: 6)

Women's sexual preferences, their enjoyment of sex, or their frigidity, have long been used to demonize them and justify their construction in the pages of the popular press as 'monsters', even when – as in Sonia Sutcliffe's case – the crimes were not hers. However, the ascription 'monster' comes most readily to the minds of journalists if the sexual preference of the woman in question is for other women. Morrissey quotes a newspaper editor (originally cited in Wilson, 1988: 55) who describes his idea of a heaven-sent news story: 'If I could get a story of a beautiful lesbian who mows down children at a kindergarten with a machine gun I would be over the moon' (2003: 18). In fact, 'real life' provided the next best thing in the form of Australian murderer Tracey Wigginton and her three co-accused – not one lesbian killer on the rampage, but four (Verhoeven, 1993)! In our *'heteropatriarchal'* (Hart, 1994) culture, lesbians, prostitutes and women who are deemed sexually promiscuous are archetypal 'outsiders'. Within a group already classified as 'other', they are *even more* other. As victims they are invisible, as offenders they are superordinate.

Millbank further elaborates on the tendency of the media to view lesbian sexuality as a 'cause' of aggressive behaviour. In the cases of two women, Tracey Wigginton who, with three friends, picked up a male stranger in her car in Brisbane, Australia, offered him sex and then murdered him, and Aileen Wuornos who killed seven men in Florida, USA, it is their sexuality that is said to have 'explained' their crimes. They were lesbian, so they hated men. But 'they also hated society and the family – represented by "the father" – so they killed men who were father figures' (Millbank, 1996: 461). Interestingly, in the Wigginton case, of the four women who were accused, only three were convicted. The fourth, who was acquitted, did not conform to cultural stereotypes of lesbians and was portrayed as being not 'properly gay', but rather a straight girl led astray (Morrissey, 2003).

As far as the media are concerned, lesbians represent an 'anomalous' category (Lévi-Strauss, 1979; Fiske, 1982) positioned precariously on the borderline of maleness and femaleness. Reliant on constructing reality within categories of binary opposition, anomalous beings draw their characteristics from both categories and consequently they have too much meaning, they are conceptually too powerful. In terms derived from cultural anthropology, lesbians 'dirty' the clarity of their boundaries and are subsequently designated taboo (Douglas, 1966; Fiske, 1982). At a psychic level, lesbians represent neither one gender nor the other, but can be superimposed onto the social division between masculinity (as active) and femininity (as passive). Quoting a tabloid, Verhoeven demonstrates the precariousness of such classifications in relation to Wigginton, whose gender was presented literally as shifting between femininity and masculinity:

> At that time [1987 – on meeting her lover Donna] Wigginton rode a motorcycle and took her lover on the pillion. She always exceeded the speed limit. But when Wigginton slipped behind the wheel of the 'loving couple's' Commodore car, her character changed completely – to that of the helpless female who always drove cautiously and never exceeded the speed limit. (*Weekend Truth*, 23 February 1991: 8, cited in Verhoeven, 1993: 114)

The unsubtle Freudian metaphors used in this piece demonstrate the extent to which psychoanalytical themes are part of the currency of popular discourse.

As an anomalous category, lesbianism is often applied to deviant women whatever the evidence (or lack of evidence) regarding their sexuality. The 'natural' harmony between lesbianism and aggression, assumed and reinforced by culture, was epitomized by press coverage of Myra Hindley eight years after her original conviction. Not content with portraying her according to multifarious, and sometimes contradictory, manifestations of evil (as we shall see in this chapter, the only derogatory stereotype the media could not pin on her was that she was 'mad' – and her apparent sanity was held against her), the press alighted on her alleged lesbianism as 'proof' of her ongoing depravity. The catalyst for this new wave of hysteria was the news that Hindley had conspired to escape from prison with the help of a prison officer, who was said to be her lover, and a fellow inmate. Hindley's biographer, ex-*Sun* journalist Jean Ritchie, took the 'jailbreak plot' to be evidence of Hindley's unsavoury promiscuity and power to manipulate others (1988; cited in Birch, 1993). Assumptions about lesbian sexual desire and violent transgression were further reinforced in 1995 when photographs appeared in the popular press showing Myra Hindley and Rose West holding hands in the high-security wing of Durham Prison (Smith, 1997; Wykes, 2001).

Another anomalous category for women is that of 'rapist', hence it is one of the most incomprehensible crimes – to the media and public at large – for women to be convicted of. While stories involving men who rape are so commonplace that they do not necessarily make the news agenda (unless, as discussed in Chapter 2, they conform to several cardinal news values), women who rape are already newsworthy, although their relative invisibility is not because they don't exist – 18 women were convicted of rape or of aiding and abetting rape between 1995 and 1999 (http://news.bbc.co.uk). Claire Marsh, who at 18 years old is the youngest woman to be convicted of rape in the UK, was not surprisingly subjected to sustained and sensationalized media coverage after she was involved in an attack on a woman in July 2000. Her co-accused, Marvin Edwards, by comparison, was given much less attention and some newspapers and broadcasts did not even name or carry photographs of him (another male accomplice convicted was too young to be legally identified). Morrissey (2003) discusses two further cases involving women – Valmae Beck and Karla Homolka – who, with their male lovers, were convicted of abducting, raping and murdering girls. She notes that the crimes of the women were shown to far outweigh those of their partners, and it was they who received most press attention. In addition, while their male partners – Barrie Watts and Paul Bernardo respectively – *were* viewed as dangerous psychopaths, they nonetheless remained comprehensible; their lusts were an extreme manifestation of 'normal' male fantasies. Their wives, on the other hand, were portrayed as sadists whose deviant sexuality stretched the public's concept of malleable femininity beyond comprehension.

If women offenders cannot be constructed as lesbians or sexual sadists, their deviance will be verified with reference to their previous sexual conduct and sexual history. Basically, if a woman can be demonstrated to have loose moral standards, the portrayal of her as manipulative and evil enough to commit a serious crime is much more straightforward. Conversely, men who commit such crimes are often reported in respectful, even romantic terms. Wykes notes how the press referred to the relationship between Fred West and two of his victims (one raped, one murdered) as 'sexual intercourse' and an 'affair'. He was also variously constructed as a good husband, a hard worker and a reliable provider, who was driven by a 'mad and terrible love' for his wife (Wykes, 1998: 238). Before his suicide in prison left Rose to stand trial alone, Fred had declared that he would take all the blame and that her everlasting love was payment enough (Sounes, 1995: 348). Another male murderer whose media portrayal evoked connotations of the 'misguided romantic' was John Tanner who, in 1991, was found guilty of the murder of his girlfriend, Rachel Maclean, a student at Oxford University. The reporting of this incident conveyed the impression that it was a crime of passion ('he loved her to death') and reports of Rachel's alleged promiscuity and infidelity were carried under headlines such as the *Daily Telegraph*'s 'Lover strangled student in jealous rage' and the *Mirror*'s 'Jealous John strangled his unfaithful girlfriend'. The inference, then, was that Tanner was not *entirely* to blame for his actions; his crime was triggered by the infidelity of his girlfriend.

Physical attractiveness

In addition to their sexuality and sexual history, women who kill are subjected to intense scrutiny regarding their physical appearance and attractiveness; a fact that is entirely in keeping with general life. In contemporary societies, the media are engaged in a very particular construction of gender whereby those aspects of femininity that are valued – youth, slenderness, decorativeness and so on are constructed to suit the 'male gaze' (Wykes and Gunter, 2004). This gendered narrative underpinning media discourses within advertising, women's magazines, tabloid newspapers and so on, extends to news discourses and includes constructions of female criminality. The degree to which media discourses are stuck in a Lombrosian view of female criminality are demonstrated by Australian newspaper reports that portrayed Tracey Wigginton as the epitome of an unfeminine, unnatural woman with 'huge buttocks and thighs' and 'a personality to match her 17-stone frame – big' (Morrissey, 2003: 124). Of her co-accused, the two who were also convicted (and sentenced to life imprisonment and 18 years respectively) were described in turn as 'heavily-built … her face fixed in a malevolent glare' and 'short and stocky' with a 'dumbfounded' expression (2003: 124). By contrast, the fourth woman who was acquitted was not only regarded as a faux-lesbian, but was described as demure and pretty, the most attractive of the accused. Physical appearance was also a factor in the press reporting of Valmae Beck, who assisted her male partner in the abduction, rape and murder of a 12-year-old girl in Queensland, Australia in 1987. Her motives, apparently, 'lay not in her own sadistic desires, but rather in her insecurity and increasing age' (2003: 151). Morrissey cites the Brisbane *Sunday Mail* (11 February 1990), who claimed that Beck's age and 'frumpish looks' made her terrified of losing her husband to the extent where she would do anything for him. Similarly, in this country, the homely appearance of Rose West inspired the *Daily Mirror* to liken her to a 'toad on a stone' (cited in Smith, 1997).

Yet women, it seems, cannot win. If conventionally attractive they will be presented as *femmes fatales* who ensnare their victims with their good looks, but are cold, detached and morally vacuous. A prime example of this characterization is convicted rapist and murderer Karla Homolka, who was presented by the Canadian media as good-looking but shallow. The media also contrived to portray Homolka in positivist terms, as the epitome of beauty and femininity, yet revealing 'traditionally masculine' traits in her enjoyment of the rapes and of sex generally (Campbell, 1995 cited in Morrissey, 2003). Similarly, British killer Tracie Andrews, who was convicted of the murder of her boyfriend, Lee Harvey, after appearing at a press conference to appeal for his 'road rage murderer' to come forward, was a former model and was, by all conventional standards, an attractive young woman. But the press described her as 'vain' and 'heavily made up' and a headline above photographs of her read 'Looks that could kill' (*Daily Star*, 30 July 1997).

Bad wives

As discussed earlier, the chivalry hypothesis has been most successfully challenged in relation to women who fit popular, mediated images of deviance, either in their dress and appearance or in their behaviour. When women do not conform to Victorian-inspired ideals of femininity and domesticity, and can therefore be judged bad wives and mothers, they are much more likely to confound a judge's idea of appropriate womanhood (Kennedy, 1992; Lloyd, 1995). By contrast, marital status, family background and children have little or no bearing on most cases involving male defendants whose conformity to conventional notions of 'respectability' rely on issues such as employment history rather than factors such as marital status (Lloyd, 1995). Ideally, women should be housewives, content to remain at home, economically and emotionally dependent on their husbands who are busy bestriding the public sphere (Worrall, 1990). Women who transgress these codes of conduct and pursue public lives of their own, are tolerated only if they continue to put their husbands and families before their careers, and occasionally appear beside their husbands as attractive trophies and further evidence of his success.

Little wonder, then, that women who kill their spouse or partner are the epitome of the 'bad wife', almost regardless of the provocation that led to the crime. Sara Thornton, convicted in 1990 of killing her violent, alcoholic husband, Malcolm, is one such case. She says, 'I've been portrayed as a woman who nagged him over his drinking, who didn't always wear knickers and who went off to a conference and left him' (Wykes, 1995). What is perhaps slightly more surprising is that women who are the victims of murder by their spouse or partner are frequently portrayed in a similarly negative light, and put on trial for their own victimization. One infamous example of the 'topsy turvey justice of patriarchal law' (Radford, 1993) concerned Joseph McGrail, who walked free from the courtroom with a two-year suspended sentence for killing his 'nagging' common-law wife. The judge, Mr Justice Popplewell, famously said that the victim would have 'tried the patience of a saint'. Ironically, this verdict came in July 1991, just two days after Sara Thornton appealed against her sentence and lost.

Feminist research has shown that, unlike men for whom there are recognizable patterns of 'lifestyle' violence involving public rituals of heavy drinking and fighting, women's violence is mostly confined to the domestic sphere (Polk, 1993; Heidensohn, 2000). Furthermore, in cases where men murder their female spouses or partners, the crimes are often precipitated by jealousy or depression (for example, when the woman threatens to leave, or leads the offender to believe she is being unfaithful to him). Women, on the other hand, tend to resort to *spousal homicide* as a response to initial violence from their male partner (Browne, 1987; Lloyd, 1995). However, it is interesting to note the extent to which recently there has been a backlash against feminist research and theory. For example, despite all evidence to the contrary, Hornby (1997) concludes that the over-representation of men in the criminal justice system must be evidence of a hugely discriminatory system. He also challenges the notion that men are more likely to be violent than women, with the glib comment that a child is more likely to be hit by its mother than its father. Of course, to say that men are more violent than women is by no means to accept that all men are violent, violence-prone or tolerant of violence, and that all women are non-violent or victims of masculine violence (Miedzian, 1991). But in some areas of research, it is arguable that anti-feminist sentiments, such as those that underpin Hornby's views, have clouded the real picture of offending and victimization. One such area is that of domestic violence, a subject which has seen vigorous attempts in recent years to cast men as its victims. But despite the salience of male victims of domestic assault in official and popular discourses, research has shown that victimized men are likely also to be perpetrators of domestic violence, especially in male–female partnerships (Gadd et al., 2003). Furthermore, men identified as 'victims' are less likely than female victims to have been repeatedly victimized or seriously injured, and are more likely to have the financial resources to allow them to leave the abusive relationship (2003). Such misrepresentations illustrate Wykes' assertion that media and legal constructions of male and female violence fit within a framework that emphasizes traditional models of family organization and femininity that is commensurate with a 'broader ideological "claw-back" of feminist "gains"' (1998: 234). The consequence of this emphasis is that traditional conservative family and gender relations are endorsed and celebrated, even when the reality of many of the crimes discussed in this chapter indicates families and marriages as sites of (largely masculine) violence, sexual abuse and murder.

Bad mothers

In a Freudian analysis, our psychological make-up means that early dependence on our mothers makes us especially vulnerable to the 'fear that an evil mother in human form can elicit' (Morrissey, 2003: 23). Not only do they kill, hurt or neglect when they are 'supposed' to care and nurture, but they also represent only a tiny fraction of serious criminals, so they frequently have a perceived 'novelty' value that guarantees media interest in them. The 'bad mother' motif is so culturally pervasive that it is ascribed to virtually *all* women, whether victims or offenders, actual mothers or non-mothers, and whether they are involved in the murder of children or commit other crimes but also happen to *be* mothers. In the latter category, Tracie Andrews was widely castigated for committing a crime that carried a life sentence, as this would entail a long separation from her daughter, although in a rare moment of empathy, the *Birmingham Evening Mail* noted that 'this 28-year-old unmarried mother of a little daughter seemed dwarfed by her surroundings ... it was painful to remember that a verdict of guilty would lead to her daughter Karla being deprived of her mother' (29 July 1997). However, we are reminded in the same article that this is no embodiment of the feminine ideal. Illustrating positivist themes already discussed, Tracie is described as a 'bruiser of a woman', a street fighter whose 'bottle blonde hair grew more tawny as the trial progressed ... sometimes obscuring all her features except the heavily-jutting jaw'. More controversially, women who lose their children in terrible circumstances may also be portrayed as bad mothers. One of the most notable cases in this respect is that of Lindy Chamberlain, who was convicted of the murder of her baby daughter in Australia in 1982 despite asserting that she had seen a dingo emerging from the tent where her daughter was sleeping. Sentenced to life imprisonment, Chamberlain had many appeals turned down until, in 1986, in the light of new evidence and mounting public concern, the case was re-examined and Chamberlain was acquitted. A less extreme, but still controversial, example of the media's inclination to portray mothers as 'guilty victims' is Denise Fergus, the mother of James Bulger, who was roundly condemned by some sections of the popular press for turning her back on her son while paying for shopping in the Bootle mall from which he was abducted. This view was later legitimated by the rather unfortunate comments of Sir David Ramsbotham, then Chief Inspector of Prisons, who informed an interviewer that Mrs Fergus would be feeling 'guilt as well as grief'. He went on: 'I don't know, but if I'd left my two-year-old when visiting a shop I'm not sure I'd feel entirely comfortable' (*Independent on Sunday*, 15 July 2001).

But the bad mother motif is most systematically and vengefully applied to female offenders who are involved in the killing of children. Rose West and Valmae Beck both presented an enigma for the media in so far as they were mothers who were involved in the abuse and murders of children (her own, as well as others', in the case of West). The following passage appeared in an Australian newspaper and is written in response to the sentencing of Beck for her part in the rape and murder of a 12-year-old girl with her partner, Barrie Watts, who was reportedly obsessed with the idea of raping a virgin. Yet it could just as easily have been written about the crimes of Rose West in this country:

> Before this case, how could anyone have believed that a middle-aged mother would be party to such a crime ... what I would like to know is this: If such a plain, ordinary-looking housewife and mother as this one can become physically involved in such a terrifying crime, then how many more ordinary men and women are out there waiting to come under the influence, as she said she was, of an evil swine like her partner in rape, torture and murder? Surely any mother would have enough compassion to be repulsed and in quick succession sickeningly enlightened when her husband said he wanted to rape a 12-year-old school-girl? ('Kavanagh on Saturday': 'Compassion? It's time for real justice'. *Courier-Mail*, Brisbane, 10 February 1990, cited in Morrissey, 2003: 148)

Mothers who rape and sexually abuse children and young women embody the 'monstrous maternal' (Morrissey, 2003: 154). Despite the notoriety of a handful of high-profile female sexual offenders such as West and Beck, society generally is not ready to come to terms with the existence of a group of individuals whose crimes challenge the firmly-held belief that women are incapable of sexual aggression. Furthermore, in cases where men sexually abuse their children, the media frequently contrive to apportion blame, in at least equal measure, on the children's mothers for allegedly colluding with the offences. In most of these cases the women concerned are also the victims of abuse at the hands of their partners and are often too frightened to report it, but this does not prevent judges and juries sentencing them as 'bad' mothers rather than abused women (Morris and Wilczynski, 1993). Perhaps the archetype of the 'bad mother' in cultural discourses on crime in the UK is Myra Hindley, not because she had children herself (she didn't) but because, as a woman who was convicted of serious crimes against children, she was deemed guilty not only of breaking the law, but also of breaking every culturally sanctioned code of femininity and womanhood. Beverly Allitt, a nurse who was convicted of murdering four children in her care, of attempting to murder three children, and inflicting grievous bodily harm on six other children, is another example of a woman who failed to measure up to the ideals of maternal care perpetuated by a patriarchal media. In Allitt's case it was her chosen profession as well as her sex that was used against her. Not only was she described as the 'angel of death' by many newspapers and the 'most monstrous woman since Myra Hindley', but an editorial in the *Daily Express* went on:

> Women should nurture, not harm. By and large they do. Even today violence is a male speciality. But nurses are supposed to be the epitome of female care. They are the angels of newspaper headlines. When women do things like this it seems unnatural, evil, a perversion of their own biology. (5 May 1993)

Arguably, then, it is women's 'natural' role as mothers and carers that makes it so difficult for society to accept that women can harm children.

Mythical monsters

The images of women that still prevail in media constructions of women who commit serious crimes derive from pagan mythology, Judaeo-Christian theology and classical art and literature. Despite the diversity of these sources, modern constructions of deviant women frequently draw on any or all of these traditions, invoking images of witches, satanists, vampires, harpies, evil temptresses, 'fallen women' and Christian notions of Original Sin, to convey female wickedness. These motifs are often used in tandem with references to lesbianism. Like lesbianism (which threatens the clarity of the gender categories 'male' and 'female'), many of these mythical monsters are similarly anomalous classifications. For example, many of the mythical and religious images drawn on to portray evil women mediate between gods and humans, while satanists and vampires straddle the categories of the living and the dead. Fitting into neither one category nor the other, but deriving from both, they are invested with too much meaning, which has to be controlled by designating it as taboo (Fiske, 1982).

Two favoured figures from Greek mythology who can be viewed as anomalous are Medea, an enchantress who, when spurned by her lover, murdered her children, and Medusa, the snake-haired monster who turned her victims to stone with a stare. Tabloid newspapers have made ample use of both symbolic figures in their coverage over the last 40 years of Myra Hindley, the reporting of whom is invariably accompanied by the famous police 'mugshot' taken at the time of her arrest in 1965. According to Helen Birch this image, a 'brooding presence' that has held a 'bizarre grip' over the public imagination for four decades, even among those too young to remember the original case, has become detached from its subject (1993: 33). It has become a symbolic representation of the 'horror of femininity perverted from its "natural" course' (1993: 34–5), an icon of female deviance. In homage to Lombroso, many writers have alighted on the peroxide blonde hair and 'hooded eyes', and drawn inferences from these physicalities ranging from haughty indifference to irredeemable evil. An editorial in the *Guardian* hints at the way the image that has become part of the cultural fabric of our country through its constant reproduction in the pages of the popular press, interpellates us via its subtle evocation of mythological monstrosity:

> Myra, Medusa. Medusa, Myra. No matter what she looked like after she was sentenced to life imprisonment in 1966, Myra Hindley was fixed forever in the public eye as the peroxide-haired gorgon of that infamous police snapshot. Look at her defiant, evil eyes, we are meant to say. Spawn of the devil, God knows, she probably had a head of snakes, covered by a blonde wig to fool us, this evil, evil woman. (Glancey, 2002)

Another monstrous motif used in narratives about female killers is that of the vampire. Most notorious in this respect is the representation of the Australian woman Tracey Wigginton who, after killing Edward Baldock in Brisbane in October 1989, was described by the Australian press as the 'lesbian vampire killer'. As several writers have noted, cultural connections have been made between vampirism and lesbianism in film and literature for more than a century, a stereotypical link that is not altogether surprising given that the lust for blood is usually equated with the vampire's role as sexual aggressor (Verhoeven, 1993; Morrissey, 2003). The psychoanalytic equation of vampiric bloodsucking with oral sex in many narratives and texts further cements the notion of the female killer as not only murderous, but also sexually deviant. In Tracey Wigginton's case, the vampire appellation came about after her accomplices claimed she killed her victim in order to feast on his blood. Despite psychiatric evidence that they were deluded in this respect, the press began to report the story as fact, revelling in stories of gothic horror, cannibalism and sexual perversion. Although there was *some* speculation in later coverage that her accomplices concocted the 'lesbian vampire' story in order to diminish their own roles in the murder and leave her to face trial on her own (Verhoeven, 1993), in general the vampire motif gave the media a fascinating 'hook' on which to hang a story that might otherwise have elicited little interest. The willingness of the public to believe the (literally) fantastic stories that were concocted about vampirism was not so surprising. As Verhoeven comments, 'if the public could believe a woman would actually kill a man at random, then it was capable of believing anything' (1993: 123–4). This willingness to believe also extended to investigating police officers, who admitted to watching vampire film *The Hunger* in an attempt to find clues as to a motive for the crime (Morrissey, 2003). The vampire motif was stretched almost to the point of incredulity when it was alleged in court that she combed the streets in search of a victim while listening to the strains of the Prince song 'Batdance' (Verhoeven, 1993). Even when psychiatrists declared that she was unfit to stand trial and should be subjected to further psychiatric treatment, their diagnosis was skewed to fit the Gothic narrative. The multiple personality disorder with which Wigginton was diagnosed was taken as further evidence of her vampirism, and subsequently allowed for a re-enactment of other mythical archetypes such as the witch, the siren and Jekyll and Hyde (Higgins, 1994, cited in Morrissey, 2003).

The depiction of female killers as vampires or other mythical monsters clearly serves to make them less woman than monster. Even the reporting of the Tracie Andrews case was humorously constructed with a nod to vampiric motifs and, echoing Tracey Wigginton's musical tastes, the *Sun* quoted a former boyfriend in the headline 'Tracie was so crazy in bed she made us do it to "Bat Out Of Hell"' (30 July 1997). In fact, most of the women discussed in this chapter have been reported in terms that emphasize their conformity to one or more of these ideological constructions of deviant femininity. Lindy Chamberlain was stereotyped as a witch who sacrificed her daughter in a satanic ritual; Aileen Wuornos, nicknamed the 'damsel of death', was a vengeful lesbian prostitute stalking innocent men to fulfil her inhuman lusts; Beverley Allitt was an 'angel of death' who cold-heartedly killed babies and children in her care; Tracey Wigginton was a 'vampire killer'; Karla Homolka was a beautiful but morally vacuous temptress; like Medusa, Tracie Andrews possessed 'looks that could kill'; Rose West was a kinky Lady Macbeth figure who dominated her husband and was the real instigator of the sordid goings-on within the 'Gloucester house of horrors' – after her husband's death, Rose became the 'black widow' in mediated discourse; Valmae Beck's confession and court testimony was evidence of her *scopophilic* desire to watch rape and murder and her sadistic enjoyment in aiding their commission. As Creed (1996) argues, motifs like these reinforce the notion of female killers as scapegoats for a phallocentric culture. A culture's deepest beliefs and darkest fears about women become entangled with childhood anxieties about supernatural monsters and creatures from the underworld passed down via legend, folklore and myth. Monstrous images of women become so firmly entrenched in the popular consciousness that it becomes almost impossible to view Myra, Rose, Tracey et al. as real women, rather than the grotesque caricatures portrayed in the media. For many feminist commentators this is a problem that is not confined to those women who are constructed via legal and media discourses, but it raises important wider issues concerning attitudes to women: 'The dichotomy between "good" and "bad" women ... serves as a means of patrolling, controlling and reinforcing the boundaries of behaviour considered "appropriate" for *all* women' (Morris and Wilczynski, 1993: 217). This brings us to another set of stereotypes which dominate 'official' discourses on women who offend; namely that *all* women are potentially mad at certain times of their lives (1993: 217).

Mad cows

While folklore and myth have created one collection of motifs of deviant women, another set of images has been supplied by science and medicine (Heidensohn, 1985). Once more, the 'findings' of 19th century male pioneers, from Lombroso to Freud, have been profoundly influential in constructing notions of female pathology as explanation for women's offending.

Most women who commit serious offences such as murder or manslaughter are advised by their lawyers to use psychiatric pleas; in other words, to plead guilty on grounds of diminished responsibility or *infanticide* (a crime that applies to women only, referring to the killing of a child under the age of 12 months by its mother when the balance of her mind was disturbed as a result of childbirth). Wilczynski (1997) notes that in cases of *filicide* (the killing of a child by its parent or step-parent), while 30 per cent of men use psychiatric pleas, over 64 per cent of women do so, resulting in women being twice as likely to receive psychiatric or non-custodial sentences (interestingly, filicide is the only type of homicide that women and men commit in approximately equal numbers). Men tend to utilize 'normal' pleas which do not require an 'abnormal' state of mind, for example, involuntary manslaughter, which requires an absence of intent to kill or seriously injure the victim (1997). Consequently, men are much more likely to receive a custodial sentence when they kill their children (even in cases where a psychiatric plea has been used). Wilczynski further argues that although men who kill their children are sometimes viewed as 'sad', they are usually regarded as 'bad': their killings are 'less surprising, and they are more in need of punishment and deterrence' (1979: 424).

These findings might, at first glance, suggest that the tendency to 'psychiatrize' women *can* lead to leniency, especially in cases where women commit infanticide or filicide (Marks and Kumar, 1993; Morris and Wilczynski, 1993; Wilczynski, 1979). But several commentators are at pains to point out that psychiatric disposals are not necessarily 'lenient' sentences. They can result in women being labelled 'psychotic' or 'psychopathic' for life, and there are many documented cases of women who have been incarcerated in mental hospitals, prisons and other institutions far longer than they might have been had their behaviour not been medicalized and had they not been prescribed drugs on which they became dependent (Lloyd, 1995; Wilczynski, 1997). The casualness with which women's crimes are medicalized is well documented (Dobash et al., 1986; Sim, 1990; Lloyd, 1995; Wilczynski, 1997) and is typified by the defence's use of Munchausens syndrome by proxy (MSBP) in the Beverley Allitt trial, an illness that few had heard of prior to this case. In simple terms MSBP – the 'caring disease' – is a condition that affects parents or carers, mostly women, who are driven by a psychological need to gain attention by being involved in the medical care of an infant. In such circumstances it might be assumed that those in the criminal justice system, and in society generally, find it much easier to accept that a woman has committed violent or heinous offences if she can be catagorized as a deluded lunatic or unstable hysteric, even if sentences do not necessarily reflect that sentiment. The word 'hysteria' comes from the Greek *husterikos*, meaning 'of the womb', and has long been employed in order to reinforce the notion of women as 'other'. Additional psychopathological states peculiar to women – for example, pregnancy, childbirth and lactation are legally sanctioned explanations of infanticide, while menstruation and menopause are also treated as inherently pathological states which 'explain' female offending (Heidensohn, 2000).

Pathologizing the female reproductive cycle also allows the 'bad mother' motif to be utilized. Treating women who commit infanticide or filicide as hormonally disturbed perpetuates the 'myth of motherhood' (Oakley, 1986) and suggests that 'normal' women are naturally maternal and find motherhood constantly fulfilling and joyful. While this is a dominant construction in mediated discourses, especially advertising, it is an image that is at odds with the stark reality that for many women motherhood can be anything but, for a variety of structural reasons (poverty, lack of support and so on) as well as physiological and psychological ones (Wilczynski, 1997). Most (in)famously, Pollack in his (1950/1961) publication, *The Criminality of Women*, argues that women's 'other' biology not only propels them into crime, but also allows them to conceal their criminality, just as they have, for centuries, concealed menstruation, pregnancy, the fatherhood of their children, menopause and sexual arousal. If women can fake orgasm, Pollack argues, they must be naturally deceitful and are thus better equipped to conceal their deviance. While Pollack has been largely discredited, especially in the feminist literature, the idea that women are ruled by their biology persists in medical, legal and media discourses about crime. The use of pre-menstrual syndrome (PMS) to explain and excuse women's violent offending is the most recent manifestation of a biological determinism that has its origins in Victorian ideas about hysterics (cf. Benn, 1993). Meanwhile, men are regarded as rational agents, ruled by their heads, not their biology. Hormonal imbalance is arguably no more likely to result in women's crime as it is men's, although few criminal cases are defended on the grounds that high testosterone levels might explain male outbursts of violence (notwithstanding that in the 1960s and 1970s some researchers did claim that violent crime was associated with a male chromosome abnormality, dubbed 'supermale syndrome'; cf. Ainsworth, 2000). The tendency to pathologize women's physiological and 'natural' traits in order to construct them as artful deceivers brings us to the broader stereotype of women as evil manipulators.

Evil manipulators

Many of the individuals mentioned in this chapter – Myra Hindley, Rose West, Karla Homolka, Valmae Beck – did not commit their crimes alone, but in partnership with their male lovers and husbands. Women who form murderous alliances with men are the most problematic for the institutions that seek to understand them and communicate their actions to the rest of society, particularly as their prey are often the archetypal 'innocent' victims – children and young women. These female offenders neither inspire sympathy as victims nor celebration as powerful avengers and, as such, they represent an enigma to mainstream academic and feminist discourses, and offer the least possibility for rehabilitation or redemption as far as the legal and media professions are concerned (Morrissey, 2003).

Women who join with their partners in killing cannot be simplistically constructed as lesbians, even if their victims are girls and young women. The media therefore struggle to employ their standard narrative of lesbianism because their relationships with their male accomplices *insists* on their heterosexuality (although it doesn't stop them from trying, as demonstrated by the image of Rose and Myra holding hands, mentioned earlier). Equally, it is usually not possible to easily construct these women as victims or avengers because rarely is there evidence that suggests either of these defences. Even if there are grounds for constructing them as victims (as in the case of Homolka, who finally went to the police after months of savage abuse at the hands of her co-accused), their involvement in such terrible crimes (in this example, the abduction, drugging, rape and murder of young women, including her 14-year-old sister, Tammy Homolka) makes it impossible for the media to elicit any sympathy for them.

The media's solution to the problem of heterosexual women who appear to be equal partners, or at least to go along unquestioningly with their men's wishes in very serious crime, is to place the burden of guilt on their shoulders. As a consequence, in all the cases mentioned above, the argument runs thus. Ian, Fred, Paul and Barrie were all evil men, capable of extreme cruelty. But without a submissive woman, a sadistic man would never act. It is only together that they become a 'lethal pair' (Morrissey, 2003: 152). It is therefore the woman who is instrumental in unleashing the violence and depravity that the man has thus far contained. As numerous commentators have pointed out, the Myra and Ian soap opera that continued to play out in the pages of the popular press years after their conviction is testament to this. Although Hindley's role in the offences was minor compared to Brady's, her culpability is somehow regarded as greater. In not resisting Brady's sado-masochistic demands, and in failing to intervene to stop his grisly crimes, it was in fact Hindley who let down their victims. As a woman, she should have shown compassion, she could have done more. The betrayal was Myra's. She was the evil manipulator, he the unfortunate bearer of a tormented psyche. This image was reinforced when, in 1985, Ian Brady was transferred from prison to a psychiatric hospital, suffering from paranoid schizophrenia. He went on hunger strike and proclaimed his wish to die. Photographs of a thin, ravaged Brady, 'his body apparently displaying the signs of inner torment' began to appear in the press and provided 'a graphic counterpoint to those of Myra, smiling, in her graduation gown at her degree ceremony, presenting a softer, prettier, happier image' (Birch, 1993: 55). As the decades rolled by, Myra's demonization only intensified, making her a larger-than-life, constantly in-your-face caricature, while Ian Brady literally and metaphorically disappeared.

The motives of women who form partnerships with men who kill, and assist them in their murderous quests, are complex and contested. Some critics argue that, for the most part, these are 'ordinary' women who happen to fall under the influence of a controlling, usually older, man and that without that fateful first meeting they would have gone on to live 'normal', suburban lives (Williams, 1967; Smith, 1997; Wykes, 1998). Others argue that this conceptualization negates the *agency* and free will of such women, and that they may actually seek out such men because they have similar desires, going along with their partners' murderous plans as a vehicle to their own empowerment (Birch, 1993; Morris and Wilczynski, 1993; Pearson, 1998; Morrissey, 2003). For these writers, the unpalatable suggestion that these women may have enjoyed their crimes is the main impediment, not only to the invisibility of their roles in the crimes in media and legal discourses, but also to an adequate feminist consideration of the cases. It is much harder to defend a person who has apparently willingly committed heinous acts of cruelty than one whose actions resulted from duress or oppression and, as such, the actual involvement of these women is 'repressed out of conscious existence' (Morrissey, 2003: 156).

Non-agents

The conclusion of increasing numbers of scholars therefore is that neither academic feminism nor society at large are ready to confront the reality that women can be cruel, sadistic and violent. The simple truth that men are more aggressive than women not only encourages a widespread cultural ignorance of the fact that women have the potential for violence, but it also serves to deny psychically the notion that women can kill *as women*. In general, women are viewed either as big children (which is how they were considered by Lombroso and Ferrero a century ago, and which still permeates clinical discourse; Morris, 1987) or as men (a view endorsed by the many examples of women who are portrayed as 'mannish' lesbians; see also Ward Jouve, 1993). Stock stereotypes such as vampires and snake-haired medusas also serve to deny women's agency. If a murderess becomes a mythical monster, she loses her humanity and is considered to have acted – but not as a contemporary human woman (Morrissey, 2003).

There are only two crimes for which women may retain their humanity and avoid the ascription of 'evil', but both imply that offending women are non-agentic. They are 'spousal homicide', where the woman can be seen as acting in self-defence against an abusive partner, and infanticide, where a woman can be viewed as a mixture of 'mad' and 'sad'. In either case, the woman concerned can be regarded as a victim who is not responsible for her actions. Morrissey reflects on constructions of victimization and their wider implications for women generally in relation to spousal murder:

> Many portrayals of women who kill depict them as so profoundly victim-ized that it is difficult to regard them as ever having engaged in an inten-tional act in their lives ... Representations of the murderess as victim, then, function to deny her responsibility, culpability, agency, and often her ratio-nality as well, in their bid to explain her behaviour and secure her sympa-thetic legal treatment. While undeniably often successful in securing reduced sentences, the disadvantages of such a strategy outweigh the benefits in terms of improving general societal attitudes to, and challeng-ing negative myths and stereotypes of, women. (Morrissey, 2003: 25)

As discussed earlier, explanations of female criminality that rely on determinis-tic assumptions about women's physiology and biology arguably have the most far-reaching implications for deviant and non-deviant women alike, and domi-nant discourses of madness most incontestably speak to the non-agency of female offenders. While the Beverley Allitt case provoked the majority of the popular media to fall back on stock notions of psychiatric disorder, augmented by their discovery of Munchausens disease, one lone, contradictory voice was reported in the *Telegraph*. Dr David Enoch, a consultant at the Royal Liverpool Hospital and an expert on Munchausens, argued that popular assumptions about Allitt were incorrect:

> She is not mad, she is not psychotic. When you are psychotic you lose insight and delude yourself, you do not know what you are doing. Those who suffer from Munchhausens *know* that they are not really ill and have insight into their actions ... she would have known what she was doing with the children. (19 May 1993)

Even women who kill their own children may not fall neatly into the category of 'irrational' or 'emotional outburst' that are so often constructed for them. As Alder and Baker (1997) explain, acts of infanticide and filicide may be perpe-trated by women who are highly emotional at the time of the offence, but these acts do not necessarily represent a sudden, irrational loss of control.

The failure of the media to acknowledge the agency of women involved in serious offences is also apparent in terms of the delicacy with which the media side-step the actual details of their offences. Selective reporting is especially evident in cases where women rape and sexually abuse. For example, the crimes of Myra Hindley continue to be held up as perhaps the most heinous ever committed in Britain, yet even many of the journalists who continue using her image in order to sell newspapers are too young to remember her trial in 1966, and may not actually be fully cognisant of her precise role in the sexual torture and murder of the victims. Despite the collective sense of horror and revulsion at her crimes, few of us know what Myra Hindley *actually did*. Similarly, legal and media constructions of Valmae Beck and Karla Homolka glossed over their participation in the sexual assaults they committed. In fact, Homolka was not convicted of sexual abuse because of the temporary absence of incriminating videotapes at the time of her trial and, in the case of Beck who *was* convicted of rape, many newspapers did not mention this important aspect of her crimes (Morrissey, 2003). And, while the media enjoyed slavering over the details of Rose West's sexual predilections, the extent to which she was involved in the sexual abuse and murder of the victims whose remains were found at Cromwell Street and elsewhere remains unclear and legally unproved (Smith, 1997; Wykes, 1998). The reticence with which the media confront women's serious sexual crimes is somewhat surprising, especially given the appetite for sex that is often attributed to the popular press and its readership. Morrissey speculates that despite incontrovertible evidence proving women's participation in sex crimes, the media are simply not able to present female protagonists who so clearly deviate from conventional hegemonic, heteropatriarchal conceptions of femininity: 'Apparently, so these news stories say, men rape and murder, women watch and help with the clean up' (2003: 153). Yet, at the same time, the prudish and partial representation of women's involvement in rape and murder encourages the public at large to dip into the cultural reservoir of symbolic representations and 'fill in the gaps'.

Honourable fathers vs. monstrous mothers: some concluding thoughts

Psychosocial approaches to 'otherness' have provided a useful framework within which to study possible explanations for the bigotry and hysteria that characterizes media and legal discourses of offending women, and shed light on the general and deep-seated cultural discomfort generated by women's wickedness. Our inability to view women who commit serious offences as anything other than – well – 'others', may relate to our psychological make-up in so far as early dependence on our mothers makes us especially vulnerable to the fear that evil women can elicit (Morrissey, 2003). Our unconscious fears of feminine evil are then picked up and reinforced by a heteropatriarchal culture that presents any female deviation as intrinsically shocking:

> Those doing the defining, by that very act, are never defined as 'other', but are the norm. Those different from the norm – in this case, women – are thus off-centre, deviant. Man is the norm, the objective standard by which others are measured. Men are perceived to be independent, rational, autonomous and responsible. The ... other, the female is therefore dependent, emotional, not entirely adult and irresponsible. She is defined in reference to men. (Lloyd, 1995: xvii)

This psychic understanding of 'otherness' is central to the differential media reporting of men who kill and women who kill. Quite simply, when we consider the narratives used to construct mediated stories about serious crimes, women are characterized as bad mothers even when they are non-mothers and/or have killed adults, not children. Men, on the other hand, whomever their victims, are rarely described as 'bad fathers' (although, as with women, stereotypes based on assumptions about class, race, age and family stability, have a bearing on the legal and media discourses constructed around men's offending). Compare the examples of deviant women discussed above with the case of Robert Mochrie who, in July 2000, battered to death his wife and four children before ingesting poison and hanging himself. In a *Cutting Edge* documentary on Channel 4 (29 July 2003), Mochrie was presented as a tragic hero. *'Familicide'* – or *'Family annihilation'* as it has been dubbed by the media – is usually carried out by middle-aged men driven to a violent last resort either by marriage breakdown or by their inability to continue providing for their family in the 'traditional' manner. To some extent, Mochrie was experiencing both: his wife was involved in a relationship with his former business partner, he was regularly visiting prostitutes and, following early retirement, he had made some bad investments and was on the verge of bankruptcy. Despite these factors which might be thought to mitigate against the depiction of a 'typical' middle-class family, the discourse constructed by the Mochrie's friends and neighbours and presented uncritically by the television documentary makers, centred entirely around that: their sheer averageness. The words that were repeatedly used to describe Robert Mochrie were 'ordinary', 'normal', 'regular', 'decent'. Cath and Robert Mochrie were 'the perfect couple' and Robert 'adored' his children. Yet in the early hours of 12 July 2000, he 'meticulously', 'calmly' and – according to Cath's best friend – 'gently' bludgeoned each member of his sleeping family to death with a hammer, sent a few text messages, cancelled the milk, and then hanged himself.

As a newspaper editorial following the documentary observed, the sympathy shown toward Robert by friends, while generous and perhaps rather surprising, is not extraordinary. It was probably a brave attempt to square the man they thought they knew with the unknowable man who took six lives, including his own (McLean, 2003). But the collusion of the programme makers is more surprising. Not only did they entirely avoid resorting to stock motifs of monsters and devilry, but they also endorsed the idea of Mochrie as a fundamentally decent man driven to the edge by some sort of heartfelt but misguided heroism. The narrator of the documentary concluded that Mochrie's motivation 'in a strange and terrifying way, was love'. Newspaper columnist Gareth McLean's comment that Mochrie's motivation was more likely to be fear than love brought about by a combination of near-psychotic depression and a 'desperate, sad, proud and defiantly macho inability to ask for help' (2003), once more demonstrates the extent to which psychoanalytic ideas have penetrated popular and media discourses. But of greater interest in the current context is the quietly forgiving response of the community at large to these tragic events. As McLean continues: 'try imagining the tsunami of loathing that would descend upon her were a woman to commit those crimes' (2003).

It is not being suggested here that all men who murder are tolerated, ignored, understood or applauded. Most men who commit terrible crimes are not treated with the empathy that was extended to Mochrie, and it is men who are most frequently portrayed by the media as 'monsters' or 'evil beasts'. But the contention is that media and public responses to women who kill and seriously harm are even more exaggerated than they are for men. Male violence is seen to exist on a continuum ranging from the non-violent to the murderous and sexually bizarre, which results in it being viewed only in terms of degrees (Naylor, 2001). Even the criminological literature on masculinity and homicide couch familicide in terms of 'misguided altruism', and as a matter of masculine honour and pride in the face of overwhelming social expectations concerning men's responsibilities for their families' wellbeing (Alder and Polk, 1996). Put simply, violence is viewed as one of the many possible behaviour patterns for men; it is not strikingly unusual, even when extreme. Consequently, when a man kills he can expect that his crime will be both imaginable and possibly – as in the case of Robert Mochrie – even seen as human. Indeed, male crime is intrinsic to the hegemonic masculine ideal. In all spheres of life – political, social, economic and, above all, cultural – masculine violence is articulated, glorified, even fetishized. Men who commit serious crimes are thus normalized to a much greater degree than women who do so, and their crimes tend not to be accompanied by a sense of collective denial. Yet in cases of women who kill, 'vilification operates to displace the offender from her society, to insist on her otherness, thereby avoiding the knowledge that she is produced *by* that society'

(Morrissey, 2003: 24). No such expulsion is required when men murder; indeed, men's crimes might be said to be but one aspect of a prevailing cultural ideology of aggressive macho values that sustains men's crimes and makes them possible (Ward Jouve, 1988).

Two factors were mentioned at the beginning of this chapter that are paramount in securing a female offender's notoriety. One is her conformity to the key journalistic news values outlined in Chapter 2. Women who murder or sexually abuse form a tiny percentage of an already small, though demonized, group of criminals. This immediately guarantees their coverage; their crimes are novel, and they are negative in essence. But in addition they frequently illustrate most or all of the 12 cardinal news values (see Chapter 2). The horror of their crimes meets the required *threshold*; a grim *predictability* is woven through the account of their crimes via the use of stock stories and familiar motifs (lesbian monster, evil manipulator and so on); their histories and motives are reduced to the *simplest* of forms (that is, that they must be 'mad' or 'bad'); their pathology is constructed as *individual* and random, the most meaningless of acts carried out by individuals in whom we are meant to trust – hence any of us (or our children) are at *risk*; their crimes are explained by reference to their *sexuality* or sexual deviance; they frequently achieve a kind of macabre *celebrity*; indeed, some gain iconic status through *graphic imagery*, such as the police mugshot of Myra Hindley, which not only identified her as the 'face of the nation's deepest fears' (Upton, 2000: 6) in the popular media long after the peroxide had grown out and the lines on her face had appeared, but also achieved further immortality in art*; the victimization of *children* in murders by women further cements their newsworthiness, and even when children are not directly involved, the anomaly of women who kill being *potential* mothers is taken as proof enough of their deviation from notions of traditional womanhood, notions that are at the heart of *conservative ideology*. Finally, murderesses become notorious by virtue of their geographical and cultural *proximity*. The generally ethnocentric nature of our media means that those cases which are culturally and geographically meaningful to a home audience – Myra, Rose, Tracie and so on will have every aspect of their lives dissected for an avaricious audience. But the women discussed by Belinda Morrissey who came from Australia, America and Canada (Tracey Wigginton, Aileen Wuornos and Karla Homolka respectively) – countries all politically,

---

*The artist, Marcus Harvey, became notorious himself when he used a cast of a child's hand as a brush to create an acrylic portrait of Hindley for a show at the Royal Academy a few years ago. It was roundly condemned by the popular press and was pelted by visitors with eggs and ink. The infamous photograph also fascinated 1980s band, The Smiths, who reproduced it on record sleeves, again creating much media furore.

economically and culturally allied to our own – barely rated a mention in the UK media.

The fears of some feminist writers that constructions of women who kill have wider implications for all women are understandable, given the evidence put forward in this chapter. Mediated understandings of deviant women do not exist in a cultural vacuum and negative, potentially damaging stereotypes based on women's appearance, sexuality and behaviour are, of course, not limited to discourses about women who commit very serious crimes. All women who are in the public eye are inclined to become the subjects of narratives that construct them in terms of their willingness, or otherwise, to conform to traditional notions of passive, heterosexual, maternal, compliant femininity. However, many commentators have noted that, when it comes to women who kill – and here, once more, we find echoes of the public response to children who kill – a deep cultural unease is provoked by the uncomfortable reality of the human capacity for depravity. Media reports might blithely attribute women's serious crimes to their *in*humanity and 'otherness', but Smith (1997) argues that society *needs* the figure of the dominant female killer luring her hapless male partner into crimes he might otherwise not have committed, however far from the reality of the cases described in this chapter that depiction might be.

With this thought in mind, it seems fitting to end this chapter with some final reflections on Myra Hindley who has been, for many in this country, a constant, powerful, yet invisible presence throughout our entire lives. Her permanence in the collective consciousness has been assured by a number of high-profile appeals through the courts of Britain and Europe against her natural life tariff. However, her status in the collective British psyche as this country's number one folk devil has been augmented by a media that has inflicted her with almost every derogatory and damaging stereotype that can be ascribed to women. Before her death inside prison in 2002, Hindley spent over 30 years being the focus of society's most profound anxieties. Helena Kennedy (1992) maintains that Hindley became such a symbolic – iconic, even – figure because she was the vessel into which society poured its dark secrets; a reminder of the depths to which human depravity can sink. Fellow barrister John Upton comments: 'she is not merely a woman who has committed a crime; rather, there is an element of criminality inherent in her womanhood' (Upton, 2000: 6). In short, our fascination with Hindley reveals deeply conservative attitudes about the role of women in contemporary culture that are rarely exposed to the light of day. She remains – even in death – the archetypal 'she-devil', a monstrous, mythical, murderess who defies all our conscious and unconscious beliefs about womanhood. Yet her crimes were not unique, far less uniquely evil, as was maintained by Lord Stein during Hindley's final, failed appeal to the House of Lords in 2000. On the continuum of lesbianism, sexual deviancy, depravity and evil, Hindley somehow encompassed all points. Yet her actual participation in sexual assault, rape, torture and murder – what she is actually guilty of – remains overlooked or side-stepped to the point where it is invisible. Women who seriously offend are thus in the curious position of being held aloft as the most depraved examples of humanity by a public who are largely unaware of their actual deviations. Such women become symbolically detached from their crimes; crimes from which we all derive a moral certainty. Myra Hindley was irredeemably evil, no further discussion is necessary. But we have to ask ourselves whether this is an appropriate response by the media, the legal, political and justice systems, or by society at large? Is the curious mixture of public apathy and outrage in the interests of anyone, not least the victims and bereaved families? The other factor noted at the start of the chapter which secures criminal notoriety is the prevailing cultural climate in which an incident occurs. In the case of women who kill and sexually abuse, it is unlikely that there will ever be a climate of opinion which views these crimes as mundane or humdrum, even in the cynical and crime-saturated times in which we live.

Summary

- This chapter has located psychological and sociological concerns with identity and difference within criminological discourses of responses to crime in an attempt to understand the origins of, and reasons for, the fear and loathing that is directed (arguably disproportionately) at a particular group of deviant 'others' – women who kill and rape.
- The cultural inclination to view women's deviance as a manifestation of their 'otherness' is compounded by its newsworthiness, which is unquestionable, and the proposition that there may never be a prevailing ideological climate that tolerates women who deviate from cultural expectations of 'appropriate' feminine behaviour.
- It has been argued that, in common with wider media and cultural constructions, women who kill are subject to intense scrutiny – both in legal and media institutions – regarding their sexual proclivities and history, and are frequently judged on their body size, shape and sexual attractiveness. Paradoxically, conventional constructions of both beauty and ugliness can be used as evidence of a woman's inherent badness, and the media borrow from a range of classical literature and mythology to evoke images of monstrous women. Women who kill (especially those who kill children and young women) are the diabolical antithesis to the myth of the good mother, and much media discourse is constructed around **'*essentialist*'** notions of women; in other words, they presuppose that the 'essence' of women is different from that of men, and that women are biologically predisposed to be caring and nurturing. Women's crimes against children are especially inexplicable and 'unreal'.

Unless an offence can be accounted for in terms of a 'sickness' that is compatible with the essential 'nature' of womanhood, it will be regarded as 'unnatural' and evil (Worrall, 1990). A degree of biological essentialism is also evident in the common theme that women who commit serious crimes – especially when they do so in partnership with a man – are the prime movers in these relationships and are, in essence, evil manipulators.

- If a woman's serious offending cannot be explained as 'madness' but appears to be a lucid and rational act, it becomes symbolically disturbing. Women who claim that they acted in an autonomous and calculated manner (as Myra Hindley did) are so transgressive of societal notions of 'proper' (that is, non-agentic) womanhood that the details of their offences are glossed over in legal and media discourses and explanations for their crimes are curiously absent from feminist readings.

- The discussion has demonstrated that psychosocial and feminist perspectives are far from incompatible, drawing on psychoanalytically informed ways of understanding gendered identities. In the cases discussed in this chapter, psychoanalytic concepts have been used in conjunction with sociologically-informed ideas from media studies and cultural studies in order to explore exactly why it is that some individuals generate a level of hysteria and vilification that is arguably disproportionate to their actual offences. In addition, it has been argued that the media have consistently represented the abuse perpetuated on women and children as extraordinary rather than as the worst outcomes of the institutions of marriage and the family which historically have enshrined unequal relations between men, women and children.

STUDY QUESTIONS

Study a range of newspapers and pay close attention to stories involving women offenders.

1   What evidence can you find for the proposition that women are constructed according to their perceived 'otherness'? What kinds of motifs and stereotypes are apparent in your chosen news report?

2   To what extent do Lombrosian ideas about 'born female criminals', whose deviance is indicated by their very physiology, permeate contemporary discourses concerning women and crime?

3   What sorts of women conform to mediated ideas about 'ideal' victims and which women are invisible in media discourses about victimization?

4   The unwillingness of media, legal and academic discourses to recognize the possibility of women's agency has arguably resulted in other 'omissions' in our understanding of female offending. Explanations which centre on women's lust, greed, revenge or sheer entrepreneurism are curiously absent from criminological inquiries (Davies, 2003). What examples of 'invisible crimes' can you think of which illustrate this observation?

FURTHER READING

There is now quite a substantial literature within criminology concerning gender and violence, and much of it draws on media representations to illustrate the circulation of ideas concerning both women's violence and victimization. A useful introduction to feminist perspectives is Gelsthorpe, L. (2002) 'Feminism and criminology' in M. Maguire, R. Morgan and R. Reiner (eds) *The Oxford Handbook of Criminology*, 3rd edition (Oxford University Press). Frances Heidensohn has also written extensively on feminist approaches to sex and violence; see, for example, Heidensohn, F. (2000) *Sexual Politics and Social Control* (Open University Press). Maggie Wykes has written about specific cases in her chapters in Dobash, R., Dobash, R. and Noaks, L. *Gender and Crime* (University of Wales Press) and in Carter et al. (see below). So has Joan Smith in the 1997 publication *Different For Girls* (Chatto and Windus). Helen Birch's (1993) *Moving Targets: Women, Murder and Representation* (Virago) is an edited collection which includes chapters on Myra Hindley, Hollywood representations of female killers, mothers who kill their children and female serial killers. Cynthia Carter et al.'s (1998) *News, Gender and Power* (Routledge) is another edited collection which covers some of the same ground, but from the perspective of gendered institutional working practices in newsrooms. Belinda Morrissey's (2003) *When Women Kill* (Routledge) is a more theoretically advanced book, and she discusses many of the cases featured in this chapter (for example, Homolka, Beck, Wigginton and Wuornos), which she interprets through a psychoanalytic lens. Philip Jenkins (1994) discusses serial killers, including female serial killers, in *Using Murder: The Social Construction of Serial Homicide* (Aldine de Gruyter).

6

Crimewatching

Chapter Contents

OVERVIEW

Chapter 6 provides:

- A discussion of the relationship between the media and public fears about crime and the rationality or irrationality of such fears.
- A comparison between 'critical criminological' and 'left realist' perspectives on fear of crime.
- A consideration of the changing role of the police and of the powerfully symbolic place of the community police officer in the British psyche, exemplified by the fictional television character *Dixon of Dock Green*.
- A discussion of the symbiotic relationship between the police and the media.
- An analysis of the origins and genre conventions of long-running 'reality' BBC series *Crimewatch UK* and its constructions of victims, offenders and the police.

KEY TERMS

critical criminology	legitimacy	representation/misrepresentation
fear of crime	police and policing	victimization
left realism	rationality/irrationality	

In the last two chapters we have seen how the media, in the absence of any alternative discourse to explain the existence of violence and cruelty (particularly in those who are 'supposed' to be pure and blameless) fall back on stock notions of 'pure evil' to describe particular individuals regarded as 'other'. This chapter is less concerned with public hysteria and more interested in the mundane, everyday level at which fear operates. Divided into three sections, the chapter will first discuss the proposition that media representations of crime make certain individuals and groups feel more vulnerable than their likelihood of actual victimization suggests they should be. In the second section, it will briefly discuss dramatized images of policing and the impact that fictional programmes (for example, *The Bill*) have on the police themselves. This part will also consider the ways in which the media and the police have become accustomed to working together, a partnership that serves to legitimate the police's power and authority, but which has been put in jeopardy following the transmission on BBC1 of an undercover documentary disclosing racism among police recruits, which some senior police officers characterized as a betrayal by the corporation. Third, and finally, Chapter 6 will discuss public fears of crime in relation to *Crimewatch UK* which consistently over-reports the most serious but statistically uncommon offences, constructs particular and polarized views of victims and offenders, and portrays the police as calm and efficient crime fighters who are unwavering in their commitment to bring criminals to justice.

The mass media and fear of crime

A number of writers (for example, Chibnall, 1977; Hall et al., 1978; Box, 1983; Schlesinger and Tumber, 1994; Kidd-Hewitt, 1995; Osborne, 1995; Slapper and Tombs, 1999) have examined the proposition that the media present crime stories (both factual and fictional) in ways which selectively distort and manipulate public perceptions, creating a false picture of crime which promotes stereotyping, bias, prejudice and gross oversimplification of the facts. Their conclusion is that it is not just official statistics that misrepresent the picture of crime (cf. Schlesinger and Tumber, 1994; Coleman and Moynihan, 1996; Muncie and McLaughlin, 2001), but that the media are also guilty of manipulation and fuelling public fears. Studies carried out in the UK and US indicate that crime reporting in the press is more prevalent than ever before, and that interpersonal crimes, particularly violent and sexual crimes, are consistently over-reported in relation to official statistics (Roshier, 1973; Graber, 1980; Ditton and Duffy, 1983; Smith, 1984; Schlesinger and Tumber, 1994; Greer, 2003a). Some studies (for example, Roshier, 1973) have also found that newspaper readers overestimate the proportion of crimes solved, and that the police sometimes reinforce journalistically produced concerns about a 'crime wave' by feeding reporters stories based on previously reported incidents (Fishman, 1981). This can sometimes provoke fear of a crime surge at a time when statistically incidents of that crime are on the decrease (cf. Schlesinger and Tumber, 1994). The reasons for the media's preoccupation with certain types of crime may be largely pragmatic and economic (they are, after all, in the business of selling newspapers and gaining audience ratings), but the dual outcomes of their portrayals of crime and violence are heightened public anxieties and a greater public mandate for increasingly punitive punishments.

Within criminology, discussions of public fears about crime tend to be polarized along theoretical lines. Marxist-inspired *critical criminologists* argue that politicians, the media and the criminal justice system set the agenda for public debate about crime and the implementation of criminal justice, and collude in perpetuating notions of 'enemies within'. These agendas then shape public perceptions, not only about their likelihood of being a victim of crime, but also about who they should fear. Steven Box (1983) suggests that the picture of crime that the public receive is manipulated by those in power, and that there is an over-concentration on the crimes of the young, the black, the working class and the unemployed, and an under-awareness of the crimes of the well-educated upper and middle classes, the socially privileged and those in power. He argues that the processes by which the public receive information about crime via the mass media result in perceptions about criminal justice being determined by very narrow legal definitions that tolerate, accept or even applaud the crimes of the privileged, while criminalizing the disadvantaged. Signorielli (1990) goes further, claiming that the way the media constructs crime and violence encourage populations to accept increasingly repressive forms of social control: 'fearful people are more dependent, more easily manipulated ... more susceptible to deceptively simple, strong, tough measures and hard-line postures ... they may accept and even welcome repression if it promises to relieve their insecurities and other anxieties' (1990: 102). In all these expressions, crime is viewed as an ideological construct; it protects the powerful and further marginalizes the powerless.

However, there is an implicit assumption in this proposal that fear of crime is **irrational** and unreasonable – that it is a kind of false consciousness produced by those in authority. **Left realist** criminologists hotly dispute this suggestion, arguing that there is a **rational** core to images of crime and to the public concerns they generate. Young, for example, claims that popular perceptions of crime and justice are largely 'constructed out of the material experiences of people rather than fantasies impressed upon them by the mass media or agencies of the State' (1987: 337). Crawford et al. concur, arguing that 'in inner city areas mass media coverage of crime tends to reinforce what people already know' (1990: 76). Of course, these are valid observations, and left realist criminologists have been right to point out that it is not just the media who are to blame for instilling fear of crime. Actual risk of **victimization**, previous experience of victimization, environmental conditions, ethnicity and confidence in the police and the criminal justice system are among many of the factors interacting through complex processes to influence public anxiety about crime. And as we have already seen in Chapter 1, the notion of passive audiences soaking up media influences in isolation of their lived experience is regarded as reductive and untenable.

Our interpretation of statistics on fear of crime may thus have to go beyond their face value. For example, the finding that the readers of popular newspapers (that is, those that report crime in a sensationalized and salient fashion) have the highest levels of **fear of crime** may simply reflect their actual risk of victimization. Readers of tabloid newspapers are concentrated in the lower socio-economic strata of society, and are more likely to live in areas, and behave in ways, that expose them to greater levels of risk of crime. To take another example, although rape is a relatively rare offence, some feminist critics have argued that within a patriarchal society, women's experience of sexual and physical violence at the hands of men can appear normal and 'ordinary', and they suggest that a common theme throughout women's descriptions of everyday encounters with men is that of powerlessness. Many women experience harassment on an everyday basis and on a level unknown to most men (Jones et al., 1986; Stanko, 1985; Dobash and Dobash, 1992; Young, 1992), which makes them attuned to the possibility of more serious sexual and/or physical assault. Furthermore, much crime against women – notably domestic assault – is hidden in the official figures and rarely makes the news. In all these respects the 2000 British Crime Survey finding that a over one-third of women do not go out alone at night because of their fear of being the victim of an assault is not that surprising and cannot be explained away as an irrational response. This figure rises to 59 per cent for women over the age of 60, but the fear expressed by older people may also be a rational response reflecting their relative weakness and vulnerability (Muncie, 2001). Conversely, the lack of fear voiced by young men may reflect a masculine bravado common to young males (Crawford et al., 1990).

But while a *specific* media effect may be difficult to isolate in a world that is increasingly characterized as 'media-saturated', the examples given above do not preclude the idea that the media play some part in the distribution of fear. Media use, while not reducible to crude 'effects' is centrally implicated in the routines and practices of everyday life and is inextricably interwoven into people's biographies and the stories they tell about themselves (Jewkes, 2002). It is impossible to separate situated experience from mediated experience and so, while women and older people may have genuine grounds for being fearful of male violence, their anxiety is constantly and pervasively reinforced by a media that recognizes and perpetuates the newsworthiness of violent crimes against women and the elderly. Quite simply, media coverage of crime and deviance is rarely grounded in fact. Crime has been exploited as commercial entertainment since the earliest days of cinema and remains the most salient theme in television dramas and 'reality' shows, which enthusiastically mix fact, fiction and titillation. Meanwhile, as we have seen in Chapter 2, news about crime and deviance has a strong social control element – 'watch and beware'. Consequently, media images of crime perpetually reinforce people's anxieties: we are, at one and the same time, fascinated by representations of crime and alarmed by them. It is little wonder, then, that those groups who become most over-sensitized to their risk of victimization are the same people whose victimization is over-reported and over-sensationalized.

Interestingly, children and young people's fears about crime are rarely discussed, although parents' fears for their offspring are part of the currency of everyday media discourse. Television is often regarded as a multi-coloured narcotic which deprives children of more healthy forms of interaction and makes them vulnerable to ideological manipulation, and music has been seen as a bad influence since Elvis Presley made his first record. But rarely is media content discussed in relation to youngsters' anxieties about crime. Bok (1998) suggests that a growing trend in the US for news reporting of child abduction, kidnapping and murder is responsible for creating a climate of fear that may be linked to an increase in child depression and suicide (cited in Keating, 2002). In both the US and the UK, concerns have been expressed about rap and other forms of music which glorify gun and drug cultures and promote homophobic and chauvinistic attitudes. In 2001 there were 21 gangster-style murders and 67 attempted murders in the UK, a figure that rose by 35 per cent in the following year (www.homeoffice.gov.uk/rds). But any link between this trend and wider cultural statements legitimating or glamorizing gang life and gun crime has not yet been adequately researched.

Fear is notoriously difficult to define. Often conceptualized as a tangible quantity which we possess in smaller or greater amounts, fear may be more accurately thought of as a mode of perception consisting of a range of diffuse anxieties about one's position and identity in the world (Sparks, 1992). Furthermore, it is very difficult to generalize about 'fear of crime "effects"'. A high-profile crime might cause people to modify their behaviour for as long as the offence is newsworthy, but this amplification of anxiety may be periodic, short-lived and confined to the environs where the crime took place (McArthur, 2002). On the other hand, the relationship between fear and the media might be best conceptualized in more subtle and pervasive terms as contributing to a cultural climate which normalizes male violence and reinforces notions of female submissiveness (Brownmiller, 1975). Ultimately, the long-term effects of exposure to mediated images of crime are virtually impossible to gauge. But as already noted, while we should be cautious when making statements about the media 'causing' fear (Sparks, 1992), it is also worth bearing in mind that fear of crime is a much more widely experienced phenomenon than victimization. Although victims of crime will probably become more fearful about the likelihood of future victimization as a result of their experiences, many more individuals will experience fear as a result of indirect contact with crime. These vicarious experiences of crime will encompass personal observations, private conversations with victims, second-, third- and fourth-hand accounts passed down through multifarious flows of communication; and, of course, the mass media (Skogan and Maxfield, 1981). Attempts to measure the impact of media reporting on public fears about crime are notoriously problematic, but it can be said with some certainty that the majority of people attribute their knowledge of the risk of crime to information received from television and newspapers (Williams and Dickinson, 1993; Surette, 1998). In a 1995 MORI poll, 66 per cent of people interviewed said they got their information from television, and 33 per cent claimed their fears about crime are increased by news and documentary coverage of crime (Keating, 2002).

According to the British Crime Survey (BCS), 'worry about crime' reached a peak in 1994 despite the fall in recorded crimes, and between 1998 and 2000, concern about crime remained relatively stable, in contrast to a 10 per cent fall in recorded crime in nearly all offence categories (McArthur, 2002). Using data from the 1996 BCS, Hough and Roberts (1998) found that, when asked how much crime involves violence, 78 per cent of those surveyed replied 30 per cent or more – Home Office statistics recorded it at just 6 per cent. Conversely, substantial underestimates were routinely made about the extent to which the courts use custodial sentences for convicted offenders. Relying on statistical measurements to gauge the extent of crime is in itself a problematic endeavour, but the key point is that public perceptions reflect the view propagated by much of the media, that is, of a continually spiralling crime rate and an over-lenient criminal justice system. Neither view is accurate, and Hough and Roberts blame the media for such public misunderstanding:

> Media news values militate against balanced coverage. Erratic court sentences make news and sensible ones do not. As a result large segments of the population are exposed to a steady stream of unrepresentative stories about sentencing incompetence. (1998: x)

While the media frequently focus on relatively uncommon issues and report them in a sensationalized, overblown manner with demands for harsher and more uncompromising punishments, local responses to anxieties about crime are often much more immediate and micro in orientation. Two examples serve to illustrate the point. In the immediate days following the murder of Damilola Taylor, the demand of local people in the area of Peckham where he lived was on community policing – an appeal for more visible patrol officers to allay people's fears. A similar response was forthcoming following the murder of Sarah Payne. Although the *News of the World*'s 'Name and Shame' campaign reported that the majority of people (76 per cent of those questioned) wanted to know if there was a convicted paedophile living in their neighbourhood, a closer look at the MORI poll on which the newspaper's campaign was based reveals a rather different picture:

> Asked what could be done to improve the safety of children in their local area, 24 per cent said more policing, 23 per cent suggested speed restrictions and 16 per cent more safe areas for children to play in. Only three per cent offered the public naming of paedophiles as a solution, the same proportion who felt more parking wardens were part of the answer. (Garside, 2001: 32–3)

The issue of community policing remains at the heart of debates about fear of crime and the public appetite for more 'bobbies on the beat' is unflagging, despite a general decline in respect and faith in the police (Newburn, 2003). Although criminological studies have repeatedly shown that providing more police officers on the streets is unlikely to reduce offending, the perception that community police officers patrolling the streets are a highly visible deterrent persists in the public imagination. It has become a key issue over which politicians fight to prove their 'tough on crime' credentials and is one of those powerfully emotive 'common sense' subjects over which it is almost impossible to publicly debate (as witnessed by Shadow Home Secretary, Oliver Letwin's, scathing attacks on academic criminologists who questioned the Conservative party's pledge to provide 40,000 new beat officers made during their party conference in 2003). The lazy and misinformed link that is popularly made between police officers on foot patrol and reductions in crime reflects the journalistic priorities that shape news reporting and the more general limitations of 'fear of crime' debates. As Downes remarks:

> That the 'fear of crime' ... remains most developed in relation to certain forms of street crime is probably more to do with collective representations of unpredictable violence than that which more frequently occurs in the home, or that which is normalized as accidental, or where victimization is indirect and dispersed, as with corporate crime. (Downes, 1988: 182)

Public demands for bobbies on the beat may be linked to unconscious fears of 'others', including immigrants, political refugees, people from ethnic minority backgrounds, travellers, pedlars and adolescents. It may be a more widespread manifestation of the 'fortress mentality' visible in many modern cities where some areas have been turned into fenced, guarded, middle-class ghettos (Minsky, 1998; cf. Chapter 7 of this volume). This would certainly help to explain why fear of crime is disproportionately felt in the relatively comfortable, low-crime areas of 'middle England' (Girling et al., 2000, 2002; Taylor, 2002). Public support for beat officers might also be taken as evidence of the critical criminological proposition that citizens are likely to support more visible and repressive forms of social control if they soothe their anxieties and insecurities about crime (Signorielli, 1990). Public demands for visible police patrols may further reflect a lack of faith in the bureaucratization of the police service. In 1990 a report was published that looked at the weakening in public confidence in the police and at Home Office plans to impose new efficiency targets. The Operational Policing Review was commissioned by the police and it was essentially designed to consider the fundamental tension that was – and still remains – at the heart of the relationship between the police and the public whom they serve, namely that the police are chasing the elusive goals of economy and efficiency, while the public are demanding more community policing, which is costly and inefficient.

The role of the police

One aspect of the Operational Policing Review was that both individual police officers and members of the public were asked to choose between two mediated ideals: a *Dixon of Dock Green* character called PC Jones, who spent most of his time working with local people in communities to prevent and solve crime, and a *Sweeney*-style PC Smith, who believed in the strong arm of the law and spent his time chasing round in fast cars arresting major criminals. It hardly needs revealing that the public favoured PC Jones, while the officers preferred to see themselves in the mould of PC Smith. But the fact that the researchers used two readily-identifiable television characters to assess attitudes towards the police is interesting, if not surprising. The police are by far the most widely covered profession on television in both factual and fictional representations, and many senior police officers are aware that fictionalized media representations of the police go beyond mere entertainment. In an age when the police have been accused of institutional racism, incompetent murder investigations and recurring corruption, dramatic portrayals of police work, and of the nature of crime and criminal justice, perform an important symbolic function and help to perpetuate a 'mythology of policing' (Manning, 1997).

For this reason, it is worth just briefly considering the role of *Dixon of Dock Green*. In recent years a surfeit of studies about media representations of the police have emerged and, for that reason, a detailed chronological analysis of media images of policing is not included here (although see suggestions for further reading at the end of this chapter). Instead, the focus will remain on the responses of public and police to mediated representations of **police** generally and the extent to which media portrayals inform perceptions of the police and produce a sense of public legitimacy for the institution of **policing**. But *Dixon* is worth mentioning on two accounts. The first is that he played a key role in shaping cultural perceptions of policing in the mid- to late 20th century and remains a looming presence in the British psyche. He first appeared in *The Blue Lamp* in 1950, an Ealing film that spawned the 20-year-long series *Dixon of Dock Green* (1955–76) on BBC1. Since that time the police have been a source of endless fascination for television producers and public alike and the ghost of Dixon continues to overshadow debates about public attitudes towards the police. In fact, despite not being a regular presence on our screens for 30 years, he is still constantly evoked by politicians, the media and the police themselves (as witnessed by the recent remarks of the Metropolitan Police Commissioner recommending a return to '*Dixon of Dock Green*-style bobbies on the beat' reported in the *Guardian*, 28 February 2003). Yet, public trust and confidence in the police is, and arguably always has been, very fragile and there has *never* been a time when the police have been universally loved and respected, nor a time when the police have conformed to the gentle, benevolent, 'firm but fair' characterization that George Dixon embodied (according to a former Chief Constable, the force in Dixon's era was 'brutal, authoritarian and corrupt'; Hellawell, 2002: 40). Indeed *The Blue Lamp*, and the television series it inspired, were extended tributes to the Metropolitan force, made with their co-operation, at a time when the police were feared to be losing public confidence and respect (Reiner, 2000).

This brings us to the other reason for dwelling momentarily on Dixon. *The Blue Lamp* tells us much about post-War attitudes to crime, criminals and the police, and illustrates many of the themes already discussed in this book. The remnants of mass society theory, anxieties about brash and immoral 'teenagers', fears about certain types of crime, namely juvenile crime and offences committed by armed gangs, and a desire to seek moral certainty in figures of authority, are all to be found in this black-and-white cinematic classic. Released at a time of heightened public anxieties over juvenile delinquency following the disruption of war, the loss of fathers, a relaxing of moral standards and so on, the film is a conventional morality tale of good versus evil. PC Dixon is portrayed as a kindly, avuncular figure who takes his role of keeping the public safe from harm very seriously. However, he lasts only 20 minutes into the film, dying after being shot during an armed robbery at a cinema by a baby-faced petty criminal played by Dirk Bogarde. The shock waves created by the depiction of the violent death of a policeman at the hands of an adolescent tearaway are hard to comprehend half a century on, but the shooting of Dixon had a wider resonance as a representation of the death of order. In other words, this plot device was entirely consistent with moral panics about youth and change in the rapidly moving society of the late 1950s (see Chapter 3). Young delinquents were regarded as a new breed of criminal who, according to a voice-over narration, lacked 'the code, experience and self-discipline of the professional thief'. They were from 'broken homes', 'a class apart' and 'all the more dangerous for their immaturity' – so unstable that they were even rejected by the established criminal underworld. Even the fact that the murder of PC Dixon takes place in a cinema is significant. In the film, cinema is contrasted with a nostalgic reference to music hall, a more traditional form of popular culture. We see a young couple on a date, quarrelling as they leave – hence the impression is reinforced that it is an appropriate place for the young delinquent with all his connotations of sex and violence (Geraghty, undated). Following the shooting, the film becomes a conventional thriller as the police pursue the feckless young villain. The audience witness Bogarde's character descending into a morass of fear and paranoia until finally he takes refuge in a greyhound stadium. The tacit understanding between the police and the criminal underworld (the decent, respectable, 'gentleman' crooks) works to track him down and together they corner him. The crowd (signifying 'the community'), who have gathered at the stadium, then close in on him and sweep him up into arms of the police, symbolically communicating society's intolerance of young offenders and their commitment to delivering criminals up to the law.

The television series *Dixon of Dock Green* continued the cosy, paternalistic and highly idealized view of the police that was established in *The Blue Lamp*, but by the time it was decommissioned in 1976 the age of innocence portrayed by Dixon was looking even more incongruous and irrelevant than it had 20 years earlier. In the previous 10 years policing had become increasingly politicized, crime rates were rising and public concerns were escalating in the wake of a number of high-profile crimes involving notorious villains, widely publicized escapes from prisons, and the abolition of the death penalty. Within this context police series became more realistic and hard-hitting and there began a procession of police officers who were portrayed not as gentlemen or heroes, but as ordinary people doing a difficult job. From *Z Cars* (BBC, 1962–78) through *The Sweeney* (ITV, 1974–78) to *The Bill* (ITV, 1984–), the police have been depicted on British television with all the human flaws and vices that any other section of the population would have. At the same time, shows ranging from *Juliet Bravo* (1980–85) and *Heartbeat* (1979–) to *Prime Suspect* (1991–) and *Between the Lines* (1992–94) and have offered diverse and sometimes contradictory images of policing. Officers have variously been portrayed as caring, controlling, corrupting and corrupted (Reiner, 2000; Leishman and Mason, 2003). In contemporary police dramas more divergent and previously neglected 'types' of officers have been introduced, including high-ranking female and ethnic minority officers and openly gay officers (ironically, such 'minority' groups are probably more represented in police dramas than in real life policing). The discourse of equal opportunities can thus be seen to operate in both fictional representations and real policing, even if much progress is still to be made in both domains (Stick, 2003).

Simultaneously throughout the last three decades the police have become increasingly visible in the factual news media, and dramatic portrayals of the police have to some extent reflected 'real life' events (many of which have been 'negative' in essence). Significant milestones in the recent, mediated history of the police include stories of police corruption (most notoriously within the West Midlands Serious Crime Squad in the 1970s, which resulted in the wrongful conviction of the 'Birmingham Six'); the inner city riots of the early 1980s, which led to a transformation in public order policing from inexperienced officers trying to protect themselves with dustbin lids to trained and 'tooled up' professionals – dubbed 'Robocops' by the media; the bungled investigation of the Yorkshire Ripper case, during which the police were led up a blind alley by a hoaxer with a north-east accent; the murder of WPC Yvonne Fletcher at the Libyan Embassy in London in 1984; the Miners' Strike of 1984 in which the police were involved in bloody clashes and mocked as 'Maggie's boys' by miners protesting at the closure of their pits by a government led by Margaret Thatcher; the inquiry into the death of black teenager, Stephen Lawrence in 1999, in which the Met were found to be 'institutionally racist'; and a BBC1 documentary shown in 2003 in which a journalist went undercover as a trainee police officer and secretly filmed racist behaviour and language among his colleagues so shocking that it led to several of the officers featured losing their jobs (see below).

There has been very little research on the extent to which media representations inform public opinions about the police, and even less about the impact that media have on the police. For example, Leishman and Mason (2003: 21) note that a 'question rarely asked ... concerns the "effects" that media images may have on the police themselves', but they do not develop this point or draw any conclusions themselves. In a small-scale study involving interviews with 12 serving police officers, Nicola Stick found that positive and negative media images of the police were influential in their decisions to join the police service. The younger, male officers talked of their 'positive' expectations of the police based on their mediated perceptions of excitement, glamour and car chases, while the older males remembered (with a rose-tinted hue) joining a *Dixon of Dock Green* style force in which their colleagues were men of pride and principle. Perhaps most surprisingly, the two female officers interviewed cited negative media portrayals as reasons for joining the police. Following damaging portrayals in documentaries which showed police officers in a poor light (for example, as racist), they decided that the service needed people, like them, 'joining with the right attitude' (Stick, 2003: 31).

This research is undeniably limited in scope – largely because the researcher (a postgraduate student) faced difficulties in access when she told her target police force the subject matter on which she wished to interview respondents; an indication of the sensitivity felt by the police regarding media representations of their work, even three months prior to the transmission of the infamous BBC documentary uncovering racism among recruits. It cannot, therefore, be said to be conclusive in its findings. However, the study does raise important questions about the symbiotic relationship between police and media. The younger officers interviewed cited fictional portrayals of the police which they enjoyed (in line with previous studies, Stick found that *The Bill* is still viewed as one of the most accurate reflections of police work), yet were dismissive of factual representations and were suspicious of the motives of journalists. Young male officers hinted at a combative relationship between themselves and the media, viewing their own role as that of 'gatekeepers', preventing the media from getting 'what they want'. They also saw themselves as 'easy targets' for a critical and scandal hunting media in contrast to 'the criminals who don't have to play by the same rules' (Stick, 2003: 33; cf. Graef, 1989; Reiner, 2000). Senior officers were more positive in their views, regarding the relationship as one of interdependency, mutual benefits and 'trust' rather than 'power'. They were more inclined to talk of the media as an effective tool to be used by the police; a position which probably reflects their more advanced training, contact with, and exposure to the media (Stick, 2003: 33).

Of course, the police are now supported by a raft of employees including press officers, marketing professionals, public relations officers and corporate identity specialists, all engaged in the business of 'image work' on behalf of the police (Mawby, 2002). According to Mawby, there is a danger that such image work could be deployed for improper motives, such as misrepresentation to mask mal-practice or to deflect responsibility. Embedded within police image work is the language of 'openness' and police forces are increasingly espousing 'open' com-munications and transparency. The rhetoric therefore suggests that the police are very happy to allow the media and the wider public to be informed about policing policy and practice (Mawby, 2002). However, Mawby is cynical, and his concern that the police may be giving an impression of democratic accountable policing, while simultaneously sustaining the restricted interests of the police service, has taken on a new significance in recent times. The police may publicly congratulate themselves on their openness and accountability, but this does not mean that they are impermeable to outside attempts to highlight their ongoing, internal, structural deficiencies. The aforementioned documentary, *The Secret Policeman*, shown on BBC1 (21 October 2003) has proved to be a public relations disaster for the police service. The programme showed the results of secret filming by an undercover journalist posing as a trainee police officer over a period of seven months at a national police training centre in Bruche, Cheshire. In an eerie echo of a simulated racist attack by the young men sus-pected of murdering Stephen Lawrence (also filmed covertly), rookie police offi-cers were shown voicing extreme racist opinions, and one was seen wearing a makeshift Ku Klux Klan hood. The police's PR nightmare began a month before transmission when a senior civil servant in the Home Office wrote to the BBC chairman accusing the corporation of deceit and demanding that they withdraw the programme from the schedules (*Observer*, 26 October 2003). Subsequently, in the days before the broadcast, the Chief Constable of Greater Manchester Police (GMP), one of the forces concerned, and the Home Office, issued defiant statements, criticizing the BBC for its methods and for going ahead with the broadcast. The day after the broadcast, however, senior officers and the Home Secretary were competing for media airtime in which to condemn the officers filmed, perhaps having had time to ingest the horror and revulsion felt by many viewers at the scenes they had witnessed.

Like all covertly filmed 'documentaries', important questions arise concerning the ethics of secret filming, the opportunities for journalists to ask leading ques-tions with the intention of 'entrapment', the processes by which hundreds of hours of film are edited down to an hour's material for broadcast, and so forth. *The Secret Policeman* shocked many, including senior officers in the Metropolitan Police, who believe they are making progress in rooting out racism from within their ranks, following the 1999 Macpherson report which highlighted institu-tional racism within the Met. But this programme demonstrated that nationally there is still a long way to go, especially in the areas of recruitment and training. Among the most surprising aspects of the exposé was that racial awareness training for new recruits appeared to consist of them being told there are four words they must not use: 'nigger', 'wog', 'paki' and 'coon'. To this extent, while superficially the programme might be interpreted as reinforcing the notion of a 'few bad apples', it actually hinted at more widespread, structural problems at the heart of the police. This impression was not helped by Mike Todd, Chief Constable of GMP, who was in America at the time of the broadcast, but who was reported as having threatened the BBC with a 'Hutton-style inquiry' if the programme went ahead. Almost a decade ago Richard Osborne wrote: 'The fear of crime is greater than the fear of an inadequate police force and as long as the police can win the media war through programmes like *Crimewatch UK* their control of the news flow is guaranteed' (1995: 39). Ironic, then, that Chief Constable Todd's most petulant shot across the bows was the threat that the police would withdraw their co-operation from the BBC's *Crimewatch UK* (*Observer*, 26 October 2003).

Crimewatch UK

The threat of the police retracting their support for *Crimewatch UK* was deemed significantly shocking to make headline news in the week following the transmission of *The Secret Policeman*, attesting to the place of *Crimewatch* in the television establishment and in the cultural identity of Britain. Frequently singled out as being a significant contributor to false ideas about crime among this country's population, *Crimewatch UK* is a long-running BBC programme that uses both dramatic reconstructions and surveillance footage of crimes to try to gain information from the public. This final section of this chapter will provide an in-depth analysis of the programme and will explore the myths that it perpetuates about crime. The discussion will pay particular attention to the programme's constructions of offenders, victims and the police.

Crimewatch UK was one of the forerunners of the television genre now known as 'reality television' and like all 'reality' programming it transgresses the conventional borderline between fact and fiction (Schlesinger and Tumber, 1994). Although different to contemporary reality programmes such as *Big Brother* in so far as much of it is shot conventionally in a television studio, it was one of the first television programmes in the UK to include dramatic reconstructions of crimes, use footage from CCTV and amateur camcorders, and also among the first to rely on audience participation. The series, which is broadcast monthly for 10 months of the year, began on BBC1 in 1984, a time of increasing political focus on issues of law and order, and mounting public concern that victims of crime were getting a raw deal (1994). Its main presenter from the beginning has been Nick Ross, although *Crimewatch* itself became the subject of media attention when, in 1999, Ross's co-presenter, Jill Dando, was the victim of a violent murder.

Crimewatch UK was inspired by sources from Britain, America and Germany. Schlesinger and Tumber offer an account of the show's origins, describing how British producers borrowed the idea and revised it slightly for a British audience. They took a concept that had already existed in this country in the form of *Police Five* (an ITV show that ran from 1962 until 1990) and extended it, adding the 'magic ingredient' of audience participation (Schlesinger and Tumber, 1994: 253). They looked to the phenomenally successful *America's Most Wanted* but rejected the overt dramatization favoured in this show, where reconstructions of crimes were filmed in slow motion and accompanied by dramatic music in order to heighten viewers' sense of suspense and excitement. They also studied the German programme *Aktenzeichen XY ... Ungelost* (*Case XY ... Unsolved*), which was closest to the format of *Crimewatch UK* and which had already been running for 17 years, but decided against the German method of filming reconstructions from the perspective of the offender, especially in relation to sexual offences such as rape (1994: 253). So successful has *Crimewatch UK* been that it has seen off a number of competitors on the rival commercial channels and spawned its own spin-offs, including *Crimewatch Unlimited*, *Crimewatch File* and *Crimewatch Solved*.

The formula of *Crimewatch UK* has remained virtually unaltered since it first aired 20 years ago. There are three or four reconstructions, usually of very serious crimes such as murder, armed robbery or rape; a segment which reveals CCTV footage of offenders with an appeal to anyone who can identify them to come forward; photographs of suspects whose names are known, but whose whereabouts are not; and updates on cases previously featured – a device that has the three-fold purposes of congratulating the audience for helping to secure convictions, making them feel absolutely integral to the show, and further giving the (inaccurate) impression that *Crimewatch* is largely responsible for solving serious crimes in the UK. In addition, recent months have seen the return of a feature previously abandoned concerning stolen property. In a blatant appeal to the legions of viewers who watch *The Antiques Roadshow*, *Bargain Hunt* and their imitators, an expert in antiquities shows off high-value art, jewellery and antiques that have been recovered by the police. Although the programme has dropped the rather tabloid-inspired titles previously used to differentiate the various items in each show ('Your Call Counts' and 'Aladdin's Cave' were once the titles used to signal updates and the item on stolen property respectively), there have been only two significant changes in content since the first broadcast two decades ago. First, the show has come to rely increasingly on CCTV footage, which is more common and of better quality than was the case in the 1980s. Accordingly, stills and moving images from CCTV cameras form a much greater part of each programme, sometimes being used to supplement dramatic reconstructions of a crime, as well as being used as free-standing items in other sections of the show. The second major new innovation is in DNA testing, which has enabled the police to reopen old files and work with the producers of *Crimewatch UK* in reconstructing cases that might otherwise have been consigned to history. Reconstructions of crimes from the 1960s and 1970s have added an interesting new element to the programme, requiring *Crimewatch* researchers to reflect the period in which the offence occurred with authentic cars, fashions and hairstyles. Like other popular television shows (*Last of the Summer Wine, Open All Hours, Heartbeat* and so on), this aspect of *Crimewatch* may appeal to audiences through discourses of memory, nostalgia and loss (Jewkes, 2002; Jermyn, 2003). Otherwise, the only variations in the programme's content have reflected commensurate changes in patterns of offending, with decreasing numbers of armed robberies on banks and building societies featured and an increase in appeals for information about terrorists and paedophiles.

Dramatized reconstructions are the trademark of *Crimewatch UK* and are the elements that have drawn most vehement criticism of the programme. The writing and filming of crime reconstructions are governed by the BBC Producers' Guidelines, which are as follows:

- Do not use reconstructions simply to attract or entertain audiences, but to convey factual information.
- Do not reconstruct detail which there is no reason to believe actually occurred.
- Filming techniques must not frighten or disturb audiences.
- Do not reveal details which could lead to copycat crimes.
- All reconstructions must be clearly signalled.
- Reconstructions must minimize the distress caused to victims of crime or their relatives.
- Do not glamorize crime or criminals.
  (Pengelly, 1999)

As we shall see through the remainder of this chapter, these guidelines are interpreted somewhat loosely by the producers of *Crimewatch UK*.

The tension between information and entertainment that lies at the heart of *Crimewatch*'s audience appeal is a source of anguish for the programme's producers – or so they claim. Angela Holdsworth, former editor of the show, says that crime is kept in context:

> We don't only focus on violent crime, but we are trying to help the police catch the more serious criminals, and a lot of serious crime involves violence. We agonise over everything we put in. We don't choose items for their entertainment value. But clearly we couldn't do something where

> television wouldn't help, where there's nothing to film. A journalistic sense must come into it. (*Guardian*, 3 September 1990)

But it is precisely this 'journalistic sense' that concerns many. Schlesinger and Tumber reflect on the fine line between documentary and drama that the programme makers have to tread, and the remarks of the show's original producer, Peter Chafer, that the emphasis is firmly on the former rather than the latter are arguably not as true in 2004 as they were in 1984 (Schlesinger and Tumber, 1994). For example, in the October 2003 broadcast (see Table 6.1 below), a reconstruction of what is described in the voice-over as an 'unprovoked ambush on a woman which could easily have killed her' starts with the sound of high-pitched screams heard over an image of a ferris wheel lit up against a dark night sky. The shrill shrieks are then revealed to emanate from a group of women enjoying a hen party at a house in Blackpool, but a grisly impression has already been conveyed and the audience's appetite for vicarious violence has been whetted. In such 'scene-setting' frames, that build-up to the commission of the offence, there is inevitably scope for dramatic interpretation. As Sparks (1992: 156) notes, it is no coincidence that these 'crime scarers' employ the 'same syntax of depiction, narration and editing as crime fictions do', and excitement, suspense and fear are the intended objectives of these techniques (cf. Kidd-Hewitt, 1995). In fact, it could be argued that the success of *Crimewatch UK* is dependent on its very capacity to frighten its audience. Just as adolescents measure the success of a film by how much it scared them, a response which is clearly associated with pleasure in many children's accounts (Buckingham, 2000), so an adult audience gets a visceral thrill from being able to watch a serious crime unfolding with their own eyes.

Although intentionally dramatic, the crime reconstructions are defended by the programme makers and the BBC on public service grounds. Schlesinger and Tumber (1994) observe that, by featuring human-interest-based tales of misfortune, *Crimewatch UK* has much in common with the popular press, and indeed nearly all the crimes selected will conform to the news values outlined in Chapter 2 of this volume. Like the popular media more generally, then, *Crimewatch* prioritizes crimes of violence and may amplify public fears that crime is spontaneous, random and indiscriminate. One of the unfortunate consequences of a television programme that relies on audience ratings, not only for its commercial success, but also to justify its self-proclaimed role in the business of crime detection, is that the producers actively seek out stories that will capture the public imagination and prick the consciences of any potential informants sufficiently to encourage them to pass on information. According to the Executive Producer in charge of BBC crime programmes (cited in Weaver, 1998), this justifies their steadfast adherence to a tried-and-tested formula that concentrates on the most violent and serious crimes, such as murder and rape, perpetrated on the most vulnerable victims; young women, girls and elderly women.

The preoccupation with danger, risk, fear, reassurance and retribution which underpins the reconstructed cases on *Crimewatch UK*, and the pleasure with which those emotions are experienced by the audience, inevitably raises ethical questions regarding victims' rights and the feelings of bereaved families. Actors' dialogue is frequently used to convey a sense of reality and encourage the viewing public to empathize with the victim, but it might be construed as titillating and taking unnecessary liberties with the truth. The BBC is a public service broadcasting company, but it still operates in a commercial environment and must produce attention-grabbing television in order to attract audiences. Barry Irving, then Director of the Police Foundation, alluded to this tension when he remarked:

> A show like *Crimewatch* is too attractive to programme makers to be eval-
> uated properly. It has everything. It panders to the British taste for a mod-
> icum of violence and nefarious activity, it's cheap to make, it promotes a
> whizz-bang action view of the police and encourages viewer participation.
> And over it all is a halo, because it is so evidently A Good Thing.
> (*Guardian*, 3 September 1990)

A further frisson of excitement is produced by the immediacy of television. In recent years, the timescale between a crime being committed and its appearance on *Crimewatch UK* has been greatly reduced, so that stories about major crimes now more frequently appear on BBC news bulletins in the same month or even week. In fact, despite the amount of work involved in producing a live pro-gramme, *Crimewatch* aims to be reactive and sometimes includes very late entries. One such broadcast was in January 1998, when two cases submitted on the day of transmission were presented as studio items. This flexibility allows *Crimewatch UK* to capitalize on existing media attention and audience familiarity with a story as part of its audience-building strategy. A successful example was a reconstruction of the kidnapping of estate agent Stephanie Slater, in 1992, after she had been released unharmed. Already the subject of intense media interest, the programme's own profile was lifted when a call by Michael Sams' ex-wife, who recognized his voice from a taped ransom demand broadcast on *Crimewatch UK*, led to the kidnapper's arrest (Schlesinger and Tumber, 1994).

The programme can thus titillate its audience with trailers prior to the monthly broadcast promising to reveal aspects of a case not previously disclosed (Schlesinger and Tumber, 1994). The suspicion that this strategy may be pri-marily designed to pander to public voyeurism and increase audience ratings is never far from the surface, particularly – as in the case of 'previously unseen' footage of murdered skydiver, Stephen Hilder, jumping out of a plane moments before plunging to his death – the new material does not actually offer new clues or move the investigation forward (*Crimewatch UK*, July 2003). A further consideration is that *Crimewatch UK* has been running for so long that it has become a flagship for the BBC, an integral part of the broadcasting establishment, snuggling alongside *The Antiques Roadshow* and *Eastenders* in terms of longevity and audience familiarity. The possibility that it could start to be seen as 'cosy' and 'safe' may have encouraged its producers to 'up the ante' with increasing use of ploys designed to encourage viewers' inquisitiveness and maximize their loyalty. One such innovation is the use of home video footage, although rarely do the programme makers obtain film of the crime moments before its dramatic denouement, as in the case of the skydiver mentioned previously. More commonly used are video clips showing the victim in 'happier times' with family or friends. Like all photographic images, video footage speaks of a moment frozen in time, but may be all the more compelling because – to borrow a phrase from Paul Willis (1982: 78) it gives us 'real, solid, warm, *moving*, and *acting* bodies in actual situations'. Moving images of murder victims in the prime of life, smiling, laughing, fooling around for the camera, are a particularly poignant reminder of the fragility of life. But they also allow the audience to 'know' the victim, to see them within their family and social contexts, and to vicariously share in their celebrations, while all the time participating in their vulnerability and mortality (Jermyn, 2003).

A content analysis of three editions of *Crimewatch UK* selected at random reveals that each features six main cases, either crime reconstructions or extended reports with photographs, CCTV footage or other graphic imagery. Cases from each of these shows will be referred to throughout the remainder of the discussion. In brief the details are as shown in Table 6.1.

Crimewatching victims

As we have already seen, the indisputable fact that *Crimewatch UK* has a mission to entertain sits uneasily with its public service remit. A content analysis of any edition of the monthly show reveals that the crimes which are statistically most uncommon (murder, rape, crimes against the person) are most frequently featured on the programme, while the crimes to which the public are most likely to be victims (crimes against property at one end of the scale; crimes committed by powerful organizations at the other) rarely, if ever, feature.

Furthermore, crimes of a violent and/or sexual nature, usually resulting in death, against girls, young women and elderly people are the mainstay of the show. Victims who fall within these groups tend to be constructed as tragic innocents whose disappearance and/or death have destroyed not only an individual life, but those of an entire family. A common device used to convey the wider impact of fatal crimes is the 'triangulation' of presenter, victim and victim's close relative (Jermyn, 2003: 185). In an openly emotional interview a bereaved

Table 6.1   *Three editions of* Crimewatch UK

February 1998

1   Reconstruction: Aggravated robbery at home. Victim white woman, suspect male of 'North African appearance'.
2   Report on fatal hit-and-run. Victim young white woman.
3   Reconstruction: Sexually motivated murder of white 15-year-old girl in Essex. No leads.
4   Report with CCTV footage. Sexual assault on 16-year-old boy on train. Appeal for information on black man with 'Jamaican accent' but no indication of whether he's wanted as a witness or perpetrator.
5   Reconstruction: Armed robbery on jewellers. E-fit of black man.
6   Report on sexual assaults on women in Highgate, North London. CCTV footage of suspect – black man.

March 2003

1   Reconstruction: Sexually motivated murder of 17-year-old girl by stranger. Suspect Asian man.
2   Report: Robbery on elderly white woman in home by two strangers. Suspects white men, filmed on a camcorder by a suspicious neighbour.
3   Reconstruction: Aggravated robbery on family in their home in the West Midlands. Young children held at gunpoint. Suspects: 'goofy white man', 'stocky black man' and 'Asian woman'.
4   Report on 'entrenched joyriding culture' in Northern Ireland. Film of relatives of hit-and-run victims and appeal for suspect (white male, named) to give himself up.
5   Reconstruction: Return to case which occurred in May 1964. Sexually motivated murder of 13-year-old girl. No leads on suspect except that he suffered from gonorrhea and owned a car (the latter being not as commonplace 40 years ago as today). DNA available. Appeal for men who lived in area of South Yorkshire where the crime occurred to come forward and give a DNA sample so they can be eliminated from inquiry; appeal to women who can put all the facts together and come forward with a name.
6   Reconstruction: Armed robbery on jewellers. Suspects three black men.

October 2003

1   Reconstruction: White, female warehouse manager abducted from her home and taken to workplace where she was tied up while a gang of at least six robbed the warehouse of computers. Three individuals involved in kidnap, two described as black, one white.
2   Reconstruction: Assault on a woman in a Blackpool street by stranger. She was talking to her police officer boyfriend on her mobile phone at the time of the attack. E-fit of suspect, male, ethnicity unclear.
3   Reconstruction: Murder of white man after an argument in McDonalds in North London. Suspect caught on CCTV, described as with a 'Mediterranean or dark skinned appearance'.
4   Reconstruction of rape of 12-year-old black girl by stranger. Suspect black male. 3D computer graphics used for the first time to illustrate the scene of the crime.
5   Reconstruction: Return to case which occurred in September 2003. Murder of 10-year-old boy. Case featured on 30th anniversary of murder, with an aim to 'bring those responsible to justice and provide closure for the family'. No DNA evidence mentioned.
6   Report on theft of giant pumpkin grown by 82-year-old man for Children In Need.

partner or parent will be interviewed in the studio with a large photograph of the victim positioned in the background, between them. As the interview progresses the camera cuts back several times to a close up on the image of the victim, while the presenter describes them as primarily a good wife and mother, or loving son and father, in such a way as to suggest that there is 'little space for any other angle or way of understanding' who the victim was (2003: 185). In the February 1998 edition this technique was used to sentimentalize and sanctify a victim of a hit-and-run. Presenter Jill Dando described her as a 'very kind and caring' mother who looked after disabled people in addition to her three young children. Her photo showed an attractive, smiling, blonde-haired young woman, and as the camera panned out from the image to her grieving widower, Dando asked him 'what kind of woman *was* Tina?', a question that had self-evidently been answered already. In addition, the programme uses home video footage and photographs from family albums to emphasize the victim's familial ties, and voice-overs and personal testimonies by loved ones reinforce the notion that this is a crime that has destroyed not just one life, but many. Victims are seen at weddings, birthday parties, on holidays and at graduation ceremonies – all quintessentially 'family' occasions (Jermyn, 2003). By allowing us into aspects of a life usually kept private, *Crimewatch* invites us not only to relate to the victim and their family, but also to imagine ourselves in their tragic circumstances. The privileging of family also underlines the conservative ideological framework that is at the heart of assumptions about a case's 'newsworthiness' and reinforces cultural stereotypes about 'deserving' and 'undeserving' victims (see Chapter 2). As Jermyn states: 'It is difficult to imagine a *Crimewatch* victim outside of the parameters of the family: to not be in a family would be to not be a proper victim' (2003: 185).

However, even 'deserving' victims who are portrayed within a loving family context are also open to censure, which implies that they were partly to blame for their victimization. In cases of sexually motivated murders of young women – one of the most commonly featured crimes on the programme despite its relative infrequency in real life – there is often implicit criticism of the victim's behaviour in both the reconstruction and narration by the studio presenter. Furthermore, despite strenuous claims to the contrary by those responsible for making the programme, the reconstructed crimes are frequently presented in a graphic and sensationalized manner, and female victims are sexualized unnecessarily. For example, Weaver (1998) describes in detail one *Crimewatch* reconstruction of the sexual assault and murder of a 17-year-old female hitchhiker in which the victim, played by an actor, is shown lying on a sunbed at a friend's house in her underwear. Its invitation to voyeurism is reinforced by the fact that the frame is shot from above with the viewer's gaze bearing down on her. The scene has no relevance to the case and does not in any sense move the plot forward, yet is pivotal in conveying to the audience an impression of the victim. Allusions to the girl's culpability in her violent end are made throughout the reconstruction: she refused a lift home from her mother, failed to contact her boyfriend who spent the evening searching for her on his motorbike, resorted to hitchhiking home from her friend's house after dark and accepted a lift from a stranger in a van. All these examples of her recklessness are crystallized in the scene where she lies on the sunbed in her bra and pants, giggling with her friend. Here we see connections graphically made between feminine vanity, the desire for an attractive body to solicit attention on her forthcoming beach holiday, and risk-taking behaviour as the audience already knows that she met her death when she left her friend without arranging transport home (Weaver, 1998).

According to Kidd-Hewitt (1995), *Crimewatch UK* is guilty of locking certain sections of the audience into a terrorizing world of fear reinforcement, a belief supported by Weaver who conducted focus group interviews with women who were shown the reconstruction of the hitchhiker's murder. A common response was that taking a lift in a car may have been preferable to walking all the way home in the dark – the 'lesser of two evils', as one participant put it (Weaver, 1998: 256). Respondents also praised the reconstruction for raising awareness of the dangers facing women who go out alone in the evening, and even the sunbed scene was endorsed by some who felt that its 'watch and beware' tone justified its titillating nature. Although Weaver's study illustrates the polysemic nature of media texts with several different, and often competing, interpretations of the reconstruction being offered by her interviewees, the overwhelming response from the women interviewed is an unproblematic acceptance of *Crimewatch*'s warning to other women against hitchhiking. Most welcomed the 'public service' element of the show and ingested the programme's implicit criticism of the victim for engaging in irresponsible behaviour. Few questioned the belief that it is women's individual responsibility to restrict and censure their behaviour in order to avoid being the victim of crime, and none criticized *Crimewatch* for failing to provide any alternative means of imagining how violent attacks on women could be prevented (see below). Weaver draws on feminist writer Susan Brownmiller (1975: 400) to conclude that her interviewees' unquestioning absorption of this gendered narrative suggests that women 'accept a special burden of self protection ... that women must live and move about in fear and can never expect to achieve the personal freedom, independence and self assurance of men' (cited in Weaver, 1998: 262).

The extent to which *Crimewatch UK* amplifies fear among its viewers – especially those least likely to be victims of serious crimes – has been a central theme of both media studies and criminology literature on the subject. Schlesinger and Tumber (1994) note that research carried out by the Independent Broadcasting Authority found that one in three viewers thought that *Crimewatch* had made them, and probably other viewers, feel more afraid of being a potential victim of crime. The BBC's own research claimed that fear was largely confined to female viewers, especially those living alone. There are also claims that the presenters' reassurances throughout each show that crime is falling and serious crime is very rare, might misfire, and may actually increase the likelihood of anxiety among certain sections of the audience (Schlesinger and Tumber, 1994). A particularly unfortunate monologue by veteran presenter Nick

Ross in the March 2003 programme followed the reconstruction of the sexually-motivated murder of 17-year-old 'A'-Level student, Hannah Foster:

> Murders of young women like Hannah make headline news for the very reason that they're pretty unusual. Two-thirds of Britain's murder victims are male and six times more people are killed each year in road accidents than in homicides. But of course there is something especially upsetting about the murders of women and these are the appeals that tend to get the biggest response from *Crimewatch* viewers.

Ross then proceeds to give updates on four similar yet unconnected murder cases, all of which occurred in the capital or surrounding area within a 12-month period (three, like the murder of Hannah, occurred in the previous two months). They were: a report on the funeral of 14-year-old Millie Dowler who disappeared the year before; the arrest of a murder suspect in the case of 23-year-old Finnish student, Suvi Aronen, murdered in March 2003 as she spoke to her mother on her mobile phone; and 'progress reports' on the cases of Marsha McDonnell, a 19-year-old student bludgeoned to death on a road close to her home in February 2003; and Margaret Muller, a 27-year-old student stabbed while jogging in Victoria Park, East London in the same month. Despite apparently trying to reassure viewers, Ross's decision to bring together reports on five young women murdered by strangers in unconnected, unprovoked, seemingly motiveless attacks, creates the impression of a terrifying crime wave and makes his cheery advice at the end of the show – 'Don't have nightmares, do sleep well!' – seem rather hollow. Furthermore, by its very nature, *Crimewatch UK* may amplify audience fears because it only reconstructs crimes that are unsolved; crimes, in fact, where the police have no significant leads and have reached the end of an investigative cul-de-sac. Hence, the viewer is denied a sense of closure – the murderer/rapist/thief is still 'out there' and ready to strike again.

Crimewatching offenders

A further problem that has been identified in relation to *Crimewatch UK* is that it may generate fear of, or hostility towards, particular groups such as people from ethnic minorities. *Crimewatch* tends to over-represent crimes involving black offenders and under-represent black victims, especially males in both categories. In the major cases included in the three editions analysed, where the ethnicity of the suspect was known, four offences involved white people, while 10 concerned non-white individuals (in two of the cases, both white and non-white offenders were involved). The programme also frequently fails to distinguish between different ethnic and national groups, homogenizing offenders' 'otherness' with phrases like 'North African appearance', 'Mediterranean appearance' or 'Kosovan appearance'. In only one serious crime was a female offender implicated (in the aggravated burglary in the March 2003 edition, an Asian woman knocked at the door of the house before the two men, one black, one white, entered the house and overpowered the family). Women offenders are more commonly featured in other parts of the programme where photographs and CCTV stills accompany their appearance as perpetrators of fraud and other financial crimes.

While victims are firmly located within family structures and are thus 'legitimized' as innocent and undeserving casualties, the same contextualization is never extended to offenders (Jermyn, 2003). Constructions of offenders are the exact antithesis to those of victims. While victims are shown within their family contexts, affirming their 'normality' and 'typicality', offenders are invariably anonymous, constructed as individuals and existing in isolation of social and familial ties. Because *Crimewatch UK* can show only cases where there are no significant leads or suspects (for fear of prejudicing a trial), the offender is frequently not seen in the reconstruction at all, or may be represented only symbolically as a figure in extreme long-shot, either walking or running near the scene of the crime or as a shadowy figure at the wheel of a vehicle. These *representations*-from-a-distance reinforce the impression of the offender as 'outsider' with no ties to domesticity or 'normality'. This is an important point in relation to public constructions of criminals, and contrasts with other television genres where knowledge about the background of offenders and the context of their crimes, elicits a very different response. For example, Gillespie and McLaughlin (2002) conducted a study which showed that, in group discussions of media narratives, respondents displayed shifts in opinion regarding offenders depending on what television genre was being discussed. In conversations about soap operas the overtly punitive opinions that many had previously expressed about offenders were challenged, and ultimately reconfigured, in line with what they 'knew' about the character. In accordance with early media studies which proposed that media content had a more significant impact on audience members if they could, in some way 'identify' with the character being portrayed, Gillespie and McLaughlin found that where respondents could empathize with the offender on the basis of what they knew about him or her, a less punitive attitude was adopted. This 'deeper knowledge' of the background of the offender and the crime is precisely what is missing from *Crimewatch UK* where sympathy, empathy or understanding are simply not options. In presenting offenders as 'others' and their crimes as senseless and random, programmes like *Crimewatch* stimulate sentiments of revulsion and repugnance towards offenders and reinforce populist ideas about punishment (Gillespie and McLaughlin, 2002).

Curiously, the 'outsider' status of the offenders who commit the heinous crimes featured on *Crimewatch* is constructed even in relation to other criminals – the 'decent', 'respectable' kind. In an echo of the reference to different classes of criminals in PC George Dixon's first incarnation more than half a century ago, Nick Ross says of the aggravated house burglary mentioned earlier: 'I suspect that *anybody* watching this, even people who are part of the criminal fraternity, have never experienced anything like this, and won't have any truck with these guys anyway' (*Crimewatch UK*, March 2003). By contrast, there is little recognition that *Crimewatch* is a media text which offers more than just a powerful tool for the police and broadcasting company, creating space for audience resistance, empowerment and the subversion of dominant media ideologies. For instance, the accusation that programmes in this genre are 'schools for crime' is not dwelt on by the programme's producers or presenters. An American study of 208 prison inmates discovered that 9 out of 10 had 'learned new tricks and improved their criminal expertise' by watching crime programmes (Hendrick, 1977, cited in Meyrowitz, 1985: 118). One of the most notorious reconstructions ever shown on *Crimewatch UK* involved a re-enactment of a complex and ingenious method of raiding building societies via access through the roof. The detail of the reconstruction was so graphic and so accurate that there were several successful 'copycat' raids following the broadcast, causing the producers of *Crimewatch* and the police to completely rethink their approach to reconstructing serious offences. Meanwhile, British studies have found that many prison inmates watch *Crimewatch UK* specifically to see if they can spot any of their friends and associates, to laugh at the police struggling to solve crimes, to **legitimate** their personas as violent criminals, and to ground themselves in 'reality' – their reality (Daniels, 1997; Jewkes, 2002; Matthews, 2002).

Crimewatching the police

When the police were first approached about co-operating with television producers on *Crimewatch* they were initially suspicious of the idea. However, *Crimewatch UK* has proved to be one of the most effective public relations exercises at the police's disposal. In fact, the benefits to them in terms of the warm feelings induced by watching the police and public working together to solve crimes arguably outweighs all other benefits of the programme. This is a fact clearly understood by the police, despite the threat by Greater Manchester Chief Constable, Mike Todd, to boycott the show. The producers of *Crimewatch UK* are at pains to point out that they maintain their autonomy from the police, but one of the main criticisms levelled at the programme is that they do not seek information from any other source and that the police have too much say in what gets broadcast. Before each programme is put together, researchers routinely call each police force to ask about major unsolved crimes and invite investigating officers on selected cases to the television studio. This may be seen in a positive or negative light. On the one hand, the production team have unique access to every detail of an investigation, and are privy to aspects of a case that may not have been revealed publicly. The flip-side is that the police can determine the conditions under which knowledge is used. Each broadcast of *Crimewatch* includes around 30 police officers from all over the UK who appear on the programme in support of their respective cases. Typically, these will include senior investigating officers who will usually take part in a live interview with one of the main presenters. Other officers operate the telephones and serve as a backdrop to the studio presentations. One notable difference in current editions of *Crimewatch* as compared with the 1980s version is that the senior investigating officers are as likely to be women as they are men, a development that reflects advances made by women within the senior ranks of the police. In addition, there are police officers who are regular presenters on the show, the longest serving of whom is Detective Sergeant Jacqui Hames, who has been part of the presenting team since 1990.

Crimewatch UK presents the police in a positive light as both professional and personable. The officer in charge of the case is invited to the studio to discuss the offence and lend the investigation a 'personal touch'. To that extent, it does not necessarily matter how 'televisual' the officer is, nor how much media training they have received (although most are relaxed and confident performers in front of the camera). The key factor is that they represent the human face of the police service and inspire confidence in potential witness or informants to telephone the incident room. In this respect the programme is undoubtedly successful, although of the calls that come in during and after each broadcast (an average of around 1,000 according to the programme's website, www.bbc.co.uk/crime/crimewatch) only two or three may be of use.

In essence, then, editorial control is a trade-off between the police, who recognize that *Crimewatch* gives them unparalleled access to potential sources of information, and the programme makers who are in the business of entertaining their audience – however voyeuristically that might be achieved. It is the alliance between the media and the police that is the key to the programme's longevity. *Crimewatch* is a safe haven for the police: unlike other media genres they are not going to be criticized or challenged here. The success of the partnership is measured in arrests. Since the first programme aired in 1984, the *Crimewatch* team claim that there have been 582 arrests as a direct result of the programme (*Independent*, 21 April 2000, cited in Leishman and Mason, 2003: 115) and Nick Ross frequently alludes to the programme's achievements in the monthly broadcasts ('nine arrests since the last programme as a direct result of *Crimewatch*', February 1998). While undoubtedly impressive, Irving points out that such claims are impossible to substantiate. He counters that most of those arrests may have occurred anyway, without the help of television, and that the arrest figures proudly reeled off by *Crimewatch*'s producers and presenters are evidence of 'exactly the crass lack of rigour that is applied to the subject'

(*Guardian*, 3 September 1990). The programme functions, then, as a vehicle for reinforcing the police's role as successful crime fighters. At the end of the October 2003 edition, Nick Ross told the viewing public that fatal shootings are down in the UK and stand at one of the lowest figures in the world, while the most recent British Crime Survey show that 'over all, British people's experience of crime is *down*, down to the lowest figure since the early 1980s'. This ringing endorsement of the police's work is underlined with an ironic twist on his usual endnote: 'So, apart from worrying about scary journalists, there's no need to have nightmares. Do please sleep well'. Even more affirming of the police's success is spin-off series *Crimewatch Solved* which, as the title indicates, reconstructs investigations that have resulted in a positive outcome and justice done. As others have noted (for example, Leishman and Mason, 2003), the simplicity and moral certainty traditionally ascribed to fictional detectives is now to be found in the realms of 'factional' representations and 'infotainment' shows. With graphics of falling crime rates, police detection rates cited as 25 per cent, and a description of the National Police Training College as home to the 'crafty' and 'ingenious', *Crimewatch Solved* (BBC1, 20 August 2003) could hardly have been more laudatory and less challenging in its portrayal of the police as heroic crimefighters (Stick, 2003).

Crimewatching crime: some concluding thoughts

It is increasingly being recognized that the medium of television is situated within, and fully interwoven with, many other social practices, to the extent where crime, criminals and criminal justice cannot be separated from their representations on television (Sparks, 1992; Ferrell, 2001). While we cannot make sweeping claims about media 'effects' or the media being responsible for 'causing' fear of crime, we can look at the ways in which media in general, and television in particular, are integral to the processes of meaning-making by which we make sense of our everyday lives (Jewkes, 2002). If, as Sparks (1992) contends, fear of crime is more likely to be governed by uncertainties than known probabilities, the issue of fear must be inextricably linked to issues of representation, interpretation and meaning (Muncie, 2001). Misrepresentations concerning the extent of certain types of crime, the likelihood of victimization, and the locations in which crime commonly occurs, are bound to create a skewed picture of the 'problem of crime' in this country.

One of the central aims of the makers of *Crimewatch UK* is to vary the cases featured on the show. They achieve this with some degree of success in relation to geographical spread (although there is still a concentration on offences that have taken place in England, as opposed to the other countries of the UK). They also adhere to the news imperative of 'novelty' to break up the running order and inject new life into the programme. For example, in the three episodes analysed for the purposes of writing this chapter, a novel approach can be found in several aspects of the show. First, producers do strive to include crimes that are not the usual staples of the show. The March 2003 programme included a report on the theft of rare birds' eggs, while the decision to end the October 2003 edition with a report on a stolen pumpkin not only located the programme in 'real time' (it being the broadcast before Halloween night), but also echoed ITN's 'And finally ...' story designed to leave viewers on an upbeat or comical note. The programme also aims for innovation in its depiction of crimes, as demonstrated by the home video footage of an elderly woman letting two burglars into her home, filmed from behind curtains by a vigilant neighbour (March 2003). A novel approach was further used in the October 2003 edition when, for the first time, 3D computer graphics were used to show the internal and external decoration of a house in which a rape took place.

However, the programme as a whole fails to diverge far from its tried-and-tested formula of representing a limited range of very serious crimes perpetrated against a restricted category of victims. A *Crimewatch* producer's comment that the programme strives for a mixture and balance of items – which he illustrates with the evidence that in one show they included a sexual assault and murder of a woman in Tonbridge Wells and then did a reconstruction /report into the Notting Hill rapist – is unlikely to convince many that *Crimewatch* represents a cross-section of crimes in Britain (cited in Schlesinger and Tumber, 1994: 261). To put it bluntly, incidents most likely to feature on *Crimewatch* are crimes against the person in which a high level of violence is involved, and crimes of a sexual nature, especially in cases involving young women and girls. Much less likely to be included are white-collar crimes, corporate or state crimes, and crimes in which the police have bungled the investigation (Schlesinger and Tumber, 1994). Also unlikely to be featured is any useful advice concerning crime prevention. The case of the young woman assaulted in Blackpool in the early hours of the morning while talking on her mobile phone is a good example of a missed opportunity to offer preventative advice. In addition to reinforcing messages about unnecessary risks taken by young women who choose to walk alone at night, the presenters might have taken the opportunity to remind female viewers of the value of carrying a rape alarm and the false sense of security that a mobile phone offers (even if the person on the other end is a police officer, especially if – as in this case – he is working in a different city at the time!). The programme could also encourage women to join forces if they have to walk at night and encourage friends to stop each other from venturing out alone, in much the same way as pub-goers are encouraged to prevent someone who is likely to be over the legally permitted alcohol level from driving home. The fact that none of this advice is offered on the television programme will inevitably ensure that questions continue to be raised about where the public service/entertainment balance of *Crimewatch UK* lies.

Summary

- The media are not solely to blame for inciting fear of crime. Actual risk of victimization, previous experience of victimization, environmental conditions, ethnicity and previous contact with the police and criminal justice system are among many factors interacting through complex mediated processes to influence public anxiety about crime. As Richard Sparks comments: 'the reception by people of media stories about crime and punishment is best grasped ... *in situ*, in which case many public responses that are commonly deprecated by criminologists and others as "irrational" or "hysterical" tend to become substantially more intelligible' (2001: 197).
- However, the media might be said to play an important role in creating a cultural climate in which certain types of criminal behaviour are portrayed more frequently, and with greater intensity, than others. This distortion may cultivate fears among certain sections of the audience, and exaggerate their risk of victimization. Given that the British Crime Survey shows that fear of crime has an inverse relationship with statistical occurrence, the media may be partially responsible, in so far as crimes against the most 'fearful' but least likely to be victimized members of society – especially young women and elderly people – are over-reported and over-sensationalized.
- Some critics argue that, as a consequence of the media's tendency to concentrate on the most atypical crimes and present them in a sensationalistic and voyeuristic manner, women and the elderly are socialized into fear and become over-sensitized to their own roles in avoiding becoming victims of crime. One of the programmes most frequently singled out for criticism in this respect is *Crimewatch UK*. In research, relatively few female viewers expressed the view that *Crimewatch* promotes a gendered agenda that encourages women to think of themselves as potential victims. This suggests that most female viewers uncritically accept their 'at risk' status and modify their behaviour accordingly. Meanwhile, in over-emphasizing sexual and/or violent offences against all women and girls that occur in public, *Crimewatch UK* emphasizes women's culpability in their victimization and implicitly endorses men's 'privileged' access to any place at any time.

- The genre conventions employed by *Crimewatch UK* not only result in an overwhelming emphasis on violent and sexual crimes perpetrated mostly on women (always constructed as 'tragic victims'), but they also serve to construct offenders and crime scenes in particular ways. Crimes featured on the show are usually committed by non-white, male strangers ('others'); in either the victim's home (a particular violation, and indicative of their vulnerability) or in public places (usually 'the streets'); which results in not just the victimization of the individual, but of their entire family who have been 'robbed' of their loved one. Like other examples discussed in this book, this structuring of events means that traditional conservative family and gender relations are endorsed and celebrated, even when the reality of sexual and violent crime suggests that the home is frequently a site of (largely masculine) violence, sexual abuse and murder. *Crimewatch* might also be said to be guilty of ignoring other forms of crime, notably those involving institutions, structures and the (relatively) powerful. For example, middle-class and white-collar crime – when featured at all – tend to be included in the short 'appeal' sections of the programme, where a photograph of a fraudster or embezzler might be shown with an appeal for their name or whereabouts. Corporate crimes are almost entirely invisible in *Crimewatch UK*, just as they are in other media genres. The dramatized reconstructions – which are the main items in the show and the primary reasons for its ongoing existence – almost invariably cover crimes of a sexual or violent and random nature.
- *Crimewatch UK* is also a prime example of the collaborative relationship between the police and the media. The issue of policing has increasingly come to be understood not simply in its political or social context, but as a set of semiotic practices enmeshed with mediated culture (Ferrell, 2001). 'Image work' is central to a police service that is increasingly coming to recognize that policing is as much about symbolism as it is about substance (Mawby, 2002).
- Thanks to programmes like *Crimewatch*, appeals from families, crime reconstructions and interviews with senior detectives requesting help from the public are now familiar communicative formats across a range of media genres. The images and language of such communications are carefully crafted and chosen by the police in an attempt to persuade potential witnesses, offenders or people who suspect someone of the offence to come forward with their information. In this respect, we have seen a return to the kindly benevolent, consensual policing epitomized by the fictional *Dixon of Dock Green*. Unfortunately, since PC Dixon walked the beat, the relationship between the police and the media has often been characterized as difficult and mutually hostile. In recent years the police have sought to embrace and exploit the media in pursuit of a positive image and an impression of legitimacy and accountability. However, the bond of trust formed between the two institutions is still fragile, as witnessed by periodic media exposés of racism and sexism within the police service.

STUDY QUESTIONS

1   It has been said that PC George Dixon has been 'exhumed and laid to rest more times than some care to remember' (Greer, 2004). What accounts for the enduring popularity of Dixon and why is his image still evoked so long after *Dixon of Dock Green* was taken off air?

2   Conduct your own analysis of an edition of *Crimewatch UK*. To what extent does it follow the conventions of news reporting (that is, 'news values') in the popular press and broadcast media? Do the reports and reconstructions in your selected edition conform to, or flout, the BBC programme guidelines?

3   In your own experience as a viewer, does *Crimewatch* amplify fears about certain types of crime and victimization? If so, are its effects long-term and diffuse or short-term and based on geographical and cultural proximity?

4   In addition to the example of *The Secret Policeman* broadcast by the BBC in October 2003, there have been a number of other cases where individuals (especially celebrities) have been covertly filmed engaging in criminal and deviant behaviour, such as accepting money to rig sporting events and dealing in, or buying, drugs. Frequently, as in the case of the BBC documentary, the individuals are set up by journalists in what amounts to entrapment. Are undercover investigation methods by journalists justified in cases where issues such as sexism, racism, corruption and crime might otherwise not be revealed?

FURTHER READING

Robert Reiner has written extensively on police and the media, including his chapter 'Media made criminality: the representation of crime in the mass media' in Maguire M., Morgan R. and Reiner R. (eds) (2002) *The Oxford Handbook of Criminology* (Oxford University Press) and 'Mystifying the police: the media presentation of policing' in Reiner, R. (2000) *The Politics of the Police* (Oxford University Press). An excellent and reasonably up-to-date analysis of the subject is provided by Leishman, F. and Mason, P. (2003) *Policing and the Media: Facts, Fictions and Factions* (Willan). Mawby, R. (2002) *Policing Images: Policing, Communication and Legitimacy* (Willan) is especially good on the 'image work' that the police now have to engage in. Given the relationship between fear of crime and issues of policing, this chapter has deliberately concentrated on a single element of the criminal justice system – the police. However, that is not to say that fears about crime are not implicitly related to other aspects of criminal justice, for example courts (especially when sentences are passed that are perceived as erratic or too light) and prisons (which might be perceived as overcrowded because of the dangerous and volatile nature of contemporary society). These other aspects of criminal justice, and their representations in the media, are explored in Jewkes, Y. (2004) 'Media Representations of Criminal Justice' in Muncie, J. and Wilson, D. (eds) *Cavendish Handbook of Criminology and Criminal Justice* (Cavendish). In addition, Mason, P. (ed.) (2003) *Criminal Visions: Media Representations of Crime and Justice* (Willan) covers several interesting topics, including Mason's own chapter on cinematic representations of prisons – a follow up to his earlier chapter, 'Prime time punishment: the British prison and television' in Kidd-Hewitt, D. and Osborne, R. (1995) *Crime and the Media: the Post-Modern Spectacle* (Pluto). The aforementioned *Criminal Visions* contains a chapter by Jermyn on *Crimewatch UK* 'Photo stories and family albums: imaging criminals and victims on *Crimewatch UK*'. Kay Weaver's chapter '*Crimewatch UK*: Keeping women off the streets' is in Carter, C. Branston, G. and Allen, S. (eds) *News, Gender and Power*. However, the best introductory analysis to *Crimewatch* remains that contained in Schlesinger, P. and Tumber, H. (1994) *Reporting Crime* (Clarendon).

7

Crime and the Surveillance Culture

Chapter Contents

OVERVIEW

Chapter 7 provides:

- A brief consideration of the dominance of the Panopticon as a metaphor for contemporary surveillance techniques.
- A discussion of the extent to which surveillance technologies and systems are linked to form carceral networks of disciplinary power.
- An exploration of the institutional rationales and motivations that have led to a dramatic expansion of surveillance over the last two decades.
- A discussion of these rationales in relation to surveillance in a specific context; the workplace.
- An analysis of the ways in which media and popular culture have helped us to conceptualize various forms of surveillance through their representation in newspapers, television, films, music, art and so on, and how the 'viewer society' that the mass media have given rise to, synthesises panoptic and synoptic models of surveillance.

KEY TERMS

carceral society	Panopticon and panopticism	surveillant assemblage
control of the body	profit	synopticism
governmentality	security	voyeurism

Over the last 15 years, Western societies have experienced a rapid growth in the use of surveillance, to the extent where most citizens have come to take for granted that they are observed, monitored, classified and controlled in almost every aspect of their public lives. At the forefront of the surveillance society is closed circuit television (CCTV): it is estimated that the average person living and working in a major city could be filmed up to 300 times a day (cf. Norris, 2003, for an overview of the history and expansion of CCTV in the UK). If one wishes to take advantage of credit, withdraw money from a bank, work for an employer, vote in an election, purchase goods, attend a football match, drive a car, catch a train, use a mobile phone or surf the Internet, it is virtually impossible to remain anonymous. Quite simply, recent years have witnessed the 'disappearance of disappearance' (Haggerty and Ericson, 2000: 619).

At the same time, surveillance has become a salient topic for academic reflection, being both fertile ground for theoretical analysis and of sufficient interest to policy-makers and commercial operators to attract funding from central and local government agencies, policing bodies, security firms and private companies. Most criminological research in this area has explored the role of CCTV, either in specific contexts (for example, Beck and Willis's 1995 analysis of CCTV in retail outlets, and Newburn and Hayman's 2001 study of the use of CCTV in a London police station) or more generally in terms of its role in, and impact on, situational crime prevention (see Clarke, 1997, for an overview). Surveillance has thus become a cornerstone of the literature on 'target hardening', 'defensible space' and victimization (Newman, 1972; Barr and Pease, 1990; Davis, 1994). Some studies have examined whether visual surveillance technologies such as CCTV are effective in cutting crime or whether they simply displace it to surrounding areas (with contradictory findings: Short and Ditton, 1995). Others have focused on the capacity for visual surveillance systems to reduce public fears about personal safety (Bennett and Gelsthorpe, 1994; Ditton et al., 1999). On the basis that these issues are dealt with at length in other criminological textbooks (for example, Coleman and Norris, 2000), this chapter will take a different approach and will discuss some of the key motivations behind the rapid expansion of surveillance and its potential for social classification and social control. The chapter will also attempt to blend voices from criminology with those of the most prominent writers in the fields of sociology and cultural studies. In line with Giddens's (1985) definition, the term 'surveillance' will be used to refer to two related phenomena: the accumulation of coded information (for example, from genetic material) which can be used to manage the behaviour of those about whom it is gathered, and the direct supervision of some individuals by others who are in positions of authority over them. But first let us consider the primary motif that unites debates about surveillance across all academic disciplines: the Panopticon.

Panopticism

In the popular consciousness, images of CCTV and other forms of surveillance are dominated by the figure of 'Big Brother', George Orwell's creation of an all-seeing, all-knowing, invisible super-power. In academic discussions of surveillance, however, the dominant metaphor has been that of the **Panopticon**, an image that lends itself especially well to discussions of surveillance technologies which allow some individuals to monitor the behaviour of others. The Panopticon, developed by 18th-century reformer Jeremy Bentham, was an architectural design that could be used for prisons, schools, factories, workhouses and any other social institutions that required the management of large groups of people by a small number of individuals with authority over them (indeed,

Bentham envisaged entire cities being developed along panoptic lines). The overtly punitive elements of the Panopticon led to it becoming most frequently associated with prison design, and although it is often written that Bentham's model was never realized, several prisons *were* constructed according to the broad principles of ***panopticism***.* In brief, Bentham's design consisted of a circular building with individual cells built around its entire circumference, and a central watchtower in which the activities of the prisoners could be constantly watched. A system of lighting that illuminated the cells but kept the inspection tower in darkness made it possible for just one person to monitor many inmates, each of whom knew they were under surveillance, but did not know exactly when. They were therefore obliged to behave as if they were being monitored at all times, and conformity and passivity were assured. The mental state of being seen without being able to see the watcher induced a fear that eliminated the need for visible deterrents or overt force. The Panopticon was subsequently appropriated by others who gave it a Foucauldian slant, taking the ideological concept behind the structure and using it to demonstrate the potential of new communication and information technologies. Writing about the plague at the end of the 17th century, Foucault (1977) describes how certain areas of a town were cordoned off and kept under continuous vigil with guards inspecting every part of the town to ensure that no-one escaped to spread the disease further. Consequently, like the inmates in Bentham's prison, the town's population were not simply observed; the surveillance of them was designed to act as a deterrent, a caution to encourage them to behave in a certain way. Thus, for Foucault, Bentham's architectural design was not only a blueprint for future surveillance technologies which would allow a small, unseen few to observe the lives of the masses, it was also a means of attaining absolute control over a conforming, docile population.

The surveillant assemblage

The pertinence of the panoptic model is obvious in relation to CCTV, but it is increasingly being used as a metaphor for other innovations, especially those used in conjunction with computers (ID cards, store loyalty cards, DNA databases, encryption, fingerprinting, hand geometry, eye scans, voice recognition, digitized face recognition and so on). In other words, advances in technology have arguably

---

*One of the most well known panoptic-style prisons was built on the Isle of Pines, Cuba, in 1932 (www.ucl.ac.uk/Bentham-Project). Photographs of it can be viewed via links provided on the UCL site.

resulted in the disciplinary gaze being extended beyond the confines of closed and controlled environments, such as the prison or the factory, to encompass society as a whole (McCahill, 2003). However, as Norris and Armstrong (1999) demonstrate, the panoptic effects of CCTV systems are limited. Three shortcomings are highlighted. First, CCTV systems that operate in public spaces, such as streets, are impossible to monitor continuously and it is relatively easy for those intent on behaving deviantly to disguise their appearance or move outside of the camera's gaze. Paramilitary groups such as the IRA have shown themselves to be particularly adept in this respect. Over the last decade, despite the increasing likelihood of CCTV cameras in areas targeted by bombs, the police in England and Northern Ireland have had relatively little success in identifying the individuals responsible. Second, even when deviance is observed, the ability to mobilize a rapid response is constrained. In most cases, CCTV operators themselves are not authorised to deal with incidents, and neither are they in a position to demand swift intervention by the police. By way of example, Norris and Armstrong note that out of a total of 600 hours of observational research conducted in three city centre CCTV control rooms, they witnessed just 45 deployments.

The third and most interesting limitation of CCTV in the current context is the fact that the disciplinary power of the panopticon is only complete when one-way total surveillance is combined with additional information about the individual being monitored. Norris (2003) suggests that despite the massive expansion of CCTV surveillance in Britain, its operators' inability to routinely link a person's image to any more detailed knowledge or information about them, places a severe limitation on CCTV as a Panopticon; such surveillance is, as Haggerty and Ericson note, 'often a mile wide but only an inch deep' (2000: 618). To put it in its simplest terms, there is not much the police can do with a recorded image of an offence that has already taken place unless further data can be gathered about the offender – name, whereabouts, address, previous convictions and so on – hence the use that the police make of television programmes like *Crimewatch UK* in appealing to the public to 'fill in the blanks'.

However, depth, or intensity, of surveillance can also be achieved via the connection of different technologies (for example, digitised CCTV systems and computer databases) and institutions (such as the police and private security companies). Haggerty and Ericson (2000) refer to this convergence of once discrete surveillance systems as a *'surveillant assemblage'*. But however sophisticated the linked surveillance systems are, they are prone to human error or ignorance. By way of example, Norris and Armstrong (1999: 221) report that two Welsh football fans were erroneously entered onto the National Football Intelligence Unit's database of suspected hooligans and were subsequently identified and arrested while at an away match in Belgium. The pair were deported and banned from travelling anywhere in Europe, despite having done nothing wrong. This raises the interesting issue of electronic identities taking precedence over 'real' identities. Once information (be it visual or textual) about a person is entered onto a linked surveillance system, their identity is 'fixed' even if it is 'false'. In much the same way as a person's legal identity is constructed from a mass of facts taken from the beginning to the end of life – birth certificate, passport, employment histories, medical and dental records, criminal record, post mortem, and so on – a cumulative mass of documents that captures and fixes them (Finch, 2003; cf. Foucault, 1977), so an individual can be captured in a web of non-documentary, visual surveillance.

Increasingly, in any major serious crime investigation both the victim and the suspect will have their movements, consumption patterns, reading tastes, personal contacts, sexual histories and various other aspects of their private lives compiled into a detailed 'dossier that reflects the history of his [sic] deviation from the norm' (Poster, 1990: 91). This coalescence of information is then frequently made public knowledge via the mass media. For example, following the murder of *Crimewatch UK* presenter Jill Dando on the doorstep of her London home in April 1999, it was revealed that 14,000 e-mails were examined, 486 names in her Filofax were investigated, and 2,400 statements were taken. Stories about Dando's relationship with her fiancé and several of her previous boyfriends appeared in the tabloid press. Further depth of knowledge was achieved by means of additional layers of surveillance. For example, after CCTV footage showed a blue Range Rover speeding south of the murder scene shortly after the killing, 1,200 cars were traced (the result of which was that seven months later the murder team arrested a man on suspicion of the theft of such a vehicle). In the week following her death, police released CCTV footage of her shopping in Hammersmith on the morning of her murder, and also revealed that their 'prime suspect' had made his getaway on a number 74 bus, speaking on a mobile phone before disembarking at Putney Bridge. A year after her murder, on 25 May 2000, Barry George was arrested following a period of intensive surveillance of his home. Yet ironically it was not a piece of high-tech gadgetry that finally led to George's arrest, but a 'dog-eared index card' stored in a West London police station which held details of the suspect's previous sex crimes and firearms offences (*The Times*, 3 July 2001, available at www.timesonline.co.uk). The card had lain undiscovered for nine months after the murder, until a police officer chanced upon it.

Another example that illustrates the depth of information which can be achieved when fragments of data are coalesced is the police hunt for 12-year-old Shevaun Pennington, who disappeared with a 31-year-old American in July 2003 after 'meeting' him in an Internet chat room. Following Shevaun's safe return home it was widely reported that, despite her family's pleas for information about their missing child and her abductor, the police had known their whereabouts all along, thanks to a GPS (global positioning satellite) system that could pick up the suspect's mobile phone transmissions. Not only did this allow the police to triangulate the phone's location to within a few metres, but they were reportedly able to activate the phone even when it was switched off. In addition, the police alerted credit card companies so that an alarm was automatically triggered when the suspect used his credit card to buy airline tickets. Meanwhile, police in his home town were examining his personal computer where they found downloaded child pornography, and his criminal records which revealed that he had previously been charged with molesting a 12-year-old child in the US (Morris and al Yafai, 2003). In Wigan, Shevaun's computer was also being examined, and it was discovered that, unbeknown to her parents, she had been in communication with the American for over a year. Perhaps most bizarrely, it was reported that the former marine had planned the abduction with military precision. Forensic analysis of his computer apparently revealed that his rendezvous and escape with Shevaun 'smacked of special forces "in-hit-out" tactics' (2003).

These are just two examples used to demonstrate that surveillance is far from a unitary technology. They happen to be two high-profile criminal cases, but even when we confine our discussion to the mundane monitoring of 'ordinary' citizens by CCTV, we are in fact referring to a nexus of cameras, computers, telecommunications and people (Norris and Armstrong, 1999). For example, in his detailed sociological study of CCTV in a northern English city, McCahill (2002) relates how people that are known to the CCTV operators – and known not just because of previous offences that have been observed and recorded, but also because they live on the same estate, were at school together, or play on the same pub darts team as the suspect's dad – may be subject to more intrusive and prolonged surveillance. Frequently the police will make use of this accumulated knowledge, and security guards may tip them off about a suspects' movements, or allow community police officers to hang around in their control room observing the monitors. Taken together, these networks of people and institutions are often said to constitute a *'carceral society'* (Foucault, 1977), whereby more and more aspects of public life are becoming subject to the kind of disciplinary power that we usually associate with the prison. In other words, the alliance of formerly discrete technologies into a surveillant assemblage is designed to create systems of discipline and domination (Haggerty and Ericson, 2000). Moreover, these systems of discipline and domination are driven by a common set of motives and desires on the part of those who instigate and operate them. In a slight modification of Haggerty and Ericson's typology, these rationales for surveillance will be further explored in this chapter under the following headings: control of the body, governance and governmentality, security, profit, and voyeurism and entertainment.

Control of the body

In *Discipline and Punish* (1977) Foucault discusses the transformation of punishment from the infliction of bodily pain and public spectacle (the book opens with a rather gruesome account of someone being hung, drawn and quartered) to a concern with the regulation of the mind. This transformation in Western European penal thinking occurred over a considerable period of time: the torture Foucault describes took place in France in 1757; the last public execution in Britain was in 1868 and abolition came only in 1969. In more recent years Cohen (1985) has observed a reverse 'master shift' in the discourse of social control from a concern with the mind back to the body; in other words, from thought and intention to observable behaviour. In contemporary society, however, the body is not the site of punishment, but rather the target of preventative crime strategies.

One aspect of this approach is that a great deal of surveillance is directed towards monitoring, codifying and **controlling the human body**. Surveillance of specifically targeted groups can be achieved via an interface of technology and corporeality that can range from direct physical contact between flesh and technological device, to more oblique or covert methods of producing information (Haggerty and Ericson, 2000). The former would include the various forms of 'electronic tagging' that are now commonplace, such as securing an electronic tag round new-born babies' wrists or ankles in hospital which not only contains personal information about the child and its medical condition, but also triggers an alarm if the infant is moved beyond a secure area. The electronic monitoring of offenders and those on probation, and the use of microchips inserted under the skin of pets to monitor their whereabouts, are also examples of the diversity of applications which exploit the flesh-technology-information amalgam (Haraway, 1991). Less direct forms of surveillance that rely on distanciated monitoring of corporeality include the computer monitoring of keystrokes to assess output and efficiency in offices and the visual surveillance of shop workers' body language to ensure that they are conveying the customer service ethos of their employer (see below).

When it comes to techniques of identification, body surveillance extends beyond individuals and discrete groups to entire populations. In this respect, identity verification is achieved by means of 'biometrics', which are identification techniques based on physical attributes – fingerprints, palm scans, retina identification, body fluids and so on. In the global surveillance society, one is no longer identified by what one has (for example, a passport or credit card), or by what one knows (for example, a personal identification number or PIN), but increasingly by what one *is* – a collection of unique body parts (Lyon, 2001). Ironically we have returned to the anthropometric preoccupations of the positivist school of criminology with their measurements of the body, skull and so on – albeit in a more sophisticated guise. There is, then, nothing intrinsically new about the 'informization of the body' (van der Ploeg, 2003: 58). Primitive forms of biometric identification have existed for centuries, and advancements in photography and fingerprinting at the end of the 19th century coincided with the centralization and bureaucratization of administration and record-keeping. In fact, fingerprinting is a good example of a form of surveillance that has lost a great deal of its stigma through familiarity and diversity of use. Once used uniquely by law enforcement agents to identify suspected criminals, with all the negative connotations that such an application would evoke, the use of finger-printing has expanded to include privileged cardholders, frequent flyers, club members and library users (2003). Meanwhile, in the sphere of forensic crime investigations, traditional fingerprinting is being superseded by 'genetic finger-printing', otherwise known as DNA testing. The speed at which a 'result' can be obtained from DNA samples has increased dramatically in recent years, and many old criminal cases that had been consigned to police files have been belat-edly 'solved' by recourse to DNA tests on items of clothing, weapons or other items touched by a suspect and which have been stored by investigators. But despite the fact that DNA provides a unique identifier that cannot be transferred between individuals, no system is foolproof. Even if an effective form of every-day personal identification incorporating DNA could be found, as with other technological advancements it is likely that the professional criminal and terrorist would remain one step ahead of the police (Jewkes, 2003a, 2003b). DNA can be cloned, 'planted' or, in the case of suicide bombers and terrorist 'martyrs', rendered irrelevant.

Governance and governmentality

An emerging theme in the criminological literature on CCTV and other forms of surveillance has been the contextualization of such systems within an 'actuarial' discourse. In other words, CCTV occupies a central role in a broad strategy of social control that has moved from being 'reactive' (that is, only activated when rules are violated) towards one that is 'proactive' (that is, tries to predict rule vio-lations before they happen) (McCahill, 2002; cf. Cohen, 1994). Visual surveil-lance systems are thus seen as just one element within a raft of risk-calculating crime control strategies which also embrace risk assessments of 'dangerousness' in relation to prisoners and those on probation, a national register for sex offenders and the notification of communities about paedophiles in their midst, community safety partnerships undertaking local crime audits, and attempts to 'design out' crime in architecture and town planning (O'Malley, 2001; Stenson, 2001). Not only do surveillance systems underpin correctional policies, then; they have created a new mode of governance. The 'rehabilitative ideal' with its promise of 'treating' the sickness that causes individuals to offend, and its evo-cation of a benevolent state concerned to eradicate poverty, deprivation and hardship, dominated criminological discourse throughout much of the 20th century (McCahill and Norris, 2002). But in recent years, as concerns about crime and the perceived failures of the criminal justice system have intensified, those in power have retreated from any pretence of liberalism and adopted the language of authoritarian populism, using phrases like 'prison works', 'zero tolerance' and 'tough on crime' (Stenson, 2001).

The new discourse of governance is also reflected in the re-emergence of 'Classical' criminological theories that view crime as opportunistic and 'normal'; in other words, requiring no particular maladjustment on the part of the offender (McCahill and Norris, 2002). The salience of these theoretical perspectives in recent years has been accompanied by a shift from policies directed at the individual offender to those aimed at 'criminogenic situations' (2002; see also Garland, 1996, 1999) including car parks, city centres at night, run-down neighbourhoods, poorly-lit streets, subways, schools and colleges, shopping centres and football stadia. While one objective of the new *governmentality* is to develop methods of situational crime control, a related aim (especially of visual surveillance such as CCTV) is to single out those who do not 'belong' in these environments and take pre-emptive action to exclude them (Naughton, 1994). Thus, rather than attempting to tolerate, understand and rehabilitate the different and the dangerous, there has been an ideological shift towards the less expensive and simpler task of displacing them from particular locations and from opportunities to obtain goods and services; of restricting mobility and behaviour; and of managing them rather than changing them (Hudson, 2001; cf. Simon, 1997; Young, 1999). These shifting attitudes are increasingly being seen not simply as attempts to govern crime but also to involve 'government through crime'; a new 'governmentality' (Simon, 1997; Stenson, 2001: 22). According to Stenson, it is targeted disproportionately at poor whites and ethnic minorities who are being increasingly segregated into ghettoized spaces that function as 'human garbage dumps, where survival, excitement and success and opportunities for entrepreneurship depend increasingly on involvement in illegal economies' (Stenson, 2001: 18; cf. Hobbs, 1995; Ferrell, 2002). Davis, writing specifically about Los Angeles, detects a similar segregation of new core business zones from the ghetto areas, a process of sequestration which, he observes, carries 'ominous racial overtones' (Davis, 1994: 4).

The move to render populations quantifiable through identification, classification and differentiation is achieved through a complex network of strategies to manage danger and predict risk transformation, and it is not difficult to see how surveillance technologies have played a crucial part. As more and more of contemporary society's ills are represented as problems of 'criminality', individuals and organizations are being encouraged to view themselves as potential victims and actively respond to the risks facing them. Government of crime is thus practised not only by police and criminal justice professionals, but also by the insurance industry, communities, employers, retail managers and so on (O'Malley, 2001). Often justified in terms of their ability to monitor 'risk' groups, who pose a significant threat to economic stability or social order, the surveillance measures adopted by these diverse bodies can quickly lead to a much broader definition of dangerousness being adopted. For example, to the concern of civil liberties groups, the UK National DNA Database, which was originally set up to aid the identification of serious offenders (that is, murderers and rapists) now includes DNA samples taken without consent from any person convicted or suspected of a recordable offence, even if subsequently found innocent. Organizations such as Liberty find it worrying enough that DNA samples and fingerprints are taken at the point of charge rather than conviction, but the Home Office plans to amend the Criminal Justice Bill to allow samples to be taken even earlier, at the point of arrest. Even more alarming for those who fear the realization of a 'Big Brother' state, there have recently been calls to extend DNA testing to every member of the British population (Radford, 2002). One of the concerns raised by this scenario is that DNA does more than establish identity; it provides a complete genetic profile and there is a growing body of research claiming that specific genes can predict future substance addiction, sexual orientation, and criminal and violent tendencies:

> As such, a system of identification based upon DNA profiling could lead to the stratification of society, creating a Brave New World based upon genetic élitism that would exacerbate the exclusionary impact of an unavoidable system of identification. At the risk of combining dystopias, such a system would also engender opposition as it would risk giving the state a Big Brother-esque omniscience by facilitating the creation of a unified and comprehensive database of information about individuals that is linked to public fears concerning the creation of an Orwellian surveillance state. (Finch, 2003: 101)

It would thus appear that the potential of DNA as a 'positive' aspect of everyday surveillance (that is, one that is acceptable to the public, for example, in reducing the growing numbers of identity thefts) is limited because, quite simply, most people recognize that a society governed by calculations of risk makes everyone a legitimate target for surveillance (McCahill and Norris, 2002).

Security

One of the outcomes of the processes of governance and capitalism outlined so far is that, as urban space has become progressively fragmented and fortified, the population that inhabits that space become subject to feelings of insecurity and paranoia. Despite the unwanted and undesirable being left in the spaces *between* the controlled urban spaces, there is a tendency for those who occupy the newly privatized public realm to nonetheless demonize them (Graham and

Clarke, 2002). As discussed in the previous chapter, when difference and diversity are not tolerated, far less celebrated, the inclination to regard some people as 'other' and fear them as a result becomes more pronounced. In such a climate, visible surveillance technologies may further increase public anxieties and contribute to the image of public spaces as dangerous places. Paradoxically, the solution most frequently put forward to counter the public insecurity that is, in part, generated by the prevalence of surveillance systems is to introduce yet more surveillance systems. Hence a greater level of exclusion is created and a 'fortress mentality' of segregation and ghettoization is reinforced. For example, personal and home security devices, including do-it-yourself CCTV systems, are increasingly commonplace in urban and rural areas alike. Architects and planners in Britain are following the American example of fortified communities, offering security to residents at both ends of the socio-economic spectrum. While the wealthy can lead hermetically sealed lives in self-contained communities protected by walls, gates and 24-hour surveillance systems, the Joseph Rowntree Foundation, a development charity, has turned two council-owned tower blocks into gated communities, complete with high fences, an intercom system and a concierge (Oaff, 2003). Meanwhile, the 2002 film *Panic Room* reflected a growing demand among affluent homeowners for indoor bunkers capable of withstanding biological, chemical and armed attack. These rooms contain a panic button to alert police, and internal CCTV monitors to allow the homeowner to view the rest of the property without risk. Although mostly found in the US, the *Observer* reports that in the UK demand is growing from businessmen, celebrities and diplomats who hail from politically volatile countries (Townsend, 2002).

There is little doubt that surveillance technologies have radically destabilized the public/private boundary, and no other issue has generated public disquiet about surveillance to the extent that fears about loss of privacy have (Lyon, 2001). Yet it is frequently claimed that, in the wake of the terrorist attacks on America in September 2001, the climate of political and public acceptability became more favourable to the idea of surveillance. For example, many governments are investigating or are on the verge of introducing identity cards. 'Smart' ID cards can hold a wide range of coded data, and could incorporate national identity card, driver's licence, health details, passport information and e-cash applications as well as eye scans or thumbprints. In the UK, as elsewhere, identity cards are presented by government as a panacea to the problems of illegal immigration, crime and terrorism. It is often assumed that technological progress has made it much more difficult for those with 'spoiled' (that is, criminal or illegal) identities to hide the unfavourable elements of their past, and that identity cards would ensure that goods and services would be allocated on the basis of entitlement (Finch, 2003; cf. Goffman, 1963). However, two somewhat contradictory issues must be borne in mind. First, it has never been easier to 'fabricate a more acceptable self' (Finch, 2003: 93). Identity theft has become a growing problem, exacerbated by the ease with which it can be achieved via the Internet (2003; Jewkes, 2003b). As Finch notes, the 'carceral network' of documentation 'fixing' the identity of the individual is, in some senses, subverted by the Internet which offers the identity thief a 'plethora of "new" identities to "try on"' (2003: 96). Furthermore, a relatively high-integrity identity can be constructed by accumulating a collection of relatively low-integrity documentation (Clarke, 1994; Finch, 2003; Stalder and Lyon, 2003). Many forms of identification can be bought via the Internet, including fake passports, driving licences, birth certificates, electronic PINs and credit card numbers (Finch, 2003; Jewkes, 2003b). As Stalder and Lyon observe, no matter how sophisticated an ID card is, it is only as reliable as the document on which it is based. Administrative identity may be established by reference to a series of documents, but the reliability of the final document, the ID card, will be defined by the weakest link in this chain of references. If a person possesses a convincing counterfeit birth certificate, they can acquire an ID card which will duplicate whatever information happens to be on this certificate. In addition, the scope for bribing officials to issue a genuine document in the knowledge that it contains incorrect information makes these systems much more vulnerable than their 'high-tech dazzle might suggest' (Stalder and Lyon, 2003: 84).

The second point to be considered is that not all criminals and terrorists have spoiled identities. Even a relatively sophisticated ID system could not have prevented the terrorist attacks on the Pentagon and World Trade Center from taking place in September 2001:

> Most of the 'terrorists' had valid visas and no criminal record of any sort. All three checks that ID cards can perform – verifying the legitimacy of the document, verifying the link between the person, and conducting a quick background check against a list of suspects – would have turned up negative because the documents were legitimate and most of the individuals were not on suspect lists. Terrorists, particularly the ones willing to kill themselves in the attack, belong to a special class of criminal. They rarely have prior convictions, thus background checks are rarely revealing. There are no repeat suicide bombers. (Stalder and Lyon, 2003: 85)

These shortcomings have done nothing to thwart the seemingly relentless drive by governments to oversee and regulate the activities of their citizens and, although surveillance as security has many and varied applications, it is state surveillance that remains of greatest concern to many commentators. While current fears about terrorism may have mollified the general public into accepting a greater degree of surveillance (and there is no convincing evidence that this is the case), many political commentators, human rights campaigners and civil liberties organizations have expressed extreme disquiet about the licence that governments take in unstable times. Certainly it is true that remote sensing and monitoring are no longer the exclusive privilege of state authorities and, indeed, Orwell's emphasis on the state as the agent of surveillance might now seem rather limited in an age where both state and non-state, central and local, institutions monitor populations (Haggerty and Ericson, 2000). For example, there was a political furore in 2002 when the British Home Secretary announced plans to permit every local authority and a number of other public bodies access to phone, e-mail and Internet data; powers that previously had been uniquely held by the police, M15, M16, GCHQ, Customs and Excise and the Inland Revenue. The fact that the government was forced to withdraw the plan in favour of one that allows for the retention of data by Internet Service Providers, may do little to allay the fears of those who believe that the Regulation of Investigatory Powers Act 2000 (RIPA) (www.hmso.gov.uk/acts/acts2000) already makes Britain the most surveilled country in Europe.

Other voices of dissent have been directed at 'Echelon', an intelligent search agent that was developed in the 1960s and is run by the US National Security Agency (NSA) and the UK Government Communications Headquarters (GCHQ). Echelon intercepts and monitors traffic on commercial communications satellites and essentially is a sophisticated 'eavesdropping' device. Justified on grounds of terrorism and crime, it has, however, been found to routinely intercept valuable private commercial data (Hamelink, 2000). In addition, 'sniffer' devices called 'Carnivores' have been installed at several internet service providers (ISPs) to monitor e-mail traffic and, if an address corresponds to a 'suspect' address, the contents of the e-mail are automatically extracted and forwarded to the FBI. While many see this as an infringement of civil liberties, in practice it is not difficult to outwit these kinds of systems. Organized criminals and terrorists use sophisticated encryption techniques, but anyone can outrun the intelligence agencies by simply changing their e-mail address frequently (Campbell, 2000). Moreover, not everyone feels secure in the knowledge that state authorities have this level of power to monitor the communications and movements of individuals, not least because they singularly failed to identify and act on a known threat to America in September 2001 (Jewkes, 2003b). More worrying for many is the ongoing 'war on terror' being waged in the wake of the attacks on New York and Washington. American governments have a long and troubled history of defining deviants, miscreants and people displaying the 'wrong kind' of patriotism, and post-9/11 fears that persons with 'Arab' or 'Muslim' backgrounds might be among the primary targets of intensive surveillance at airports or border checkpoints have not receded (Lyon, 2003; cf. Lyon, 2001: Chapter 6 for a detailed examination of the dominance of the American NSA in global surveillance strategies).

Of course, surveillance does not necessarily rely on technology. The disciplinary and repressive character of the Panopticon was exemplified by its ability to influence behaviour and transform selves. Using only a fairly primitive lighting system the panoptic prison engendered a climate of fear and paranoia. History shows that the most oppressive political regimes do not necessarily require high-tech methods to achieve the same aim. For example, the Romanian dictator Nicolae Ceaucescu (who ruled between 1965 and 1989, when he and his wife were overthrown and executed) created a culture of enforced eavesdropping that effectively amounted to a total surveillance society. Similarly, following the 'liberation' of Iraq from Saddam Hussein's control in 2003, the British media reported how the Iraqi leader created an equally low-tech climate of fear. For over two decades, the Iraqi people were encouraged to inform on their friends, relatives and neighbours, and Saddam's secret police routinely used rudimentary forms of torture to ensure that self-imposed censorship was upheld. But for some, the monitoring of communications by governments in the West is no more lawful for all its high-tech gloss and covert methods. As communications intelligence has moved its operations from narcotics trafficking, money laundering and terrorism to intercepting 'ordinary' citizens' personal and commercial telex messages, mobile phone communications, e-mails and Internet traffic, notions of what is 'acceptable' in the interests of security are once again coming under scrutiny.*

Profit

One of the most significant drives behind the expansion of surveillance comes from the companies who manufacture the hardware and software, many of which were once suppliers of military equipment, but have had to adapt to a changing global market. As the technology becomes more sophisticated, the commercial market for surveillance equipment sets to grow even further, with manufacturers of biometric access controls and facial recognition software among the most profitable. CCTV systems also remain big business. It is estimated that there are currently 2.8 million CCTV cameras operating in the UK (although McCahill and Norris, 2003, put the figure as high as 4.25 million), and the security market here is currently valued at £2,744 million (Ball, 2003). In the 1990s, the government invested 75 per cent of its crime prevention budget in CCTV schemes (2003) and in the 10 years to 2002 committed over a quarter of a billion pounds of public money to its expansion through the City Challenge Competition and Crime Reduction Programmes (Norris, 2003). Further money

---

*Also of interest in this context is Gilliom's (2001) comment that the elaborate computerized system for those on welfare in the US has supplanted rather than replaced the traditional system of 'rat calls' as a means of gleaning information. In the UK, the government regularly run television advertisements encouraging viewers to inform the Department of Social Security if they suspect someone of being a 'dole cheat'.

comes from partnerships between local authorities and businesses who contribute towards the running costs of 'public' schemes that help protect private property and public space. In total, it has been estimated that around £3 billion has been spent on the installation and maintenance of CCTV systems, excluding the monitoring costs associated with them (2003).

The drive for profit has social implications. As indicated earlier, the image of surveillance that occupies the popular consciousness frequently resembles an Orwellian dystopia where a compliant population is controlled by an invisible totalitarian power. Interestingly, in *Nineteen Eighty Four* it is the upper and middle classes who come under the intense scrutiny of the 'thought police'; the working-class masses, or 'proles', were perceived as much less of a threat, and were largely left to their own devices (Haggerty and Ericson, 2000). However, when Foucault (1977) developed his vision of surveillance as a form of hierarchical social control, he emphasized the power that panoptic surveillance techniques had over the masses, stating that surveillance did more than observe and monitor people. For Foucault, panoptic surveillance targets the soul, hegemonically disciplining the working populace into a form of self-regulation designed to meet the requirements of the developing factory system (Haggerty and Ericson, 2000). Taking a different view, Bauman (1992) has argued that surveillance is becoming less about discipline and repression, and more to do with classifying individuals according to their conspicuous wealth and consumption patterns, seducing those deemed 'desirable' into the market economy. There are two potential outcomes of this process. First, surveillance can be used to construct and monitor consumption patterns in order that detailed consumer profiles can be put together. These profiles can then be used to predict future consumption habits, lure customers to a rival organization, or even encourage people to buy items they may not otherwise have purchased, on the basis that they fit in with a pre-existing aspect of their lives. The second, related consequence is that surveillance can be used to differentiate between populations, limiting the movements of some on the basis of their identity profiles, consumption habits or spending power. The meeting of certain criteria might then determine anything from preferential credit ratings to rapid movement through customs (Haggerty and Ericson, 2000).

These processes combine to create what Gandy (1993) terms the 'panoptic sort'; a situation in which individuals are continuously identified, assessed and sorted into hierarchies which are then used to manage and control their access to goods and services. Furthermore, they have taken place against a backdrop of changes that have resulted in the supremacy of conspicuous consumption and the commodification of the city. No longer are Western cities characterized by industrialization and an emphasis on welfare. Now big budgets are made available for advertising the virtues of cities, and the role of CCTV has been recast as not simply a means of deterring criminals, but also as a friendly eye in the sky promoting the 'feel good factor' for those who work, visit or are at leisure there (McCahill and Norris, 2002). At the same time, shopping centres or malls have become the cathedrals of the age, the monuments to an era, in just the same way as train stations were in the Victorian age, and castles and defensive city walls in a much earlier epoch (Shields, 1992). And like these previous embodiments of cultural priorities, the shopping mall says much about how power and privilege are secured in everyday practices and behaviour as populations are assessed, divided and categorized on the basis of whether they look like legitimate consumers or not. In order to better understand these processes, and the role of surveillance in them, it is instructive to combine sociological and criminological approaches with contributions from other fields. Like other recent publications (Bannister et al., 1998; McCahill and Norris, 2002; McCahill, 2003), the following analysis will draw on urban geography, but its primary reference point will be the cultural studies literature on consumption.

The genealogy of shopping centres can be traced back to the luxury arcades built for the European upper classes in the 19th century (Shields, 1992), although malls as we know them today, with familiar stores selling mass produced goods, first appeared in Western societies in the 1970s and 1980s. Built on out-of-town sites, typically at motorway junctions and near large centres of population, these developments frequently resulted in an almost immediate dereliction of many town and city centres. Poverty became more visible than it had been for half a century as the homeless and unemployed came out of the urban shadows and dark slums and demanded access to the new 'glittering shopping paradises' (Christie, 1993: 66). Their reason for visiting these paradises was not to purchase goods, for their economic status precluded them from doing so. If they were young, their desire was to hang out, to see and be seen. If they were old or poor, their aim was more likely to be to escape from the weather and enter the cool or warmth of the heated/air-conditioned, controlled atmosphere (Fiske, 1989; Bocock, 1993). Many may simply have yearned to be part of a crowd, to feel the tactile pleasure of 'belonging', and – ironically – to escape the surveillance of others; for example, parents and teachers in the case of adolescents, the police and other 'officials' empowered to move them on in the case of vagrants and the homeless. But while shopping malls were constructed as palaces of consumption they were, from the start, designed with a darker touch of the panoptic prison where visibility and surveillance prevailed (Langman, 1992; Shields, 1992).

A number of writers have adopted de Certeau's cultural theories of everyday life to develop this theme. For example, Langman combines de Certeau's belief that subjectivity and power are to be found in routine consumption practices with a Foucauldian critique of the Panopticon. He notes that the mall's primary defining characteristic is that it is an enclosed aggregation more or less isolated from the larger environment. Moreover, within its boundaries, everything, from temperature to the movement of people and the shop displays, is rigorously controlled to permit consumption of an unending stream of spectacles. In other words, in the mall control is subtle and multifarious. Not only is it evident in the CCTV cameras and other security measures, but it is manifest in the scrupulous organization of spatial settings and the allocation of fantasy and pleasure (Langman, 1992; cf. de Certeau, 1984).

Developing this theme beyond panopticism, Fiske (1989) argues that shopping malls, and the cultural practices that take place within them, are key sites of struggle at both economic and ideological levels. Also influenced by de Certeau, Fiske notes that within these cathedrals of capitalism, the weak create their own 'spaces', inflicting damage on the strategic interests of the powerful. De Certeau (1984) uses the language of warfare, arguing that subordinates are like guerrillas, appropriating space as a means of resistance; an apt metaphor for the 'mall rats' who gather in shopping centres. Presdee also elaborates on this subject in his study of unemployed youth in a South Australian town, 80 per cent of whom visit the local shopping mall at least once a week, aggressively 'invading the space' of those with a legitimate right to be there (Presdee, 1986: 13). These 'outsiders' are tricking the system, consuming images, warmth and places of consumerism, without any intention of buying its commodities. At the same time, they offend 'real' consumers and security personnel by asserting their difference within, and different use of, the glittering palaces (Presdee, 1986; Fiske, 1989). Presdee's research details the various ways in which the young unemployed appropriate the space for subversive performance and resistance, including illegal drinking, provoking security guards and crowding round shop windows, preventing 'real' customers from seeing the displays or entering the stores. Little wonder, then, that the 'policing' of malls has become progressively more rigid and uncompromising in recent years, a trend that has been assisted by the almost universal introduction of CCTV cameras into retail environments. And as we have already seen, 'policing' in this context must be viewed in its broadest sense. The desire to remove 'undesirables' from shopping centres may be primarily a decision made by the mall owners and rent-payers rather than the police force: 'the malls are there to make profits, to sell goods and services, not to provide environments for "deviants" who refuse to spend or who cannot afford to spend' (Bocock, 1993: 107).

The drive to exclude some individuals from certain public spaces raises questions about the kind of society that is left as a result. There is a danger that the moral engineer has replaced the social engineer (Stenson, 2001) as 'difference' is eliminated and those who do not conform are displaced to the dark, and often dangerous, corners of the city where their capacity to 'convey a negative image' is less material (Norris and Armstrong, 1999: 45). Numerous writers have drawn on themes of cleanliness and dirt in attempting to characterize the ordering of contemporary public spaces. For example, Mulgan (1989) describes how CCTV is used to purify space of the homeless and alcoholics in order to create a convivial atmosphere for those who conform to the demands of the consumerist environment. Lyon (2003: 22) further notes that the poor are 'cleaned away' from cities for tourism. Meanwhile Bauman (1997: 14) refers to the 'new impure' who are prevented from responding to the enticements of the consumer market and are thus dismissed as 'the dirt of post-modern purity' (cf. McCahill and Norris, 2002). These analogies recall the work of anthropologist Mary Douglas, who argues that the elimination of 'dirt' is a positive effort to organize the environment; dirt invites social control because it is perceived as a threat to order. There has also been, in recent years, a more literal manifestation of this idea, with restrictions in many city centres on litter dropping, alcohol consumption, smoking and traffic. McCahill further notes that in the city centre shopping mall he observed, banned activities included walking a dog, pushing a bicycle, eating, sitting on the floor and lying down. When CCTV operatives observed these kinds of behaviours, a patrol guard would be deployed to request that the miscreant 'position their body in a way conducive to the commercial image of the mall' (McCahill, 2002: 128). In this respect, the flawed consumers who come under surveillance in shopping malls are, quite simply, 'matter out of place' (Douglas, 1966: 2).

Voyeurism and entertainment

While many commentators argue that recent developments in systems of surveillance and social control have augmented an intensification of panopticism (where the few observe the many), an emerging theme in the sociological and criminological literature on surveillance has been that of *'synopticism'* (where the many observe the few) (Mathiesen, 1997; Boyne, 2000; McCahill, 2003). As McCahill notes, the trend towards synopticism is evident in the development of the mass media, and is exemplified by the 'reality television' boom that has taken place in recent years. With reference to Mathiesen's (1997) notion of the 'viewer society' in which panopticism is intimately fused with synopticism in a process that simultaneously permits both top-down scrutiny by authority figures and bottom-up observation by the masses, McCahill (2003) argues that television shows such as *Big Brother* and its many imitators are both panoptic and synoptic. In other words, these programmes are designed to allow the few to see the many (the programme producers in the studio gallery who observe the activities of the contestants 24-hours a day), while simultaneously and synoptically allowing millions of viewers to watch both participants and, occasionally, the 'watchers' themselves. Synopticism has also been accelerated by the proliferation of video cameras, which have led to a number of instances where members of the public have filmed events that were not 'meant' to be seen, and then sold the footage to national television networks for broadcast around the world. For some, this is the essence of synopticism's appeal: 'surveillance footage represents one of the crudest satisfactions of the scopophilic drive, a sense of power at being privileged to see that which was meant to remain unseen: the point at which the private ... goes public' (Dovey, 1996: 127).

In fact, the drive is not only to look, but to be looked at. In the 21st century, to be watched elicits a positive as well as a negative response, a synoptic development which suggests that CCTV and camcorder footage is as much about entertainment as it is control (Leishman and Mason, 2003). In addition, the 'reality TV' genre that surveillance and camcorder technologies have given rise to has revolutionized television. Where television documentaries and news-based programmes were once 'normal, safe, middle class and secure', surveillance footage of serious and spectacular crimes as they happen have taken these formats into the realm of the extraordinary, the 'raw' and the dangerous (Dovey, 1996: 129).

Other media genres similarly exploit the information and entertainment potential of surveillance technologies. As we saw in Chapter 6, CCTV clips are an increasingly integral component of news broadcasts and interactive programmes like *Crimewatch UK*, as well as light entertainment shows such as *Police! Camera! Action!* and *Rogue Traders*. In the postmodern quest for the hyperreal, the desire to be part of the 'action' may be satisfied by the ability to see it played out as it was caught on camera. Although clearly a more second-hand experience than actually being there, it may constitute the 'next best thing'; or arguably the 'best thing' in so far as one can 'witness' a criminal, dangerous or spectacular event from the safety of one's home. Not only do news programmes, documentaries and populist entertainment shows routinely make use of both CCTV and domestic video footage of everything from high-speed police car chases to air disasters, but there is a burgeoning trade for such material on video and on the Internet. Newspapers also use stories involving CCTV footage to fill their pages. In a study of three British newspapers, McCahill (2003) finds that CCTV constitutes a 'good news story' because it illustrates many of the key journalistic news criteria and 'adds value' to already newsworthy stories. As we saw in Chapter 2 the mass media frequently deal in binary oppositions, and McCahill finds that this is no less true in the reporting of CCTV-related stories than any other news event. He discovers that the central discursive reporting strategy is that of a polarization between 'respectable' or 'powerful' targets of CCTV and deviant 'others'. The press have thus created an 'us' and 'them' divide, with 'us' embodied by the figure of the modern motorist at the mercy of the most expansive network of speed cameras in Europe and being hammered unfairly by a revenue-hungry government, and 'them' being the legitimate targets for surveillance; muggers, robbers, terrorists and the like.

So, surveillance is a common theme in mediated culture. Indeed, in a wide ranging analysis of this subject, Gary Marx (1995) considers the extent to which art, science fiction, comic books, jokes and cartoons, film, advertising and popular music have anticipated and even inspired surveillance systems and their applications (the *James Bond* films, *Star Trek* and *Spider Man* are just a few of the examples credited with this; the latter is said to have spurred a judge in New Mexico to implement the first judicial use of electronic location monitoring equipment!). Marx suggests that these cultural materials can further help us understand surveillance by providing an alternative language of visual metaphors (for example, Sting's 'classic' pop song 'Every Breath You Take' offers a plethora of metaphors for omnipresent and omnipotent surveillance; 1995: 114). They remind us that the meaning of surveillance is contested and is often about power (Charlie Chaplin's 1927 film *Modern Times* contains surveillance themes to illustrate the relationship between controller and controlled, manager and worker). Many cultural artefacts convey the profound ambivalence of our culture toward surveillance technologies which can both protect and violate (take two Bob Dylan songs – 'Subterranean Home Sick Blues' and 'Talkin' John Birch Paranoid Blues' – by way of example). Yet we can often see that the meaning is not in the object but in the context and in how it is interpreted (most people would agree that the song 'Santa Claus is Coming to Town' – Santa knows where you are sleeping, he knows when you're awake, he knows if you've been bad or good, so be good for goodness sake' – is an illustration of benign panopticism). There is, as several commentators have observed, nothing inherently threatening or sinister in the technology itself (Pratt, 2002; Lyon, 2003). Finally, cultural material raises new questions for social research, such as: what is the effect of popular media creating an environment that welcomes, tolerates or opposes new surveillance? Does constant media exposure normalize, routinize, domesticate or trivialize surveillance? (Marx, 1995: 106ff).

Marx reminds us that cultural material must be viewed against the backdrop of the times, and a detailed analysis such as his can tell us much about technological evolution and public attitudes to surveillance. For example, Hitchcock's dark depiction of **voyeuristic** surveillance, *Rear Window* (1954), was released at the height of the Cold War when a climate of suspicion prevailed and people distrusted even their neighbours. The television series *The Prisoner* (1967) was broadcast at a time when fears about technological progression collided with the ubiquity of the gadget-laden secret agent in popular fiction, television and cinema. Following the period of McCarthyism when political attention was directed toward the enemy within, as opposed to the enemy without, *The Prisoner* both reflected this theme and anticipated the impending Watergate scandal, perfectly encapsulating the escalating conspiracy theories of the period. More recently, films such as Spielberg's *Minority Report* (2002) reflect current developments in face and eye recognition techniques, as well as underlying concerns about the potential applications of new surveillance technologies. Set in a police state, circa 2054, *Minority Report* seamlessly combines current allegiances to proactive crime strategies with an equally contemporary faith in 'new age' prescience to raise questions about the ethics of taking predictions as 'facts' (a point that brings to mind the newly-proposed charge of 'grooming', which is causing concern among civil liberties groups because it is designed to target adults who meet a child after contact has been made on the Internet but *before* any offence has taken place; this 'real life' example raises the same question as Spielberg's movie, that is, whether *thinking* about criminal acts is the same as committing them: Jewkes, 2003c).

In short, perhaps what Marx's analysis demonstrates most forcefully is that over the last century, surveillance has been consistently viewed, at best, with ambivalence, and at worst with paranoia and hostility; indeed, all the examples discussed link oppression and exploitation with technologies of seeing. Surveillance technologies and their uses may have evolved to an extent that George Orwell could only have nightmares about, but the sentiments with which they are viewed by society at large show a significant degree of cultural continuity (Marx, 2002).

From the Panopticon to surveillant assemblage and back again

Of course, these categories – control of the body, governance, security, profit and entertainment – are far from mutually exclusive. A brief consideration of recent developments in workplace surveillance serves to illustrate the constitutive nature of surveillance rationales. Originally justified by the fear of external threats, surveillance technologies have inevitably been turned inwards, and workers in a wide range of employment sectors now come under the scrutiny of their managers. The notion of trust – once regarded as an essential element of the management–staff relationship – has arguably been displaced by surveillance systems which are now in regular use to deter theft, monitor areas that were previously the responsibility of supervisors, assess training needs, ensure that the correct organizational procedures are followed, monitor compliance with health and safety regulations, check that goods are not being damaged during loading and unloading procedures, observe workers taking unauthorized breaks, and encourage punctual time-keeping (cf. McCahill, 2002: 153 ff.). In all these practices, the governance–security–profit alliance can be discerned in various guises and formations. Moreover, it is not just employees, but also *potential* employees who are vulnerable to forms of surveillance. As I discuss elsewhere (Jewkes, 2003a), there now exists software capable of sifting through any written communication and spotting when the writer is lying or confused about the facts. One of the potential applications of this high-tech lie detector is for companies to recognize embellished or false CVs, which they can then reject on principles very closely aligned to the governance–security–profit motives discussed above.

But it is arguably surveillance that targets the body as an object to be monitored and controlled that is most alarming to the majority of employees. Examples of surveillance technologies that are being introduced in work environments around the world are toilet bowls that automatically check for drugs and CCTV cameras in cubicles that then film the people who test positive, sensors monitoring whether workers wash their hands after visiting the washroom, smart badges that track employees' movements, high-tech clocking-on procedures, and various 'Big Brother' systems that check the performance quality of staff in call centres and other telephone-based work environments – including the number of calls taken and the number of calls with a 'successful' outcome in a given time period (Hamelink, 2000; Jewkes, 2003a). Even more insidious are the workplace surveillance systems that monitor employees' presentation of self; for example, ensuring that service industry workers are always smiling and using appropriate body language. In these circumstances, the employee becomes the 'bearer of their own surveillance' and the panoptic model is once again recalled:

> In the enclosed and controlled setting of the workplace CCTV can easily become an instrument of disciplinary power exercised through the architecture of the panopticon, allowing management to see everything without ever being seen themselves … In the name of 'customer service' employees' gestures, facial expressions and body language all become subject to the disciplinary gaze … The anticipatory conformity that this induces in employees who recognize that they are always potentially under surveillance presents management with an extremely powerful managerial tool. (McCahill, 2002: 162–3)

And if there seems little voyeuristic entertainment value in these workplace examples, consider the case in 1996 of the Australian police officers caught on camera having sex, drinking alcohol and taking drugs while at work, a series of misdemeanours made more embarrassing by the fact that they were subsequently broadcast on several television networks in Australia and round the world. Or closer to home is the case of Claire Swire who, in July 2001, was severely reprimanded by her employer when she sent a risqué message from her work e-mail address to her boyfriend at a different company. In a short space of time the offending e-mail was forwarded to an estimated 10 million people, several of whom were themselves disciplined or suspended from work; a series of personal misfortunes that inspired a BBC television series called *E-mails You Wish You'd Never Sent.*

'Big Brother' or 'Brave New World'?: some concluding thoughts

Much of this chapter has been concerned with the ways in which surveillance systems are bound up with wider relations of power and discipline, reinforcing existing inequalities along traditional lines of class, gender, ethnicity and age. This stance is in line with most critical criminologists who have been generally sceptical (if not downright hostile) to the idea that surveillance technologies liberate, empower and comfort the general citizenry. The panoptic model of top-down scrutiny is exemplified by Coleman and Sim's (2000) analysis of CCTV in Liverpool city centre, in which the authors argue that the gaze of the surveillance camera is turned almost continuously downward on those who are already disenfranchised. By contrast, they say, there is a virtual absence of 'upward' surveillance of the powerful, 'whose often socially detrimental and harmful activities remain effectively beyond scrutiny and regulation' (2000: 637). While this may be true of CCTV, it cannot be said of surveillance more generally; indeed, those most subject to many forms of surveillance are the most privileged who use credit cards, mobile phones and computers (Marx, 2002). Several commentators have taken exception to the idea that the powerful are exempt from the watchful gaze and argue that power does not entirely reside in the hands of those at or near the top of social and occupational hierarchies. Haggerty and Ericson (2000: 617) concede that the targeting of surveillance *is* differential, but assert that it has nonetheless 'transformed hierarchies of observation', allowing for the scrutiny of the powerful by both institutions and the general population. Examples of 'bottom-up' surveillance include the introduction of CCTV systems into police custody suites and cells, allowing the activities of custody officers to come under just as much scrutiny as those of the inmates (Newburn and Hayman, 2001), and the global proliferation of video cameras that has resulted in numerous recordings of police brutality and government abuses of human rights (Dovey, 1996). In addition, it has been suggested that surveillance contributes to 'the political pluralism central to democracy by making ... [its] tools ... widely available so that citizens and competing groups can *use them against each other*, as well as government, to enhance accountability' (Marx, 2002: 22, emphasis added). Dovey (1996: 126) expands on this notion of 'lateral, intrasocial surveillance', noting that police issue members of Neighbourhood Watch groups with camcorders, neighbours film each other's anti-social behaviour to use as evidence in court, and parents surveil their kids for drug abuse. Returning to a familiar theme, he says: 'here's a panopticon where the warders in the all-seeing tower can go home, safe in the knowledge that the inmates are all busy trying to record each others' misdemeanours on video tape' (1996: 126).

It is not just bottom-up or lateral surveillance that may enhance due process, fairness and legitimacy (Marx, 2002). Those who operate conventional top-down

CCTV systems have also been known to resist the 'higher' authority of the police in a show of solidarity with their subjects. McCahill notes that many of the security personnel in the shopping centre he observed were from the same part of town as the people they spent their days observing and monitoring; they went to school together, played on the same football team, knew each other's families. This degree of familiarity between the observers and the observed is interesting for three reasons. First, it endorses Gillespie and McLaughlin's (2002) findings (discussed in the previous chapter) that a less punitive attitude to 'offenders' is adopted when a 'deeper knowledge' of their background is known. Second, it challenges the notion implicit in the moral panic thesis that exaggerated public responses to deviants are magnified when the perceived threat is 'close to home' (see Chapter 3). Third, the fact that watchers and watched are known to each other inevitably places limits on the disciplinary potential of the surveillance systems:

> [Some] security officers are not always willing to co-operate with the police. For instance, the local beat officer has given the security person-nel a list of 'wanted' persons and asked them to give him a ring ... if they see any of these suspects on camera. However, whether or not this infor-mation reaches the beat officer depends upon the degree of familiarity between the security officers and the local 'surveilled' population ... Recall, for example, the security officer who said, 'I wouldn't grass ... on Tommo 'cause he's all right, he's never given me any bother. Anyway, he's off the smack now'. (McCahill, 2002: 199)

Even in the workplace, the notion of surveillance as panopticism is not univer-sally endorsed. Zureik (2003: 44 ff.) summarizes several studies that challenge the view that all surveillance by managers of workers is exploitative and disem-powering. One report, by Mason et al. (2000), provides evidence from several work environments to support their argument that both workers and unions generally accept surveillance as an extension of traditional monitoring in the workplace, and have no problems with it as long as it is transparent, based on collective agreement, and does not contravene the law (cited in Zureik, 2003). In fact, many workers welcome the 'electronic supervisor' because it provides protection against unfair work distribution, violence and bullying, and accusa-tions of negligence or poor productivity. On the whole, though, a distinction is drawn between surveillance of work, and surveillance of the worker, with only the former being deemed acceptable (Marx, 1999). For example, a report from the Office of the Data Protection Commissioner (2000: 28) recommends that monitoring should not violate trust nor be excessive and 'should not intrude unnecessarily on employees' privacy and autonomy' (cited in Zureik, 2003). Marx believes that this recommendation is not being heeded by many employers, and that the 'information-gathering net' is constantly expanding to encompass aspects of workers' private lives, personal characteristics, appearance and so on. Genetic testing and screening are being introduced into the workplace to allow employers to assess the behavioural dispositions of potential employees and their propensity to certain illnesses. Because they claim to rely on precise scientific evidence, they have been characterized as 'total surveillance' (Regan, 1996: 23); a feature that makes these forms of surveillance qualitatively different to the CCTV cameras and their operators in McCahill's English shopping centre.

It might be argued, then, that discussions of surveillance have a tendency to flatten the terrain of power, control and the role of individuals in social systems, and that a more finely nuanced approach is required. The Panopticon has been a useful metaphor for the notion of surveillance as social control and has given rise to several theoretical developments of the original concept: synopticism (Mathiesen, 1997), 'super-panopticism' (Poster, 1990) and 'post-panopticism' (Boyne, 2000) to name a few. But the main limitation of the panoptic thesis is that it overstates the power of systems, institutions and processes and underplays the importance of the individual actor. The human element is often forgotten or ignored (a response known as 'technological determinism'), but as Lyon reminds us, socio-technical surveillance systems are 'affected by people complying with, negotiating, or resisting surveillance' (Lyon, 2003: 14). One of the foremost commentators on surveillance and social sorting, Lyon has always argued that surveillance is ambiguous and that technologies which permit surveillance can be positive and beneficial, enabling new levels of mobility, efficiency, productivity, convenience and comfort. In the contemporary everyday world of telephone transactions, Internet surfing, affordable domestic as well as international air travel, street-level security and work, the metaphors of Big Brother and the Panopticon may indeed seem increasingly less relevant. What is more, a general ethos of self-surveillance is encouraged by the availability of home testing kits and do-it-yourself health checks, allowing people to test for alcohol level, pregnancy, AIDS and hereditary or potentially fatal medical conditions (Marx, 2002). Such innovations empower people and offer them personal choice (for example, whether to have a child if there is risk of it being born with a congenital illness) on an unprecedented scale.

The subject of surveillance thus remains contradictory and contested. In the pursuit of the goals discussed in this chapter – control, governance, security, profit and voyeuristic entertainment – surveillance would seem to go hand in hand with suspicion, segregation and, occasionally, seduction. But as Pratt points out, most of us barely notice the extent to which we are at the centre of a surveillance society, so easily have we internalized the changes in our conduct (using swipe cards instead of keys to access our workplaces, banking by telephone or computer rather than 'in person' and so on). And to take two examples from the same area of experience: speed cameras on roads have become as 'normal' to us today as global positioning systems (GPS) fitted inside every car to trigger automatic payments for speeding, use of 'toll roads' and so on, may tomorrow ('Black box in car to trap speed drivers', *Observer*, 3 August 2003: 1). What is clear is that, like any technological innovation, surveillance must be viewed as part of a network of systems that operate within a wider context of political, cultural and economic shifts, the long-term trajectory of which remains uncertain. Dystopia or utopia? In the words of the other (Channel 4) Big Brother – you decide!

Summary

- The exponential growth of surveillance techniques in most areas of contemporary life have led some commentators to suggest that the primary advantage of technological advancement is the potential that arises for risk management at a distance. Discussions of surveillance have been dominated by pessimistic images of 'Big Brother' and the Panopticon, metaphors that have helped to perpetuate the notion that surveillance technologies are linked to insidious and repressive forms of regulation and social control. However, in recent years the idea of the 'Synopticon' has emerged to challenge this cynical and despairing view. Views of surveillance systems are now split between those who hold that technologies such as CCTV constrain people's activities, restrict their behaviour, and are used to regulate demonized 'others', and those who characterize surveillance as essentially liberating and democratizing.
- It has been suggested that we are increasingly witnessing the convergence of once disconnected systems to the point that we can now speak of a 'surveillant assemblage' (Haggerty and Ericson, 2000). The systems of discipline and domination that make up this convergence of once discrete systems are driven by five principal motives: control of the body, governance, security, profit and entertainment, all of which have significant social and cultural implications. An analysis of surveillance in the workplace has served to illustrate these motives *in situ*, and has demonstrated the arguments for and against the regulation and monitoring of individuals.
- The subject of surveillance remains an ideological battleground, but whatever view one takes of its purposes and outcomes, it must be remembered that technologies such as CCTV do not exist in a cultural vacuum, and are inextricably entwined with the human motives, values and behaviour of both observers and observed.

STUDY QUESTIONS

1 Due to limitations of space this chapter has only discussed in detail a few of the systems and practices that can broadly be defined as 'surveillance'. How many other applications of surveillance (in both its guises as coded data collection and visual monitoring) can you identify in contemporary Britain?

2 Gary Marx (1995) demonstrates that surveillance motifs are pervasive in popular culture. They range from themes of erotic fantasy (of secret watching) to political paranoia about the 'enemy within'. What are the impacts of the widespread cultural treatment of surveillance as entertainment on the public at large? Do they help to 'normalize' surveillance and make it acceptable, or do they increase public fears and anxieties about crime?

3 The UK DNA database currently stores over two million profiles, but there are discussions about whether it should be extended. What are the pros and cons of keeping samples taken from the entire population on a national DNA database? Would such a move reduce discrimination (as has been argued by Sir Alec Jeffreys, the UK scientist who discovered genetic fingerprinting) or might it create 'at risk' categories which reinforce racial and ethnic stereotypes (Nelkin and Andrews, 2003)?

4 From your reading of this subject, would you say that on the whole, surveillance systems empower or constrain?

FURTHER READING

All the chapters in Lyon's *Surveillance As Social Sorting* (2003) are worth reading. Of particular note is the chapter by Nelkin and Andrews ('Surveillance creep in the genetic age'), which charts the expansion of DNA testing and banking and discusses some of the ethical problems that arise from the increasing reliance on DNA as a form of identification. Lyon has himself written extensively on the subject of surveillance. See, for example: *The Information Society* (Polity, 1988); *The Electronic Eye: The Rise of Surveillance Society* (Polity); and *Surveillance Society: Monitoring Everyday Life* (Open University Press, 2001). Norris, C. and Armstrong, G. (1999) *The Maximum Surveillance Society: The Rise of CCTV* (Berg) is excellent, as is McCahill, M. (2002) *The Surveillance Web: The Rise of Visual Surveillance in an English City* (Willan). Bogard, W. (1996) *The Simulation of Surveillance* (Cambridge) is a fascinating discussion that takes the subject of surveillance beyond the concrete and into the realms of the hyperreal, but it is theoretically sophisticated and is perhaps therefore to be recommended for advanced level study.

Finally, Bright, M. 'They're watching you', in Y. Jewkes and G. Letherby (2002) sheds further light on some of the surveillance technologies most commonly used in workplaces. There is now an e-journal devoted to surveillance, which can be found at www.urbaneye.net, and *Crime, Media, Culture: An International Journal* also embraces new research on surveillance technologies as well as other 'new' and alternative media.

Stigmatization, Sentimentalization and Sanctification: Concluding Thoughts

Although ostensibly a book about the relationship between media and crime, this volume has touched on many wider issues which continually circulate in media discourse and partially define contemporary British society – among them, the sexual exploitation of children, the different cultural responses to men and women who kill, racism and bigotry within the police, and the threat of the 'outsider'. This latter concern is perceived as sufficiently troubling to legitimate the demonization of certain individuals and groups – on the basis of age, ethnicity, style and a range of other, usually visible, indicators – and to justify the repressive surveillance of public spaces. The examples discussed throughout the book indicate a clear selectiveness in the mediated constitution of offenders and offences as well as victims who capture the public imagination. In our increasingly individualized culture, where offending is regarded as the inflicting of harms by some individuals onto other individuals, mediated articulations of crime and punishment can still be seen as vehicles for connecting people (Sparks, 2001). As noted in Chapter 4, stories about crime and justice perform a similar role to royal weddings, state funerals and 'must see' television events, in bringing communities together and mobilizing common responses. Yet even the most extreme crime, murder, is subject to differing levels of interest, with only certain murders (of certain victims) containing sufficient human interest to touch everyone with the emotional intensity required to constitute a climate of public vilification and mourning (Greer, 2003b). Appealing to the consensual values of an 'imagined community' (Anderson, 1983), the media stigmatize offenders, sentimentalize victims and sanctify those deemed particularly vulnerable or tragic. And, in relation to the latter, it is not just victims of serious and violent offences that attain such elevated status, but in some cases (for example, Neville and Doreen Lawrence MBE) their relatives too.

While it does not claim to provide all the answers, this book has attempted to shed light on some of the most troubling questions which continue to vex scholars of media and crime. Why do only certain criminal events become thrust into the public sphere with sufficient vigour and emotional intensity to shape public fears of victimization? Why do some crimes invoke a public reaction so forceful that they become embedded in the cultural fabric of society, while other, almost identical, incidents fail almost to register on the media radar, still less capture the collective imagination? Why do some very serious crimes cast a much longer shadow than others, and some offenders become iconic representations of pure evil while others fade into quiet obscurity? Why is it, for example, that Harold Shipman, who was almost certainly the most prolific serial killer in British history, was not constantly vilified by the popular media and ascribed the kind of motifs applied to Myra Hindley or Robert Thompson and Jon Venables? And why do paedophiles who target children unknown to them merit such extreme hostility that the deep, enraged seething that bubbles quietly under society's surface occasionally erupts into violent, bloody and frequently indiscriminate action, when the level of abuse occurring within families is largely ignored?

While I didn't set out to write a book about 'self' and 'other', the finished project has had much to say about the ways in which 'we' – the audience – in an ever expansive mediascape, are influenced in our understandings of those who transgress legal and moral boundaries. I have concentrated on some of those crimes that are most sensationalized by the media and, as a consequence, have a peculiarly strong hold on our national culture and identity. But there are many 'outsiders' – 'the threatening outcast, the fearsome stranger, the excluded and the embittered' (Garland, 1996: 461) – who provide the 'others' against whom we measure ourselves. As Foucault (1988) suggests, we judge the criminal, not the crime, and for all our 'postmodern' sophistication, the beginning of the 21st century finds us still falling back on the positivist discourses of 19th-century criminology. Attributing irrationality, oversensitization and lesser reasoning to women, children, adolescents, the dangerous classes, those who lead 'unconventional' lifestyles, people from different ethnic backgrounds to our own and people with mental illnesses, it is perhaps not surprising that these 'lesser mortals' are the very groups who are considered to be most susceptible to media 'effects'. It is also they who are most consistently demonized by the media as these ascribed attributes then become the lens through which we view crime and violent behaviour. No-one who lives in today's media-saturated society is immune to the winner–loser/self–other/insider–outsider culture – little wonder, then, that to many of Britain's citizens the police and criminal justice system are viewed as, at best, ineffective and, at worst, threatening (Reiner et al., 2001).

It has long been established that the media is not a window on the world, but is a prism subtly bending and distorting our picture of reality. In most versions of this argument, the reader, viewer or listener is characterized according to varying degrees of passivity, unarmed and ill prepared to cognitively filter out the prejudices, biases and slants that may be subtly conveyed or overtly apparent. But in this book, I have argued that the relationship between media and audience in defining the parameters of social (in)tolerance and social control is not only complex, but is one of collusion. To be blunt, crime is constructed and consumed in such a way as to permit the reader, viewer or listener to side-step reality rather than confronting or 'owning up' to it. Many of the cases discussed in this volume have been described as the unthinkable and unknowable, but perhaps they simply alert us to our collective unwillingness to think and to know. I have suggested that the crimes which conform to journalistic perceptions of 'newsworthiness' elicit a deep cultural unease that we, as a society, can only confront if we detach ourselves from the perpetrator(s) emotionally, morally and physically. Through a process of alienation and demonization we establish the 'otherness' of those who deviate and (re)assert our own innocence and normality (Blackman and Walkerdine, 2001).

Our pre-modern responses to postmodern problems is also evident in the media's overwhelming tendency to denounce acts as 'evil' (Stokes, 2000). Since Cohen popularized the notion of the **'folk devil'** three decades ago, the symbolic potency of that image has been weakened and has, in recent times, been replaced by a more powerful icon – the 'evil monster'. When very serious offences are committed, the evil nature of the act is projected onto the perpetrators and 'evil' comes to be seen not as the element that sets this crime apart as an abnormal and isolated event, but as the common factor in all crimes that can be reported as components of a single moral panic (Franklin and Petley, 1996; Stokes, 2000). Thus, children who kill – in breaching our ideal of childhood innocence – and women who commit very serious crimes – in challenging traditional notions of acceptable femininity – become doubly vilified. Meanwhile, paedophiles are universally condemned as unequivocal folk devils, set apart from 'normal' society, inherently evil and incapable of reform (Critcher, 2003; Greer, 2003a). The commonly felt emotions of guilt, denial and repression that characteristically follow serious crimes perpetrated by women and children, and by **paedophiles**, give their crimes a superordinancy that lifts them above other, equally horrible, crimes and secures for them a powerful symbolic place in the collective psyche. Constructed as evil monsters or sub-human beasts, their complexity can be denied and their evil can be exorcised by their exclusion from society (Kitzinger, 1999; Critcher, 2003).

It is, then, precisely for this reason that the crimes of Dr Harold Shipman, extreme and terrible as they were, failed to spark the interest of the media and public. Although sentenced to 15 consecutive life sentences, and excluded from society in that sense, Shipman did not face the level of fear and loathing that might have been anticipated when his crimes first came to light. The sheer number of victims involved suggests that this should have been one of the most infamous and talked about mediated events in our lifetimes. Up to 350 victims, most of them elderly, were killed in their own homes or in his small surgery in a suburb of Manchester. In either case, these were environments in which his victims were at their most defenceless and vulnerable, yet felt they were in safe hands. Shipman was so respected and trusted in his community that, even after his conviction, many of his former patients were protesting his innocence and integrity. But Shipman was unmitigatingly ordinary, bland even. He went to work, took holidays abroad, enjoyed a pint at his local, spent time with his family, just like all of us. As Heidkamp puts it, in relation to a different case which involved medical professionals 'putting to sleep' their elderly patients: 'how could murder have become banal, normal?' (1993: 220). The point, then, is this. Crimes like those of Dr Shipman do not become the stuff of media sensation precisely because the constitutive features of the case (a middle-class, professional male perpetrator; elderly, mostly female victims; non-violent means of death) cannot be consigned to the unknown and unknowable margins. They invite society to recognize that it is not simply 'evil' or 'mad' people who are capable of killing, and this is an unpalatable truth that society is simply not ready to contemplate.

It would also seem that media-orchestrated infamy is shaped by the representational resources available to report a case. Since the infamous 'Watergate' tapes that brought down an American president, mediated sounds and images have themselves frequently become part of a crime story, and help not only to elevate public awareness at the time, but also to ensure that a crime remains in the collective imagination long after the trial is over. There are many examples of chilling-with-hindsight snippets and snapshots from audio tape, film, camcorder and CCTV which help to explain the potent symbolic resonance of certain crimes. The audio tape played in court of one of the child victims of Ian Brady and Myra Hindley crying and begging to go home; the hoax tapes broadcast on national television that taunted police investigating the 'Yorkshire Ripper', and led them to focus their inquiries almost exclusively on suspects with a 'Geordie' accent; the Bootle shopping centre CCTV footage of toddler James Bulger holding hands with the little boys who would kill him; the amateur video film of Rodney King being brutally beaten by the LA police; the photographs of Holly Wells and Jessica Chapman in their matching Manchester United shirts standing in front of a kitchen clock, literally frozen in time; the television footage shot from a police helicopter of O.J. Simpson driving slowly down the highway trying to evade the LA police which was seen on television by approximately 100 million viewers; the 14-minute tape played in court of Nicole Brown Simpson pleading for help from a 911 emergency operator as O.J. could be heard in the background threatening and abusing her. All these haunting moments are seared on the memories of those who have witnessed them. Of course, this is not to suggest that crime stories must have these media adjuncts in order to be deemed newsworthy. Many of the criminal cases discussed in this volume have no such audio-visual 'extras'. Nonetheless it has become virtually impossible in contemporary society to separate the real from the mediated, and every 'true crime' that comes to public attention becomes inseparable from the media discourses and images that communicate it. There is no CCTV footage of the murder of Stephen Lawrence, but that case is virtually impossible to imagine without recourse to the memories of the *Daily Mail*'s (14 February 1997) front page carrying the photographs of the five men who were acquitted, under the one-word headline 'Murderers', or of the same five men snarling and jeering at the crowd and television cameras as they left the Macpherson inquiry.

As a final thought, it must be remembered that in order to construct offenders as 'others', their 'outsider' status must be unequivocal and incontestable. All mediated discourses are narrative devices, but there are always counter-narratives, even if they are not represented by the media. Revenge is a common theme in the defences of many notorious killers and many claim that they acted out of a sense of grievance which they perceive as legitimating their crimes. Tracey Wigginton claimed that her murder of a man she had never previously met was not the act of a blood-seeking vampire, but a consequence of her violent and abusive childhood. Aileen Wuornos's explanation for her murder of seven men was that she had acted in self-defence; Thomas Hamilton who, in March 1996, massacred 16 children and their teacher in a primary school in Dunblane, Scotland, was said to have acted out of revenge against a community from which he felt persecuted and ostracized. Timothy McVeigh, who killed 168 people when he planted a bomb in a government building in Oklahoma, described it as a 'retaliatory strike, a counter attack' against the US government for their botched raid on a cult headquarters in Waco, Texas, and their treatment of Iraqis and their own troops through the use of chemicals (*Observer*, 6 May 2001). Numerous perpetrators of crimes which are, at one and the same time, so horrific that they result in life prison sentences, yet so mundane (because committed by men against women and children) that they barely register a flicker of interest from the media, were either neglected in childhood or grew up in care and, in either case, were frequently the victims of sexual and physical abuse by adults in whom they should have been able to trust. Even Jon Venables and Robert Thompson, while not mature enough at the time of their trial to offer a motive for killing James Bulger, might be said to have had extenuating circumstances which included dysfunctional and, in the latter's case, violent home lives. They formed an alliance which gave them a feeling of power in lives in which cruelty was the norm, and their two-year-old victim may have been a surrogate for their loathing of their siblings or the vessel on to which they projected all their feelings of disappointment and rage (Morrison, 1997).

Of course, all these defences can be read as cynical ploys by the actors involved, or their supporters, to shift their status from that of offender to that of victim. But the crucial point is that, in downplaying their defences, the media demonstrate the profound discomfort and denial with which our culture views these counter narratives. Whether this denial arises from a fear of the potential for 'evil' that is within all of us, or more generally of the unwillingness to accept that, sometimes, horror lies beneath the most ordinary facades is debatable. But the fact remains that the truly 'unthinkable' and 'unknowable' are those crimes that take place behind closed doors and never reach public attention.

References

Abrams, M. (1959) *The Teenage Consumer*, London: Routledge and Kegan Paul

Ainsworth, P.B. (2000) *Psychology and Crime: Myths and Reality*, Harlow: Pearson

Alder, C.M. and Baker, J. (1997) 'Maternal filicide: more than one story to be told', *Women and Criminal Justice*, 9 (15): 39

Alder, C.M. and Polk, K. (1996) 'Masculinity and child homicide', *British Journal of Criminology*, 36 (3): 396–411

Aldridge, M. (2003) 'The ties that divide: regional press campaigns, community and populism', *Media, Culture & Society*, 25: 491–509

Anderson, B. (1983) *Imagined Communities: Reflections on the Origins and Spread of Nationalism*, London: Verso

Ashenden, S. (2002) 'Policing perversion: the contemporary governance of paedophilia', *Cultural Values* 6 (1 and 2): 197–222

Ball, K. (2003) 'Editorial. The labours of surveillance', *Surveillance and Society*, 1 (2): 125–37, http://www.surveillance-and-society.org

Bannister, J., Fyfe, N. and Kearns, A. (1998) 'Closed circuit television and the city', in C. Norris, J. Moran and G. Armstrong (eds) *Surveillance, Closed Circuit Television and Social Control*, Aldershot: Ashgate

Barak, G. (ed.) (1994a) *Media, Process, and the Social Construction of Crime*, New York: Garland

Barak, G. (1994b) 'Media, Society, and Criminology', in G. Barak (ed.) *Media, Process, and the Social Construction of Crime*, New York: Garland

Barr, R. and Pease, K. (1990) 'Crime placement, displacement and deflection', in N. Morris and M. Tonry (eds) *Crime and Justice: A Review of Research*, Vol. 12, Chicago: University of Chicago Press

Barthes, R. (1973) *Mythologies*, London: Paladin

Baudrillard, J. (1981) *For A Critique of the Political Economy of the Sign*, St Louis: Telos

Baudrillard, J. (1983) *Simulations*, New York: Semiotext(e)

Bauman, Z. (1992) *Intimations of Postmodernity*, London: Routledge

Bauman, Z. (1997) *Postmodernity and its Discontents*, Cambridge: Polity Press

Bazelon, D. (1978) 'The hidden politics of American criminology', in J. Conrad (ed.) *The Evolution of Criminal Justice*, Newbury Park, CA: Sage

Beck, A. and Willis, A. (1995) *Crime and Security: Managing the Risk to Safe Shopping*, Leicester: Perpetuity Press

Beck, U. (1992) *Risk Society*, London: Sage

Becker, H. (1963) *Outsiders: Studies in the Sociology of Deviance*, New York: Free Press

Benedict, H. (1992) *Virgin or Vamp*, Oxford: Oxford University Press

Benn, M. (1993) 'Body talk: the sexual politics of PMT', in H. Birch (ed.) *Moving Targets: Women, Murder and Representation*, London: Virago

Bennett, T. and Gelsthorpe, L. (1994) *Public Attitudes to CCTV in Cambridge: A Report to the Safer Cambridge Steering Group*, Cambridge: Cambridge City Council

Berman, M. (1983) *All that is Solid Melts into Air: the Experience of Modernity*, London: Verso

Birch, H. (1993) 'If looks could kill: Myra Hindley and the iconography of evil', in H. Birch (ed.) *Moving Targets: Women, Murder and Representation*, London: Virago

Blackman, L. and Walkerdine, V. (2001) *Mass Hysteria: Critical Psychology and Media Studies*, Basingstoke: Palgrave

Blumler, J. (1991) 'The new television marketplace', in J. Curran and M. Gurevitch (eds) *Mass Media and Society*, London: Arnold, pp. 194–215

Bocock, R. (1993) *Consumption*, London: Routledge

Bok, S. (1998) *Mayhem: Violence as Public Entertainment*, Reading, MA: Addison-Wesley

Bowling, B. and Phillips, C. (2002) *Racism, Crime and Justice*, Harlow: Longman

Box, S. (1983) *Power, Crime and Mystification*, London: Tavistock

Boyd-Barrett, O. (2002) 'Theory in media research', in C. Newbold, O. Boyd-Barrett and H. van den Bulck (eds) *The Media Book*, London: Arnold

Boyne, R. (2000) 'Post-panopticism', *Economy and Society*, 29 (2): 285–307

Bright, M. (2002) 'The vanishing', *Observer Magazine*, 15 December

Brown, D (2002) '"Losing my religion": reflections on critical criminology in Australia', in K. Carrington and R. Hogg (eds) *Critical Criminology: Issues, Debates, Challenges*, Cullompton: Willan

Brake, M. (1980) *The Sociology of Youth Cultures and Youth Subcultures*, London: Routledge

Browne, A. (1987) *When Battered Women Kill*, New York: Macmillan/Free Press

Brownmiller, S. (1975) *Against Our Will: Men, Women and Rape*, London: Secker and Warburg

Buckingham, D. (2000) *After the Death of Childhood: Growing Up in the Age of Electronic Media*, Cambridge: Polity

Burke, R. and Sunley, R. (1996) *Hanging Out in the 1990s: Young People and the Post-Modern Condition*, Crime, Order and Policing Occasional Paper Series (11), Scarman Centre, University of Leicester

Burney, E. (1990) *Putting Street Crime in its Place: A Report to the Community/Police Consultative Group for Lambeth*, London: Goldsmiths College

Cameron, D. and Frazer, E. (1987) *The Lust to Kill: A Feminist Investigation of Sexual Murder*, Cambridge: Polity Press

Campbell, D. (2000) 'Echelon: world under watch, an introduction', 29 June www.zdnet.co.uk/news/specials/2000/06/echelon/

Campbell, M. (1995) 'Partnerships of perversion under study', *The Globe and Mail* [Toronto], 9 February

Cantril, H. (1997) 'The invasion from Mars', in T. O'Sullivan, T. and Y. Jewkes (eds) *The Media Studies Reader*, London: Arnold. Originally published in 1940 as *The Invasion from Mars: A Study in the Psychology of Panic* with H. Gaudet and H. Herzog (Princeton University Press)

Carter, C. (1998) 'When the "extraordinary" becomes "ordinary": everyday news of sexual violence', in C. Carter, G. Branston and S. Allen (1998) *News, Gender and Power*, London: Routledge

Cavender, G. and Mulcahy, A. (1998) 'Trial by fire: media constructions of corporate deviance', *Justice Quarterly*, 15 (4): 697–719

Chadwick, K. and Little, C. (1987) 'The criminalisation of women', in P. Scraton (ed.) *Law, Order and the Authoritarian State*, Buckingham: Open University Press

Chermak, S. (1994) 'Crime in the news media: a refined understanding of how crimes become news', in G. Barak (ed.) *Media, Process, and the Social Construction of Crime*, New York: Garland

Chibnall, S. (1977) *Law and Order News*, London: Tavistock

Christie, N. (1993) *Crime Control as Industry*, London: Routledge

Clarke, R. (1994) 'Human identification in information systems: management challenges and public policy issues', *Information Technology and People*, 7: 6–37

Clarke, R. (1997) *Situational Crime Prevention: Successful Case Studies*, 2nd edn, Albany, NY: Harrow and Heston

Cloward, R.A. and Ohlin, L.E. (1960) *Delinquency and Opportunity: A Theory of Delinquent Gangs*, New York: Free Press

Cohen, A. (1955) *Delinquent Boys: The Culture of the Gang*, New York: Free Press

Cohen, N. (1999) *Cruel Britannia: Reports on the Sinister and the Preposterous*, London: Verso

Cohen, S. (1972/2002) *Folk Devils and Moral Panics: The Creation of Mods and Rockers*, London: MacGibbon and Kee; 3rd edn with revised Introduction, London: Routledge

Cohen, S. (1980) *Folk Devils and Moral Panics: The Creation of Mods and Rockers*, Oxford: Martin Robertson; 2nd edn with revised Introduction

Cohen, S. (1985) *Visions of Social Control: Crime, Punishment and Classification*, Cambridge: Polity Press

Cohen, S. (1994) 'Social control and the politics of reconstruction', in D. Nelken (ed.) *The Futures of Criminology*, London: Sage

Cohen, S. and Young, J. (1973) *The Manufacture of News: Deviance Social Problems and the Mass Media*, London: Constable

Coleman, C. and Moynihan, J. (1996) *Understanding Crime Data: Haunted by the Dark Figure*, Buckingham: Open University Press

Coleman, C. and Norris, C. (2000) *Introducing Criminology*, Cullompton: Willan

Coleman, R. and Sim, J. (2000) '"You'll never walk alone": CCTV surveillance, order and neo-liberal rule in Liverpool city centre', *British Journal of Criminology*, 41 (4): 623–39

Connell, R. (1985) 'Fabulous powers: blaming the media', in L. Masterman (ed.) *Television Mythologies*, London: Comedia

Coward, R. (1990) 'Innocent pleasure', *New Statesman & Society*, 13 April: 12–14

Cowburn, M. and Dominelli, L. (2001) 'Masking hegemonic masculinity: reconstructing the paedophile as the dangerous stranger', *British Journal of Social Work*, 31: 399–415

Craib, I. (1998) *Experiencing Identity*, London: Sage

Crawford, A., Jones, T., Woodhouse, T. and Young, J. (1990) *Second Islington Crime Survey*, London: Middlesex Polytechnic

Creed, B. (1996) 'Bitch queen or backlash? Media portrayals of female murderers', in K. Greenwood (ed.) *The Things She Loves: Why Women Kill*, Sydney: Allen & Unwin

Critcher, C. (2003) *Moral Panics and the Media*, Buckingham: Open University Press

Croall, H. (2001) *Understanding White Collar Crime*, Buckingham: Open University Press

Cullen, D. (2003) 'Child porn list leaked to Sunday Times', www.theregister.co.uk

Daly, K. (1994) *Gender, Crime and Punishment*, New Haven, CT: Yale University Press

Daniels, A. (1997) *What Access do Prisoners in English Prisons have to the Media of Mass Communications and What Use do they Make of them?* Unpublished MA dissertation, Centre for Mass Communications Research: University of Leicester

Davies, P. (2003) 'Women, crime and work: gender and the labour market', *Criminal Justice Matters*, 53, Autumn: 46–7

Davis, M. (1994) *Beyond Blade Runner: Urban Control – the Ecology of Fear*, Open Magazine Pamphlet series, New York: The New Press

Debord, G. (1967/1997) *The Society of the Spectacle*, London: Verso

De Certeau, M. (1984) *The Practice of Everyday Life*, California: University of California Press

Ditton, J., Bannister, J., Gilchrist, E. and Farrall, S. (1999) 'Afraid or angry? Recalibrating the "fear" of crime', *International Review of Victimology*, 6 (2): 83–99

Ditton, J. and Duffy, J. (1983) 'Bias in the newspaper reporting of crime news', *British Journal of Criminology*, 23 (2)

Dobash, R. and Dobash, R. (1922) *Women, Violence and Social Change*, London Routledge

Dobash, R., Dobash, R. and Gutteridge, S. (1986) *The Imprisonment of Women*, Oxford: Blackwell

Dobash, R., Dobash, R. and Noaks, L. (eds) (1995) *Gender and Crime*, Cardiff: University of Wales Press

Douglas, M. (1966) *Purity and Danger: An Analysis of Concepts of Pollution and Taboo*, London: Routledge and Kegan Paul

Dovey, J. (1996) 'The revelation of unguessed worlds', in J. Dovey (ed.) *Fractal Dreams: New Media in Social Context*, London: Lawrence & Wishart

Downes, D. (1988) 'The sociology of crime and social control in Britain, 1960–87', in P. Rock (ed.) *A History of British Criminology*, Oxford: Oxford University Press

Downes, D. and Morgan, R. (2002) 'The skeletons in the cupboard: the politics of law and order in the new millennium', in M. Maguire, R. Morgan and R. Reiner (eds) *The Oxford Handbook of Criminology*, 3rd edn, Oxford: Oxford University Press.

Downes, D. and Rock, P. (1988) *Understanding Deviance: A Guide to the Sociology of Crime and Rule Breaking*, Oxford: Oxford University Press

Durkheim, E. (1893/1933) *The Division of Labour in Society*, Glencoe, IL: Free Press

Durkheim, E. (1895/1964) *The Rules of Sociological Method*, New York: Free Press

Ericson, R., Baranek, P. and Chan, J. (1987) *Visualising Deviance: A Study of News Organisations*, Buckingham: Open University Press

Ericson, R., Baranek, P. and Chan, J. (1989) *Negotiating Control: A Study of News Sources*, Buckingham: Open University Press

Ericson, R., Baranek, P. and Chan, J. (1991) *Representing Order: Crime, Law and Justice in the News Media*, Buckingham: Open University Press

Ericson, R.V. and Haggerty, K.D. (1997) *Policing the Risk Society*, Oxford: Oxford University Press

Fenwick, M. and Hayward, K.J. (2000) 'Youth crime, excitement and consumer culture: the reconstruction of aetiology in contemporary theoretical criminology', in J. Pickford (ed.) *Youth Justice: Theory and Practice*, London: Cavendish

Ferrell, J. (2001) 'Cultural criminology', in E. McLaughlin and J. Muncie (eds) *The Sage Dictionary of Criminology*, London: Sage

Ferrell, J. (2002) *Tearing Down the Streets: Adventures in Urban Anarchy*, New York: Palgrave/St Martins

Ferrell, J. and Hamm, M. (1998) *Ethnography at the Edge*, Boston, MA: Norteastern University Press

Ferrell, J. and Sanders, C.R. (eds) (1995) *Cultural Criminology*, Boston, MA: Northeastern University Press

Ferrell, J. and Websdale, N. (1999) *Making Trouble: Cultural Constructions of Crime, Deviance and Control*, New York: Aldine De Gruyter

Finch, E. (2003) 'What a tangled web we weave: identity theft and the Internet', in Y. Jewkes (ed.) *Dot.cons: Crime, Deviance and Identity on the Internet*, Cullompton: Willan

Fishman, M. (1981) *Manufacturing the News*, Austin, TX: University of Texas Press

Fiske, J. (1982) *Introduction to Communication Studies*, London: Routledge

Fiske, J. (1989) *Reading the Popular*, London: Routledge

Foucault, M. (1977) *Discipline and Punish*, London: Allen Lane

Foucault, M. (1988) *Politics, Philosophy, Culture: Interviews and Other Writings, 1977–1984*, London: Routledge

Fowler, R. (1991) *Language in the News*, London: Routledge

Franklin, B. and Petley, J. (1996) 'Killing the age of innocence: newspaper reporting of the death of James Bulger', in J. Pilchar and S. Wagg (eds) *Thatcher's Children? Politics, Childhood and Society in the 1980s and 1990s*, London: Falmer Press

Frayn, M. (1965) *The Tin Men*, London: Collins

Freeman, M. (1997) 'The James Bulger tragedy: childish innocence and the construction of guilt', in A. McGillivray (ed.) *Governing Childhood*, Aldershot: Dartmouth

Frith, S. (1983) *Sound Effects: Youth, Leisure and the Politics of Rock 'n' Roll*, London: Constable

Furedi, F. (1997) *Culture of Fear: Risk-Taking and the Morality of Low Expectation*, London: Cassell

Gadd, D., Farrell, S., Dallimore, D. and Lombard, N. (2003) 'Male victims of domestic violence', *Criminal Justice Matters*, 53, Autumn

Galtung, J. and Ruge, M. (1973) 'Structuring and selecting the news', in S. Cohen and J. Young (eds) *The Manufacture of News: Deviance, Social Problems and the Mass Media*, London: Constable

Gandy, O. (1993) *The Panoptic Sort*, Boulder, CO: Westview Press

Garland, D. (1996) 'The limits of the sovereign state: strategies of crime control in contemporary society', *British Journal of Criminology*, 36 (4): 445–71

Garland, D. (1999) '"Governmentality" and the problem of crime', in R. Smandych (ed.) *Governable Places: Readings on Governmentality and Crime Control*, Aldershot: Ashgate

Garside, R. (2001) 'Putting the emotion back into crime: or how we can start to win the war of the headlines', *Criminal Justice Matters*, 43, Spring: 32–3

Gauntlett, D. (1995) *Moving Experiences: Understanding Television's Influences and Effects*, Luton: John Libbey

Geertz, C. (1983) *Local Knowledge: Further Essays in Interpretive Anthropology*, New York: Basic Books

Gelsthorpe, L. (2002) 'Feminism and criminology', in M. Maguire, R. Morgan and R. Reiner (eds) *The Oxford Handbook of Criminology*, 3rd edn, Oxford: Oxford University Press

Gelsthorpe, L. and Morris, A. (eds) (1990) *Feminist Perspectives in Criminology*, Buckingham: Open University Press

Geraghty, C. (undated) www.frameworkonline.com/42cg.htm

Gergen, K.J. (1991) *The Saturated Self*, New York: Basic Books

Giddens, A. (1985) *The Nation State and Violence*, Cambridge: Polity Press

Giddens, A. (1991) *Modernity and Self-Identity: Self and Society in the Late Modern Age*, Cambridge: Polity Press

Gillespie, M. and McLaughlin, E. (2002) 'Media and the making of public attitudes', *Criminal Justice Matters*, 49, Autumn: 8–9

Gilliom, J. (2001) *Overseers of the Poor*, Chicago: University of Chicago Press

Girling, E., Loader, I. and Sparks, R. (2000) *Crime and Social Change in Middle England: Questions of Order in an English Town*, London: Routledge

Girling, E., Loader, I. and Sparks, R. (2002) 'Public sensibilities towards crime: anxieties of affluence', in A. Boran (ed.) *Crime: Fear or Fascination*, Chester: Chester Academic Press

Glancey, J. (2002) 'Image that for 36 years fixed a killer in the public mind', *Guardian*, 16th November

Goffman, E. (1963) *Stigma: Notes on the Management of Spoiled Identity*, New Jersey: Prentice-Hall

Golding, P. and Murdock, G. (2000) 'Culture, communications and political economy', in J. Curran and M. Gurevitch (eds) *Mass Media and Society*, revised 3rd edn, London: Arnold

Goldson, B. (2003) 'Tough on children ... tough on justice'. Paper presented to *Tough On Crime ... Tough on Freedoms*, The European Group for the Study of Deviance and Social Control Conference, Centre for Studies in Crime and Social Justice, Edge Hill College, Liverpool, 22–24 April

Goode, E. and Ben-Yehuda, N. (1994) *Moral Panics: The Social Construction of Deviance*, Oxford: Blackwell

Graber, D. (1980) *Crime, News and the Public*, New York: Praeger

Graef, R. (1989) *Talking Blues*, London: Collins

Gramsci, A. (1971) *Selections from Prison Notebooks*, London: Lawrence & Wishart

Greer, C. (2003a) *Sex Crime and the Media: Sex Offending and the Press in a Divided Society*, Cullompton: Willan

Greer, C. (2003b) Response to paper by Claire Valier, Cultural Criminology Conference, University of London, 9–10 May

Greer, C. (2003c) 'Media representations of dangerousness', *Criminal Justice Matters*, 51, Spring

Greer, C. (2004) Review of F. Leishman and P. Mason (2003) *Policing and the Media: Facts, Fictions and Factions*, Cullompton: Willan, *British Journal of Criminology*, 44 (2)

Groombridge, N. (1999) 'Perverse criminologies: the closet of Dr Lombroso', *Social and Legal Studies*, 8 (4): 531–48

Haggerty, K.D. and Ericson, R.V. (2000) 'The surveillant assemblage', *British Journal of Sociology*, 51 (4): 605–22

Hall, S. (1978) 'The treatment of football hooliganism in the press', in R. Ingham (ed.) *Football Hooliganism*, London: Inter-Action

Hall, S., Critcher, C., Jefferson, T., Clarke, J. and Roberts, B. (eds) (1978) *Policing the Crisis: Mugging, the State and Law and Order*, London: Macmillan

Hall, S., Held, D. and McGrew, T. (1992) *Modernity and its Futures*, Cambridge: Polity Press

Hall, S. and Jefferson, T. (eds) (1975) *Resistance Through Rituals: Youth Subcultures in Post-War Britain*, London: Hutchinson

Halloran, J. (1970) *The Effects of Television*, London: Panther

Halloran, J., Elliott, P. and Murdock, G. (1970) *Demonstrations and Communication: A Case Study*, Harmondsworth: Penguin

Hamelink, C.J. (2000) *The Ethics of Cyberspace*, London: Sage

Haraway, D. (1991) *Simians, Cyborgs and Women: The Reinvention of Nature*, New York: Routledge

Hart, L. (1994) *Fatal Women: Lesbian Sexuality and the Mark of Aggression*, London: Routledge

Hartley, J. (1982) *Understanding News*, London: Routledge

Hartman, P. and Husband, C. (1974) *Racism and Mass Media*, London: Davis Poynter

Hebdige, D. (1979) *Subculture: The Meaning of Style*, London: Routledge

Hebdige, D. (1989) 'After the masses', *Marxism Today*, January

Heidensohn, F. (1985) *Women and Crime*, New York: New York University Press

Heidensohn, F. (2000) *Sexual Politics and Social Control*, Buckingham: Open University Press

Heidkamp, B. (1993) '"Angels of death": the Lainz Hospital murders', in H. Birch (ed.) *Moving Targets: Women, Murder and Representation*, London: Virago

Hellawell, K. (2002) *The Outsider*, London: HarperCollins

Hendrick, G.H. (1977) 'When television is a school for criminals', *TV Guide*, 29 January: 118

Henry, S. and Milovanovic, D. (1996) *Constitutive Criminology*, London: Sage

Herman, E. and Chomsky, N. (1992) *Manufacturing Consent: The Political Economy of Mass Media*, New York: Vintage

Hetherington, A. (1985) *News, Newspapers and Television*, London: Macmillan

Higgins, C. (1994) 'Tales of gothic horror', in J.N. Turner and P. Williams (eds) *The Happy Couple: Law and Literature*, Sydney: Federation Press

Hillyard, P. and Percy-Smith, J. (1988) *The Coercive State: The Decline of Democracy in Britain*, London: Fontana

Hobbs, D. (1995) *Bad Business: Professional Crime in Modern Britain*, Oxford: Oxford University Press

Hogg, R. (2002) 'Criminology beyond the nation state: global conflicts, human rights and the "new world order"', in K. Carrington and R. Hogg (eds) *Critical Criminology: Issues, Debates, Challenges*, Cullompton: Willan

Hornby, S. (1997) *Challenging Masculinity in the Supervision of Male Offenders*, Social Work Monograph 157, University of East Anglia, Norwich

Horton, D. and Wohl, R. (1956) 'Mass communication and para-social interaction', *Psychiatry*, 19: 215–19

Hough, M. and Roberts, J. (1998) *Attitudes to Punishment*, Home Office Research Study no. 179, London: HMSO

Howe, A. (1994) *Punish and Critique: Towards a Feminist Analysis of Penality*, London: Routledge

Hudson, B. (2002) 'Social control', in M. Maguire, R. Morgan and R. Reiner (eds) *The Oxford Handbook of Criminology*, 3rd edn, Oxford: Oxford University Press

Hughes, G. with Langan, M. (2001) 'Good or bad business?: exploring corporate and organized crime', in J. Muncie and E. McLaughlin (eds) (2001) *The Problem of Crime*, 2nd edn, London: Sage

James, O. (1995) *Juvenile Violence in a Winner–Loser Culture: Socio-Economic and Familial Origins of the Rise of Violence against the Person*, London: Free Association

Jefferson, T. (2002) 'For a psychosocial criminology', in K. Carrington and R. Hogg (eds) *Critical Criminology: Issues, Debates, Challenges*, Cullompton: Willan

Jenkins, P. (1992) *Intimate Enemies: Moral Panics in Contemporary Great Britain*, New York: Aldine de Gruyter

Jenkins, P. (1994) *Using Murder: The Social Construction of Serial Homicide*, New York: Aldine de Gruyter

Jenkins, P. (2001) *Beyond Tolerance: Child Pornography on the Internet*, New York: New York University Press

Jermyn, D. (2003) 'Photo stories and family albums: imaging criminals and victims on *Crimewatch UK*', in P. Mason (ed.) *Criminal Visions: Media Representations of Crime and Justice*, Cullompton: Willan

Jewkes, Y. (1999) *Moral Panics in a Risk Society: A Critical Evaluation*, Crime, Order and Policing Occasional Paper Series (15), Scarman Centre, University of Leicester

Jewkes, Y. (2002) *Captive Audience: Media, Masculinity and Power in Prisons*, Cullompton: Willan

Jewkes, Y. (2003a) *Dot.cons: Crime, Deviance and Identity on the Internet*, Cullompton: Willan

Jewkes, Y. (2003b) 'Policing the net: crime, regulation and surveillance in cyberspace' in Y. Jewkes (ed.) *Dot.cons: Crime, Deviance and Identity on the Internet*, Cullompton: Willan

Jewkes, Y. (2003c) 'Policing cybercrime', in T. Newburn (ed.) *Handbook of Policing*, Cullompton: Willan

Jewkes, Y. and Letherby, G. (eds) (2002) *Criminology: A Reader*, London: Sage

Jewkes, Y. and Sharp, K. (2003) 'Crime, deviance and the disembodied self: transcending the dangers of corporeality', in Y. Jewkes (ed.) *Dot.cons: Criminal and Deviant Identities on the Internet*, Cullompton: Willan

Jones, T., MacLean, B. and Young, J. (1986) *The Islington Crime Survey: Crime, Victimization and Policing in Inner-City London*, Aldershot: Gower

'Kavangh on Saturday' 'Compassion? It's time for real justice', (1990) *Courier-Mail* [Brisbane], 20 October

Keating, M. (2002) 'Media most foul: fear of crime and media', in A. Boran (ed.) *Crime: Fear or Fascination*, Chester: Chester Academic Press

Kennedy, H. (1992) *Eve Was Framed*, London: Chatto & Windus

Kidd-Hewitt, D. (1995) 'Crime and the media: a criminological perspective', in D. Kidd-Hewitt and R. Osborne (eds) *Crime and the Media: A Post-Modern Spectacle*, London: Pluto

Kidd-Hewitt, D. and Osborne, R. (eds) (1995) *Crime and the Media: The Post-Modern Spectacle*, London: Pluto

Kitzinger, J. (1999) 'The ultimate neighbour from hell? Stranger danger and the media framing of paedophiles', in B. Franklin (ed.) *Social Policy, the Media and Misrepresentation*, London: Routledge

Knopf, T. (1970) 'Media myths on violence', *Columbia Journalism Review*, Spring: 17–18

Lacey, N. (1995) 'Contingency and criminalisation', in I. Loveland (ed.) *Frontiers of Criminality*, London: Sweet & Maxwell

Laming, Lord (2003) 'Victoria Climblié ... does the deliberate harm of children matter?', *Criminal Justice Matters*, 53 (Autumn): 46–7

Langman, L. (1992) 'Neon cages: shopping for subjectivity', in R. Shields (ed.) *Lifestyle Shopping: The Subject of Consumption*, London: Routledge

Lea, J. and Young, J. (1984) *What is to be Done about Law and Order?* Harmondsworth: Penguin

Lea, J. and Young, J. (1993) *What is to be Done about Law and Order? Crisis in the Nineties*, London: Pluto Press

Leacock, V. and Sparks, R. (2002) 'Riskiness and at-risk-ness: some ambiguous features of the current penal landscape', in N. Gray, J. Laing and L. Noaks (eds) *Criminal Justice, Mental Health and the Politics of Risk*, London: Cavendish

Lees, S. (1997) *Ruling Passions*, London: Sage

Le Bon, G. (1895/1960) *The Crowd: A Study of the Popular Mind*, New York: Viking

Leishman, F. and Mason, P. (2003) *Policing and the Media: Facts, Fictions and Factions*, Cullompton: Willan

Lemert, E. (1951) *Social Pathology: A Systematic Approach to the Theory of Sociopathic Behaviour*, New York: McGraw-Hill

Lévi-Strauss, C. (1979) *The Raw and the Cooked*, London: Cape

Leyton, E. (1989) *Hunting Humans: The Rise of the Modern Multiple Murderer*, Harmondsworth: Penguin

Lloyd, A. (1995) *Doubly Deviant, Doubly Damned: Society's Treatment of Violent Women*, Harmondsworth: Penguin

Lombroso, C. (1876) *L'uomo delinquente* (*The Criminal Man*), Milan: Hoepli

Lombroso, C. and Ferrero, W. (1895) *The Female Offender*, London: Unwin

Lyon, D. (2001) *Surveillance Society: Monitoring Everyday Life*, Buckingham: Open University Press

Lyon, D. (2003) 'Surveillance as social sorting: computer codes and mobile bodies', in D. Lyon (ed.) *Surveillance As Social Sorting: Privacy, Risk and Digital Discrimination*, London: Routledge

McArthur, S. (2002) 'Representing crime: an exercise in fear', in A. Boran (ed.) *Crime: Fear or Fascination*, Chester: Chester Academic Press

McCahill, M. (2002) *The Surveillance Web: The Rise of Visual Surveillance in an English City*, Cullompton: Willan

McCahill, M. (2003) 'Media representations of surveillance', in P. Mason (ed.) *Criminal Visions: Media Representations of Crime and Justice*, Cullompton: Willan

McCahill, M. and Norris, C. (2002) *Literature Review: Working Paper No. 2*, at www.urbaneye.net/results/ue_wp2.pdf

McCahill, M. and Norris, C. (2003) 'Estimating the extent, sophistication and legality of CCTV in London', in M. Gill (ed.) *CCTV*, Leicester: Perpetuity Press

McKay, C. (1841) *Extraordinary Popular Delusions and the Madness of Crowds*, Michigan: Three Rivers Press [reprinted 1995]

McLaughlin, E. and Muncie, J. (eds) (2001) *The Sage Dictionary of Criminology*, London: Sage

McLean, G. (2003) 'Family fortunes', *Guardian*, 30 July

McNair, B. (1993) *News and Journalism in the UK*, London: Routledge

McNair, B. (1998) *The Sociology of Journalism*, London: Arnold

McQuail, D. (2000) *Mass Communication Theory: An Introduction*, 4th edn, London: Sage

McQueen, D. (1998) *Television: A Media Student's Guide*, London: Arnold

McRobbie, A. (1994) *Postmodernism and Popular Culture*, London: Routledge

Mander, J. (1980) *Four Arguments for the Elimination of Television*, New York: Harvester

Manning, P. (1997) *Police Work*, 2nd edn, Prospect Heights, IL: Waveland Press

Manning, P. (2001) *News and News Sources: A Critical Introduction*, London: Sage

Marks, M. and Kumar, R.C. (1993) 'Infanticide in England and Wales', *Medicine the Law*, 33/4: 329–39

Marx, G.T. (1995) 'Electric eye in the sky: some reflections on the new surveillance and popular culture', in J. Ferrell and C.R. Sanders (eds) *Cultural Criminology*, Boston: Northeastern University Press

Marx, G.T. (1999) 'Measuring everything that moves', *Research in the Sociology of Work*, 8: 165–89

Marx, G. T. (2002) 'What's new about the "new surveillance"? Classifying for change and continuity', in *Surveillance & Society* 1 (1): 9–29. Available at: www.surveillance-and-society.org

Mason, D., Button, G., Lankshear, G. and Coats, S. (2000) *On the Poverty of a Priorism: Technology, Surveillance in the Workplace and Employee Responses*, pre-publication draft, Plymouth: University of Plymouth

Mathiesen, T. (1997) 'The viewer society: Michel Foucault's "Panopticon" Revisited', *Theoretical Criminology*, 1 (2): 215–34

Matthews, R. (2002) *Armed Robbery*, Cullompton: Willan

Matza, D. (1964) *Delinquency and Drift*, New York: Wiley

Mawby, R. (2002) *Policing Images: Policing, Communication and Legitimacy*, Cullompton: Willan

Messerschmidt, J. (1986) *Capitalism, Patriarchy and Crime*, Totowa, NJ: Rowman & Littlefield

Merton, R.K. (1938) 'Social structure and anomie', *American Sociological Review*, 3: 672–82

Meyrowitz, J. (1985) *No Sense of Place: The Impact of Electronic Media on Social Behaviour*, Oxford: Oxford University Press

Miedzian, M. (1991) *Boys Will Be Boys: Breaking the Link Between Masculinity and Violence*, New York: Anchor

Millbank, J. (1996) 'From butch to butcher's knife: film, crime and lesbian sexuality', *Sydney Law Review*, 18 (4): 451–73

Minsky, R. (1996) *Psychoanalysis and Gender: An Introductory Reader*, London: Routledge

Minsky, R. (1998) *Psychoanalysis and Culture: Contemporary States of Mind*, Cambridge: Polity Press

Morley, D. (1992) *Television Audiences and Cultural Studies*, London: Routledge

Morris, A. (1987) *Women, Crime and Criminal Justice*, Oxford: Blackwell

Morris, A. and Wilczynski, A. (1993) 'Rocking the cradle: mothers who kill their children', in H. Birch (ed.) *Moving Targets: Women, Murder and Representation*, London: Virago

Morris, S. and al Yafai, F. (2003) 'Shevaun flies home to family as US marine arrested in Germany', *Guardian*, 17 July, www.guardian.co.uk

Morrison, B. (1997) *As If*, London: Granta

Morrison, W. (1995) *Theoretical Criminology: From Modernity to Postmodernism*, London: Cavendish

Morrissey, B. (2003) *When Women Kill: Questions of Agency and Subjectivity*, London: Routledge

Mulgan, G. (1989) 'A tale of two cities', *Marxism Today*, March: 18–25

Muncie, J. (1987) 'Much ado about nothing? The sociology of moral panics', *Social Studies Review*, 3 (2): 42–7

Muncie, J. (1999a) *Youth and Crime: A Critical Introduction*, London: Sage

Muncie, J. (1999b) 'Exorcising demons: media, politics and criminal justice', in B. Franklin (ed.) *Social Policy, the Media and Misrepresentation*, London: Routledge

Muncie, J. (2001) 'The construction and deconstruction of crime', in J. Muncie and E. McLaughlin (eds) *The Problem of Crime*, 2nd edn, London: Sage

Muncie, J. and McLaughlin, E. (eds) (2001) *The Problem of Crime*, 2nd edn, London: Sage

Murdock, G. (1997) 'Reservoirs of dogma: an archaeology of popular anxieties', in M. Barker and J. Petley (eds) *Ill Effects: the Media/Violence Debate*, London: Routledge

Naughton, J. (1994) 'Smile, you're on TV', *Observer Life*, 13 November, in Y. Jewkes and G. Letherby (eds) (2002) *Criminology: A Reader*, London: Sage

Naylor, B. (2001) 'Reporting violence in the British print media: gendered stories', *Howard Journal*, 40 (2): 180–94

Nelkin, D. and Andrews, L. (2003) 'Surveillance creep in the genetic age', in D. Lyon (ed.) *Surveillance As Social Sorting*, London: Routledge

Newburn, T. (1996) 'Back to the future? Youth crime, youth justice and the rediscovery of "authoritarian populism"', in J. Pilcher and S. Wagg (eds) *Thatcher's Children*, London: Falmer

Newburn, T. (2002) 'Young people, crime, and youth justice', in M. Maguire, R. Morgan and R. Reiner (eds) *The Oxford Handbook of Criminology*, 3rd edn, Oxford: Oxford University Press

Newburn, T. (2003) 'Introduction: understanding policing', in T. Newburn (ed.) *Handbook of Policing*, Cullompton: Willan

Newburn, T. and Hayman, S. (2001) *Policing, Surveillance and Social Control: CCTV and Police Monitoring of Suspects*, Cullompton: Willan

Newman, O. (1972) *Defensible Space: People and Design in the Violent City*, London: Architectural Press

Newson, E. (1994) 'Video violence and the protection of children', University of Nottingham (reprinted as Memorandum 13 in House of Commons Home Affairs Committee, *Video Violence and Young Offenders*, Session 1993-4, 4th Report, London: HMSO, pp. 45–59)

Norris, C. (2003) 'From personal to digital: CCTV, the panopticon, and the technological mediation of suspicion and social control', in D. Lyon (ed.) *Surveillance As Social Sorting: Privacy, Risk and Digital Discrimination*, London: Routledge

Norris, C. and Armstrong, G. (1999) *The Maximum Surveillance Society: The Rise of CCTV*, Oxford: Berg

Oaff, B. (2003) 'Is Britain about to close the gates?' *Guardian*, 15 March, www.guardian.co.uk

Oakley, A. (1986) *From Here to Maternity: Becoming a Mother*, Harmondsworth: Penguin

Office of the Data Protection Commissioner (2000) *The Use of Personal Data in Employer/Employee Relationships*, draft report, Winslow: ODPC

O'Malley, P. (2001) 'Governmentality', in E. McLaughlin and J. Muncie (eds) *The Sage Dictionary of Criminology*, London: Sage

Osborne, R. (1995) 'Crime and the media: from media studies to post-modernism', in D. Kidd-Hewitt and R. Osborne (eds) *Crime and the Media: The Postmodern Spectacle*, London: Pluto

Osborne, R. (2002) *Megawords*, London: Sage

Osgerby, B. (1998) *Youth in Britain Since 1945*, Oxford: Blackwell

O'Sullivan, T. and Jewkes, Y. (eds) (1997) *The Media Studies Reader*, London: Arnold

Pearson, G. (1983) *Hooligan: A History of Respectable Fears*, Basingstoke: Macmillan

Pearson, P. (1998) *When She Was Bad: How and Why Women Get Away With Murder*, Toronto: Random House

Pengelly, R. (1999) 'Crimewatch: a voyeur's paradise or public service?', *Police Magazine*, January, www.polfed.org/magazine/01_1999/01_1999_voyeurs.htm

Petley, J. (1997) 'In defence of video nasties', in T. O'Sullivan and Y. Jewkes (eds) *The Media Studies Reader*, London: Arnold. Originally published in 1994 in *British Journalism Review*, 5 (3): 52–7

Philo, G. (ed.) (1995) *The Glasgow University Media Group Reader, Vols. I and II*, London: Routledge

Pilger, J. (1999) 'Blood on our hands', *Guardian*, www.guardian.co.uk

Polk, K. (1993) 'Homicide: women as offenders', in P. Easteal and S. McKillop (eds) *Women and the Law*, Canberra: Australian Institute of Criminology

Pollak, O. (1950/61) *The Criminality Women*, New York: Perpetua

Poster, M. (1990) *The Mode of Information*, Chicago: University of Chicago Press

Postman, N. (1985) *Amusing Ourselves to Death*, London: Methuen

Potter, G.W. and Kappeler, V.E. (1998) *Constructing Crime: Perspectives on Making News and Social Problems*, Prospect Heights, IL: Waveland Press

Pratt, J. (2002) 'Critical criminology and the punitive society: some new "visions of social control"', in K. Carrington and R. Hogg (eds) *Critical Criminology: Issues, Debates, Challenges*, Cullompton: Willan

Presdee, M. (1986) *Agony or Ecstasy: Broken Transitions and the New Social State of Working-class Youth in Australia*, South Australian Centre for Youth Studies Occasional Paper

Presdee, M. (2000) *Cultural Criminology and the Carnival of Crime*, London: Routledge

Punch, M. (1996) *Dirty Business: Exploring Corporate Misconduct*, London: Sage

Radford, L. (1993) 'Pleading for time: justice for battered women who kill', in H. Birch (ed.) *Moving Targets: Women, Murder and Representation*, London: Virago

Radford, T. (2002) 'DNA database "has to cover everyone"', *Guardian*, 13 September, www.guardian.co.uk

Regan, P.M. (1996) 'Genetic testing and workplace surveillance: implications for privacy', in D. Lyon and E. Zureik (eds) *Computers, Surveillance and Privacy*, Minneapolis: University of Minnesota Press

Reiner, R. (2000) *The Politics of the Police*, 3rd edn, Oxford: Oxford University Press

Reiner, R. (2001) 'The rise of virtual vigilantism: crime reporting since World War II', *Criminal Justice Matters*, 43, Spring

Reiner, R., Livingstone, S. and Allen, J. (2001) 'Casino culture: media and crime in a winner–loser society', in K. Stenson and R.R. Sullivan (eds) *Crime, Risk and Justice: the Politics of Crime Control in Liberal Democracies*, Cullompton: Willan

Roshier, B. (1973) 'The selection of crime news by the press', in S. Cohen and J. Young (eds) *The Manufacture of News*, London: Constable

Sarri, R.C. (1983) 'Gender issues in juvenile justice', *Crime and Delinquency*, 29: 381

Schlesinger, P. and Tumber, H. (1994) *Reporting Crime: the Media Politics of Criminal Justice*, Oxford: Clarendon

Schlesinger, P., Tumber, H. and Murdock, G. (1991) 'The media politics of crime and criminal justice', *British Journal of Sociology*, 423: 397–420

Scraton, P. (2003) 'The demonisation, exclusion and regulation of children: from moral panic to moral renewal', in A. Boran (ed.) *Crime: Fear or Fascination*, Chester: Chester Academic Press

Shields, R. (1992) 'Spaces for the subject of consumption', in R. Shields (ed.) *Lifestyle Shopping: The Subject of Consumption*, London: Routledge

Short, E. and Ditton, J. (1995) 'Does closed circuit television prevent crime? An evaluation of the use of CCTV surveillance cameras in Airdrie town centre', *The Scottish Office Central Research Unit Research Findings*, (8): 4.

Signorielli, N. (1990) 'Television's mean and dangerous world: a continuation of the cultural indicators project', in N. Signorielli and M. Morgan (eds) *Cultivation Analysis: New Directions in Media Effects Research*, Newbury Park, CA: Sage

Sim, J. (1990) *Medical Power in Prisons*, Buckingham: Open University Press

Silverman, J. and Wilson, D. (2002) *Innocence Betrayed: Paedophilia, the Media and Society*, Cambridge: Polity

Simon, J. (1997) 'Governing through crime', in G. Fisher and L. Friedman (eds) *The Crime Conundrum: Essays on Criminal Justice*, Boulder, CO: Westview Press

Skogan, W. and Maxfield, M. (1981) *Coping With Crime*, London: Sage

Slapper, G. and Tombs, S. (1999) *Corporate Crime*, London: Longman

Smith, J. (1997) *Different for Girls: How Culture Creates Women*, London: Chatto & Windus

Smith, S.J. (1984) 'Crime in the news', *British Journal of Criminology*, 24 (3)

Soothill, K., Francis, B. and Ackerley, E. (1998) 'Paedophilia and paedophiles', *New Law Journal*, 12 June: 882–3

Soothill, K. and Walby, S. (1991) *Sex Crime in the News*, London: Routledge

Sounes, H. (1995) *Fred and Rose*, London: Warner Books

South, N. (1997) 'Late-modern criminology: "late" as in "dead" or "modern" as in "new"?', in D. Owen (ed.) *Sociology After Postmodernism*, London: Sage

Sparks, R. (1992) *Television and the Drama of Crime: Moral Tales and the Place of Crime in Public Life*, Buckingham: Open University Press

Sparks, R. (2001) '"Bringin' it all back home": populism, media coverage and the dynamics of locality and globality in the politics of crime control', in K. Stenson and R.R. Sullivan (eds) *Crime, Risk and Justice: the Politics of Crime Control in Liberal Democracies*, Cullompton: Willan

Stalder, F. and Lyon, D. (2003) 'Electronic identity cards and social classification', in D. Lyon (ed.) *Surveillance As Social Sorting: Privacy, Risk and Digital Discrimination*, London: Routledge

Stanko, E.A. (1985) *Intimate Intrusions: Women's Experience of Male Violence*, London: Routledge

Stenson, K. (2001) 'The new politics of crime control', in K. Stenson and R.R. Sullivan (eds) *Crime, Risk and Justice: the Politics of Crime Control, in Liberal Democracies*, Cullompton: Willan

Stevenson, N. (1995) *Understanding Media Cultures: Social Theory and Mass Communication*, London: Sage

Stick, N. (2003) 'An examination of the nature and influence of media representations of policing on the police themselves'. Unpublished MA thesis, University of Hull

Stokes, E. (2000) 'Abolishing the presumption of *doli incapax*: reflections on the death of a doctrine', in J. Pickford (ed.) *Youth Justice: Theory and Practice*, London: Cavendish

Surette, R. (1994) 'Predator criminals as media icons', in G. Barak (ed.) *Media, Process, and the Social Construction of Crime*, New York: Garland

Surette, R. (1998) *Media, Crime and Criminal Justice*, Belmont, CA: West/Wadsworth

Taylor, I. (1999) *Crime in Context*, Cambridge: Polity

Taylor, I., Walton, P. and Young, J. (1973) *The New Criminology: For a Social Theory of Deviance*, London: Routledge & Kegan Paul

Taylor, S. (2002) 'Much ado about nothing', *Criminal Justice Matters*, 49 (Autumn): 15

Taylor, S. (undated) www.SteTay.com (accessed 1st November 2003)

Thomson, K. (1998) *Moral Panics*, London: Routledge

Tierney, J. (1996) *Criminology: Theory and Context*, Harlow: Pearson

Tomlinson, J. (1997) '"And besides, the wench is dead": media scandals and the globalization of communication', in J. Lull and S. Hinerman (eds) *Media Scandals*, Cambridge: Polity

Townsend, M. (2003) 'Panic-room is a must-have for rich and famous', *Observer*, 23 June

Upton, J. (2000) 'The evil that women do', *Guardian*, 17 October: 6

van der Ploeg, I. (2003) 'Biometrics and the body as information: normative issues of the socio-technical coding of the body', in D. Lyon (ed.) *Surveillance As Social Sorting: Privacy, Risk and Digital Discrimination*, London: Routledge

Verhoeven, D. (1993) 'Biting the hand that breeds: the trials of Tracey Wigginton', in H. Birch (ed.) *Moving Targets: Women, Murder and Representation*, London: Virago

Waddington, P.A.J. (1986) 'Mugging as a moral panic: a question of proportion', *British Journal of Sociology*, 37 (2)

Walklate, S. (2001) *Gender, Crime and Criminal Justice*, Cullompton: Willan

Ward Jouve, N. (1988) *The Street-Cleaner: the Yorkshire Ripper Case on Trial*, London: Marion Boyars

Ward Jouve, N. (1993) 'An eye for an eye: the case of the Papin sisters', in H. Birch (ed.) *Moving Targets: Women, Murder and Representation*, London: Virago

Watney, S. (1987) *Policing Desire: Pornography, Aids and the Media*, London: Methuen

Weaver, C.K. (1998) '*Crimewatch UK*: keeping women off the streets', in C. Carter, G. Branston and S. Allen (eds) *News, Gender and Power*, London: Routledge

Whiteacre, K. (undated) *The Cultural Milieu of Criminology and Drug Research*, www.lindesmith.org/docUploads/milieu.pdf (accessed 1st November 2003)

Wilczynski, A. (1997) 'Mad or bad? Child killers, gender and the courts', *British Journal of Criminology*, 37 (3): 419–36

Willis, P. (1982) 'Male school counterculture', in *U203 Popular Culture*, Milton Keynes: Open University Press

Wilkins, L. (1964) *Social Deviance: Social Policy, Action and Research*, London: Tavistock

Williams, E. (1967) *Beyond Belief*, London: Hamish Hamilton

Williams, P. and Dickinson, J. (1993) 'Fear of crime: read all about it?', *British Journal of Criminology*, 33 (1)

Wilson, J.Q. and Herrnstein, R.J. (1985) *Crime and Human Nature*, New York: Simon & Schuster

Wilson, P. (1988) 'Crime, violence and the media in the future', *Media Information Australia*, 49: 53–7

Wood, B. (1993) 'The trials of motherhood: the case of Azaria and Lindy Chamberlain', in H. Birch (ed.) *Moving Targets: Women, Murder and Representation*, London: Virago

Worrall, A. (1990) *Offending Women*, London: Routledge

Wykes, M. (1995) 'Passion, marriage and murder' in R. Dobash, R. Dobash and L. Noaks (eds) *Gender and Crime*, Cardiff: University of Wales Press

Wykes, M. (1998) 'A family affair: the British press, sex and the Wests', in C. Carter, G. Branston and S. Allen (eds) *News, Gender and Power*, London: Routledge

Wykes, M. (2001) *News, Crime and Culture*, London: Pluto

Wykes, M. and Gunter, B. (2004) *Looks Could Kill: Media Representation and Body Image*, London: Sage.

Young, J. (1971) *The Drug Takers: The Social Meaning of Drug Use*, London: MacGibbon and Kee/Paladin

Young, J. (1974) 'Mass media, drugs and deviance', in P. Rock and M. McKintosh (eds) *Deviance and Social Control*, London: Tavistock

Young, J. (1987) 'The tasks facing a realist criminology', *Contemporary Crises*, 11: 337–56

Young, J. (1992) 'Ten points of realism', in J. Young and R. Matthews (eds) *Rethinking Criminology: the Realist Debate*, London: Sage

Young, J. (1999) *The Exclusive Society*, London: Sage

Younge, G. (2002) 'The politics of partying', *Guardian*, 17 August, www.guardian.co.uk

Zureik, E. (2003) 'Theorizing surveillance: the case of the workplace', in D. Lyon (ed.) *Surveillance As Social Sorting: Privacy, Risk and Digital Discrimination*, London: Routledge

Glossary

adultification – a term that hints at the ill-defined and variable nature of childhood, referring to the tendency to see children and young people as possessing similar capacities of reasoning and knowledge as adults. While this may be to their advantage in human rights terms, it also leads to an inclination – in the UK, at least – to criminalize children at a very young age.

agency – the notion that individuals act independently out of a sense of moral choice and free will, as opposed to being 'acted upon' by social forces and structures.

agenda-setting – the ways in which those who work within the media decide what is important enough to be reported and what is ignored, thus setting public agendas of debate. Crime is a particularly striking example of the agenda-setting process because it is considered to be inherently **newsworthy** – although certain types of crimes, offenders and victims are more prominent on the news agenda than others.

anomie – a concept deriving from the work of Durkheim and developed by Merton, who suggests that anomie characterizes certain groups who experience a conflict between culturally desired goals (for example, material wealth) and legitimate means of attaining such goals. It is sometimes held that the media and culture industries are among the primary culprits in creating a desire for success, wealth and so on, which is unobtainable by means other than criminal or deviant.

audience – the assumed group at whom media **texts** are aimed. Recent media theory has reconceptualized the notion of audience from an agglomeration of individual receivers who are fragmented and passive, to one of sophisticated and active meaning-makers. In the light of developments in 'reality television', it might be argued that the lines between producers and audiences are becoming increasingly blurred.

behaviourism – an empiricist approach to psychology developed by J.B. Watson in the early years of the 20th century. Becoming the dominant perspective in psychology in the 1960s, this school is concerned with the objective study of observable behaviour and represents an antithetical challenge to psychoanalysis.

binary oppositions – the notion that the media (picking up on a human inclination to do the same) presents the world through polarized constructions of **difference** which are fixed and immutable – man/woman, black/white, good/evil, **tragic victim/evil monster** and so on. The media's tendency to deal largely in binary oppositions is said to further entrench biased or prejudiced public attitudes towards marginalized groups.

carceral society – the idea (derived from Foucault, 1977) that systems of surveillance are extending throughout society so that many more areas of social life are becoming subject to observation, categorization and control, resulting in an increasingly compliant population.

celebrity – one of the 12 cardinal **news values** of the late 20th/early 21st century referring to a person who is globally famous. Celebrity is said to carry cultural weight as a key signifier of how media culture operates (Osborne, 2002), and it intersects with crime in so far as celebrities who commit offences, or who are victims of crime, are eminently **newsworthy**, while some 'ordinary' offenders and victims become celebrities by virtue of the crimes associated with them.

children – a relatively neutral term (compared to the more negative ascriptions 'adolescents' and juveniles'), which nonetheless is inclined to take on somewhat sinister undertones in the aftermath of serious crimes committed by the very young.

consensus – the achievement of social unity through shared agreement. **Critical criminologists** suggest that, far from being conceived in terms of consensus, societies are actually characterized by *conflicts* between social groups and classes whose interests are opposed and incompatible. Some of these groups exercise power and hold positions of advantage over others. In this interpretation, consensus is seen as constructed and imposed in order to maintain the privileged position of dominant groups. Consensus might thus be achieved subtly and **hegemonically**.

control of the body – an aspect of surveillance achieved via an interface of technology and corporeality that can range from direct physical contact between flesh and technological device, to more oblique or covert methods of monitoring and codifying the body.

crime – conventionally crime is a violation of the law, but this is not a unitary concept and it has been extended to incorporate social harms. Its meaning is historically and culturally relative, and depends to a large extent on the theoretical position adopted by those defining it.

criminalization – the application of the label 'criminal' to particular behaviours or groups, this term reflects the state's power – transmitted via the media, among other institutions – to regulate, control and punish selectively.

critical criminology – a Marxist-inspired, 'radical' school of criminology that emphasizes the relationship between routine, everyday life, and the surrounding social structures. Critical criminology has parallels with the political economy approach within media studies in their common emphasis on the connections between class, state and crime control.

cultural criminology – an emerging approach that embraces postmodernism's concerns with the collapse of meaning, immediacy of gratification, consumption, pleasure and so on, and emphasizes the cultural construction of crime and crime control, and the role of image, style, representation and performance among deviant subcultures.

crime news – news stories about **crime** are ubiquitous in modern society and are invariably 'novel' and 'negative' in essence. In addition, crime news conforms to 12 **news values** which not only help us to understand the relationship between journalists, editors and the **audience**, but also tell us much about prevailing cultural and ideological assumptions.

dangerousness – a term that sums up widespread fear of individuals and groups who appear to pose a significant threat to order or to individuals' personal safety (references to the 'dangerous classes' were common in 19th century Britain), but is increasingly supplanted by the actuarial and politically-charged concept of **risk**.

demonization – the act of labelling individuals or groups whose norms, attitudes or behaviour are seen to constitute 'evilness'. Those who are demonized are traditionally characterized as **folk devils** and are the subjects of **moral panic** (Cohen, 1972/2002), although it is arguable that ascriptions of 'pure evil' are becoming more salient than the rather less potent image of folk devilry.

deviance – a social, and usually moral (as opposed to legal), concept to describe rule-breaking behaviour.

deviancy amplification spiral – the moral discourse established by journalists and various other authorities, opinion leaders and moral entrepreneurs, who collectively demonize a perceived wrong-doer (or group of wrong-doers) as a source of moral decline and social disintegration, thus setting off a chain of public, political and police reaction.

difference – a concept often used in a negative sense to encapsulate cultural diversity, whereby the patterns of behaviour of certain groups are identified as 'differing' from some presumed norm. Cultural difference – most unequivocally expressed in **binary oppositions** – is frequently seen as the key factor in designating some groups as 'others', 'outsiders' or 'strangers', all of which can lead to **criminalization** and **demonization**.

doli incapax – the principle that children under a certain age are incapable of understanding the difference between right and wrong, and therefore cannot be held criminally responsible for their actions.

'effects' research – a tradition of research that focuses on the impact or effects of media texts on audience attitudes or behaviour. Although a popular explanation for serious and juvenile crime (particularly and, somewhat ironically, within the media), much effects research has been discredited for isolating media influence from all other variables.

essentialism – the belief that behaviour is determined or propelled by some underlying force or inherent 'essence'. Essentialism informs many 'common sense' views on crime and criminality and provides the basis of a great deal of stereotyping about offenders.

evil monsters – a (post)modern version of **folk devils** whereby media, political and legal discourses intersect to construct serious offenders in **essentialist** terms as absolute **others** and beyond the normal values that bind the **moral majority** together.

familicide or **family annihilation** – reported to be an increasingly common phenomenon whereby a man is driven by fear of failure to kill himself and his family. It is often characterized as 'misguided alturism', or a matter of masculine honour and pride in the face of overwhelming social expectations concerning men's responsibilities for their families' wellbeing. The relatively sympathetic coverage afforded by the media to men who commit familicide is in contrast to media reporting of women who kill, and demonstrates public tolerance to men's violence.

fear of crime – a state of anxiety or alarm brought about by the feeling that one is at risk of criminal victimization. Much discussion of individuals' fear of crime centres on whether such fear is rational (that is, that there is some tangible basis to the fear, such as previous experience of victimization) or irrational (that is, that fear is engendered by overblown and sensational media reporting of serious but untypical crimes).

feminism – in criminology, feminism emerged in the 1970s to challenge traditional approaches and their inhability, or unwillingness, to explore the relationship of sex/gender to crime or criminal justice systems. Feminist criminologies are diverse and evolving, and have been instrumental in introducing theories from psychoanalysis and cultural studies into criminology. One recent concern has been the portrayal of offending women as active agents exercising choice and free will, rather than simply as passive victims of male oppression.

filicide – the killing of a child by its parent or step-parent, filicide is the only type of homicide that women and men commit in approximately equal numbers.

folk devils – the term popularized by Cohen (1972/2002) to describe an individual or group defined as a threat to society, its values and interests, who become the subjects of a media-orchestrated **moral panic**. Folk devils are frequently young people who are stereotyped and scapegoated in such a fashion as to epitomize them as *the* problem in society.

functionalism – a theoretical perspective associated with Durkheim and Parsons that characterizes societies in terms of 'social systems' which ideally function to maintain consensus and order. Social systems and institutions are valued for the function they perform for the social 'whole' so, for example, the mass media are examined for their function in maintaining equilibrium and consensus, and their interrelationship with other social systems.

governmentality – Foucault coined this term to describe the growing inclination of the state to intervene in the lives of its citizens, not only via overt forms of regulation such as surveillance systems, but also through the dynamic relations of power and knowledge circulated intellectually and liguistically across institutions.

hegemony – a concept derived from Gramsci that refers to the ability of the dominant classes to exercise cultural and social leadership and thus to maintain their power by a process of consent, rather than coercion. The notion of hegemony is typically found in studies which seek to show how everyday meanings and representations (for example, to be 'tough on crime') are organized and made sense of in such a way as to render the class interests of the dominant authorities into a natural, inevitable and unarguable general interest, with a claim on everybody.

heteropatriarchy – a society in which the heterosexual, male/masculine is assumed to be the norm, and anyone or anything that differs from this is defined as '**other**' and is subject to censure or discrimination.

hypodermic syringe model – an unsophisticated model of media **effects** whereby the media are seen as injecting ideas, values and information directly into the passive receiver, thus producing a direct and unmediated effect.

ideology – a complex and highly-contested term referring to the ideas that circulate in society, and how they represent and misrepresent the social world. Ideology is often reduced to the practice of reproducing social relations of inequality in the interests of the ruling class.

imagined community – a term suggesting collective identity based on, and encompassing attitudes to, class, gender, lifestyle and nation. An imagined community is sustained via its representation, expression and symbolization by various social and cultural institutions, including the media.

infanticide – the homicide of an infant under 12 months by its mother while she is affected by pregnancy or lactation.

infantilization – while recent times have seen a certain '**adultification**' of children, particularly in legal and criminal discourses, they have simultaneously been subjected to a much greater degree of protective control and regulation than in former times. In addition, social, political and economic forces have resulted in many young people having to delay the 'rites of passage' (marriage, home ownership and so on) that have traditionally marked the transition from adolescence to adulthood, thus condemning them to a prolonged period of infantilization.

labelling – a sociological approach to crime and deviancy made famous by Becker (1963) that refers to the social processes by which certain groups (politicians, police, the media and so on) classify and categorize **others**. Deviance is thus not inherent in any given act, but is behaviour that is so labelled.

left realism – a 'radical' criminological perspective that emerged in Britain in the 1980s which views crime as a natural and inevitable outcome of class inequalities and patriarchy, and which proposes to take both **crime** and **fear of crime** seriously.

legitimacy – the process by which a group or institution achieves and maintains public support for its actions. For example, **critical criminologists** have argued that while the media frequently construct violence by protesters as unacceptable and deviant, violence on the part of the police is legitimated on the grounds that it is seen as necessary and retaliatory.

Marxism – a theoretical approach that proposes that the media – like all other capitalist institutions – are owned by the ruling bourgeois élite and operate in the interests of that class, denying access to oppositional or alternative views. Crime is regarded as one of the ways in which class conflicts are played out within a stratified society.

mass media – the term used to describe the means of mass communication via electronic and print media made popular following the rise of the mass circulation newspaper in the 19th century and fully realized with the growth of radio in the 20th century. 'Mass media' encapsulates the notion of large numbers of individuals being part of a simultaneous audience, hence – in this book – it has been used sparingly. In the postmodern media environment, the plurality of media **texts** available and the increasing move towards 'narrowcasting' rather than 'broadcasting', makes the notion of a 'mass' media increasingly untenable.

mass society – a term from sociology suggesting that in industrial/capitalist societies individuals are directly controlled by those in power, and are atomized and isolated from traditional bonds of locality or kinship, making them particularly susceptible to the harmful **effects** of the **mass media**.

mediated – in general usage, to mediate is to connect, not directly, but through some other person or thing. In this book the term 'mediated' is used throughout to mean 'mediated via the media'. While semantically incorrect, this avoids, using the clumsier, but perhaps less ambiguous, 'mediated'.

moral majority – a term that encapsulates the **imagined community** to which the popular press address themselves. Encompassing notions of conservativeness, respect for the law and its enforcers, and a certain version of 'Britishness', it assumes **consensus** on the part of the readership and can be summed up as the *Daily Mail* view of the world.

moral panic – hostile and disproportional social reaction to a condition, episode, person or group defined as a threat. According to some, crime has moved so emphatically to the centre of the media agenda, and has become so commercialized, that a virtual permanent state of moral panic exists.

newsworthiness – a term that encapsulates the perceived 'public appeal' or 'public interest' of any potential news story. Newsworthiness is determined by **news values**; the more news values a potential story conforms to, the more newsworthy it is perceived to be.

news values – the professional, yet informal, codes used in the selection, construction and presentation of news stories.

otherness – the term 'other' denotes a symbolic entity (for example, one or more individuals) located outside of the self. Otherness involves the perception of the self as distinct from the not-self, the latter being a vast category subdivided according to learned **differences**. Otherness is frequently used as an explanation for the **demonization** and **criminalization** of those who differ in background, appearance and so on from oneself or 'us' and relies on notions such as **moral majority, imagined community** and so forth to provide the norm against which others are perceived and judged.

paedophiles – a term used almost exclusively (by the media at least) to refer to adult men who are sexually aroused by children, and applied indiscriminately to denote both 'lookers' (for example, those who download abusive images of children from the Internet) and 'doers' (those who actually abuse children themselves).

Panopticon and panopticism – the Panopticon was a prison design, created by Jeremy Bentham, that has been used as a blueprint for analysis of surveillance, social control and the exercise of power within society as a whole. Panopticism can be summed up as 'the few observing the many'.

paradigm – a shared set of ideas; the dominant pattern of thinking at any given time. Movements in theoretical understanding (for example, from modernity to postmodernity or from Marxism to pluralism) are often referred to as 'paradigm shifts'.

persistent offending – the notion that a small group of (usually young) offenders is responsible for a disproportionately large amount of crime in a given locale.

pluralism – an idea, deriving from sociology, suggesting that all opinions and interests should be equally represented and equally available. The promotion of a plurality of ideas has led some to criticize pluralism as a factor in the 'dumbing down' of culture.

police and **policing** – the term 'policing' refers to a diverse array of tasks, skills and procedures involving monitoring, regulation, protection and enforcement. Even 'the police' themselves are becoming part of a more diverse assortment of bodies with such functions, and the array of activities we term 'policing' is increasingly diffuse. Policing has come to be understood as a set of semiotic practices enmeshed with mediated culture; an activity that is as much about symbolism as it is about substance.

political economy – a sociological tradition that analyses society and social phenomena, including the media, in terms of the interplay between politics, economics and ideology.

positivism – the 19th century theoretical approach that argues that social relations can be studied scientifically and measured using methods derived from the natural sciences. In criminology it draws on biological, psychological and sociological perspectives in an attempt to identify the causes of crime which are generally held to be beyond the individual's control. In media studies, positivism has also been influential in the development of experimental, especially **behaviourist**, research, and has been particularly central to studies of media **effects**.

postmodernism – postmodernism embraces a rejection of claims to truth proposed by the 'grand theories' of the past and challenges us to accept that we live in a world of contradictions and inconsistencies which are not amenable to objective modes of thought. Postmodernism is arguably most prominent in cultural studies where it is used to emancipate meanings from their traditional usage, and emphasize pleasure, feelings, carnival, excess and dislocation. Within criminology, postmodernism implies an abandonment of the concept of crime and the construction of a new language and mode of thought to define processes of criminalization and censure.

profit – in the context of this book, 'profit' has been highlighted as a key term in relation to surveillance and social control. Surveillance and **security** represent big business and are driven largely by profit-motivated corporations who want to make their products attractive to the 'right kind' of consumer.

psychoanalysis – a theoretical approach developed by Freud and more recently popularized through the work of Lacan, psychoanalysis studies people's unconscious motivations for their actions and has been especially influential as a theory of constructions of sexuality and of masculinity/femininity.

psychosocial explanations – perspectives that draw on both **psychoanalytical** and social/sociological understandings, particularly in the pursuit of knowledge about gendered identities. It is often useful to employ psychoanalytic concepts in conjunction with sociologically-informed ideas from, for example, feminism, media studies and cultural studies, in order to explore why some individuals generate a level of media-orchestrated and publicly-articulated hysteria and vilification disproportionate to their actual crimes.

public appeal/public interest – two related but different concepts that are frequently confused. 'Public appeal' can be measured quantitatively in sales figures and ratings and is frequently used to justify the growing dependence on stories with a dramatic, sensationalist or celebrity component. 'Public interest' may involve qualitative assessments of what the public should and should not be made aware of. It therefore connotes intereference from corporations or, more commonly, politicians.

rationality/irrationality – in debates about public fear of crime, it has frequently been proposed that such fears are irrational because the crimes that people fear most are those they are least likely to fall victim to. However, in recent years **left realists** and **cultural criminologists** have argued that there is a rational core to most people's anxieties. For example, the former suggest that people will fear crime if they have previously been victimized, while the latter argue that the modern media are so saturated with images of, and discourses about, crime, that it is increasingly difficult to separate the 'real' from the 'mediated'.

reception analysis – an alternative term for 'audience research' that has taken an increasingly sophisticated view of the 'receivers' of media **texts**. No longer are **audiences** conceived in terms of what the media *do* to them but, rather, the concern of reception analysts is 'what do audiences *do with* the media?'.

representation/misrepresentation – the ways in which meanings are depicted, communicated and circulated. Although the media are sometimes conceptualized as a mirror held up to 'reality', in fact they are arguably more accurately thought of as a means of representing the world within coherent, if frequently limited and inaccurate, terms.

right realism – a school of criminology popularized in the 1980s that was less interested in discovering the causes of crime and more in developing effective means for its control.

risk – a concept that emerged to dominate discussions of late modernity in the 1990s, the term 'risk society' was coined by Beck to denote the social shift from the pre-industrial tendency to view negative events as random acts of God or nature, to the post-industrial preoccupation with man-made dangers and harms. The media are frequently conceptualized as the most prominent articulators of risk (and thus the primary source of people's **fear of crime**) because of their seeming obsession with health scares, panics over food and diet and, of course, **crime**.

scopophilia – the pleasure of looking; the desire to see the unseeable.

security – one of the five aspects of surveillance that has significant social and cultural implications. Paradoxically, surveillance technologies may make people feel both more secure and more paranoid about their personal safety.

social constructionism – a perspective that emphasizes the importance of social expectations in the analysis of taken-for-granted and apparently natural social processes. Constructionism avoids the conventional **binary opposition** of **representation**/reality by suggesting that there is not intrinsic meaning in things, but that meaning is conferred according to shared cultural references and experiences.

social reaction – the social process characterizing responses to crime and deviance. Encompassing public, political, criminal justice and media reactions, the term is often used to signify the processes of **labelling**, **stereotyping** and **stigmatizing** of certain individuals and groups.

spousal homicide – the unlawful killing of an individual by their spouse or partner, this offence has led to a great deal of research, especially within **feminist** criminology, regarding the mediating factors that have to be taken account of in studies of offending and **victimization**.

stereotyping – the process of reducing individuals or groups to over-simplified or generalized characterizations resulting in crude, and usually negative, categorizations.

stigmatizing – the process by which an individual or group is discredited because of some aspect of their appearance or behaviour. Stigmatization helps to explain why some perceived **deviants** are subjected to marginalization and social exclusion and are the recipients of hostile reporting and censure by the media.

subculture – generally used to describe groups of young people whose apearance, norms and behaviour differ from those of the mainstream or 'parent' culture.

surveillant assemblage – the depth, or intensity, of surveillance that is achieved via the connection of different and once discrete technologies (for example, digitised CCTV systems and computer databases) and institutions (for example, the police and private security companies) (Haggerty and Ericson, 2000).

synopticism – an emerging theme in the sociological and criminological literature on surveillance, synopticism describes a situation where the many observe the few (as opposed to **panopticism** where the reverse is true). The late modern trend towards synopticism is evident in the development of the **mass media** and is exemplified by the 'reality television' boom that has taken place in recent years.

text – a media text is any media product (for example, film, advertisement, television programme, Internet home page, radio jingle, newspaper article) in which meaning is inscribed, and from which meaning can be inferred.

tragic victims – the term frequently used in **binary opposition** to that of **evil monsters**, whereby the innocence and vulnerability of a victim of crime becomes the primary aspect of their representation in the media to the point of sentimentalization and sanctification.

unconscious – the term used in **psychoanalysis**, and central to the work of Freud, to refer to that which is repressed from consciousness.

victimization – the experience of being a victim of crime. The study of the relationship between the victim and the offender – or 'victimology' – has become a key concern and might be said to constitute a sub-discipline within criminology.

voyeurism – orignally used to describe the act of watching the sexual activities of others, voyeurism is now used more widely to describe spectatorship of what is usually held to be a private world.

youth – the imprecise period between infancy and adulthood. In media reporting of crime, youth tends to be more frequently linked to offending than victimization.

Index